DEEPER MAN

J. G. BENNETT

Deeper Man

**Complied and edited by
Anthony Blake**

This edition published by the J.G. Bennett Foundation
2019
First published 1978 by Turnstone Press
Second edition 1994 by Bennett Books
© The Estate of J.G. Bennett and Elizabeth Bennett

ISBN: 9781077845114

CONTENTS

PART ONE - MAN

PART TWO-LAWS

PART THREE - WORLDS

LIST OF DIAGRAMS

INTRODUCTION

This book is for those who want to discover how to live, and what human life is for. The how of life is in working with the energies of which we are made. Discovery of the why of life comes through understanding that will is not an exclusively human property.

Nearly all contemporary education deals with functions and things. There is hardly anything available in schools, colleges, universities, or training courses that can help us to manage our existence as beings or understand the purpose we can have. Anything that is not a function or a thing is felt to be mysterious, subjective, and incapable of investigation. The idea of the 'shadow' in psychoanalysis is a very accurate image of how we have come to feel about the worlds which are not composed of things.

This is not the whole story. The contemporary world is being deluged with information from the past, which tells about the nature of man, how he is composed, what he can become, where he comes from, and what his place in life is. At the same time, we are deluged with the revelations of science, which give us new glimpses of the universe. The two streams of information hardly mix, let alone combine. What has been transmitted to us from the past includes information of a particular kind.

It is very probable that the kind of mentation that is developed by ordinary education is incapable of assimilating ancient knowledge. It is easy enough to pick up the words and even believe in this or that doctrine, teaching, or image, but assimilation is something different. Assimilation is where we bring it into our lives. In spite of appearances, most of us have hardly assimilated any of the information made available. This is true of both ancient or traditional knowledge and contemporary scientific and historical knowledge. This book represents information of a special kind, combining the ancient and the modern. It is the work of J.G. Bennett, a pupil of G.I. Gurdjieff, but it is not the work of one man in isolation.

Baha ad-din Naqshbandi, the fourteenth-century Sufi, who was the spiritual head of a great order that eventually spread throughout the world and involved millions of people, said, 'There are things to be believed that have been transmitted by reliable informants but only in a summary way. The clarification of practical wisdom, *marifāt*, consists in showing people how to discover them in their own personal experience'.[1]

Out of the spirit of this tradition came the twentieth-century master Gurdjieff, whose message to the West was part of a new opportunity for men and women to find a genuine education in the worlds beyond the ones we know.

Gurdjieff bluntly declared, 'Man cannot do' and 'Man is asleep'. This is a statement of our attachment to the world of things, in which we are merely things, out of touch with energy and purpose.

In comparison with those who made attempts to reestablish the metaphysics of the 'perennial philosophy', the ancient wisdom, he appeared as a monumental barbarian, introducing the feeling of a dynamic universe and an uncertain existence, satirizing and ridiculing the idea of a safe and holy creation suitable only for people content to sleep in their piety. His vision was immense, and innumerable thinkers and writers of the twentieth century came under his spell, even though this did not appear until after 1950, when Gurdjieff's own book, *Beelzebub's Tales to His Grandson*, was first published. He saw, more than fifty years ago, the need for a science of ecology and a totally different understanding of human responsibility. The disintegration of the modern world has been an unintentional verification of his ideas.

One of Gurdjieff's most powerful urges was to convey to people the guts of a creative life. Nothing was to be taken for granted. Everything was to be personally verified. At the heart of it all, the individual man or woman had to 'work on themselves' and transform the very substances of which they were made.

Many people who have heard about these ideas have developed a wrong picture of what 'work on oneself' means. The picture we have of 'work' is derived from what we do to things, but in a world of things nothing can change what it is.

Gurdjieff insisted that first we must study the phenomena of the inner world in our own experience at firsthand. It is only then, when we are able to recognize different kinds of 'doing', that our efforts can be useful. What doing or effort or action is, is quite different in the different worlds. The ordinary human life in its labors and sufferings probably contains the complete range of possibilities, but the vast majority of the opportunities that come are wasted. Gurdjieff studied the possibilities of action, their con-

---

1 J. G. Bennett. *The Masters of Wisdom*, Turnstone Books 1977, p. 181.

ditions of arising and their mutuality, and created a method of intentional life.

Among his followers was an Englishman of extraordinary intellect and determination, J.G. Bennett. He saw that one could not stay still with Gurdjieff's ideas: they were to be worked with. They were a means of discovery and not an end point. Often in great self-doubt and uncertainty, he set himself to learn in a practical way about the transformation of man indicated by Gurdjieff, and sought out other people who might really know something of this action. Along his way, he gathered hundreds of people who leaned on his strength of purpose. Often they would look to him for answers, whereas in reality his center of gravity lay in questions.

Towards the very end of his life, Bennett was at last able to say, 'Now I can educate people in the way of transformation'. He set up a school, the International Academy for Continuous Education, in 1971, and set himself the task to start this action within people in just ten months. For some observers ten months was ridiculously long; for others it was ridiculously short. For those who understand something of the labors of Gurdjieff at his own center at the Prieuré in France almost fifty years earlier, what Bennett achieved was truly remarkable. But we can hardly judge events which really have to do with other worlds.

He lived for just over three years of the five years of the existence of the Academy. During this time, he was able to establish 'conditions of work' that could be sustained by ordinary people such as myself over the remaining time. He also tried by every means to share his understanding of *marifāt,* practical wisdom. Part of his effort was in many series of talks that dealt with a completely new understanding of the universe and man, and penetrated into the meaning of Gurdjieff's own writings.

He took as his province all knowledge. He determined that the only thing that could make sense was the whole, and he had ever before his mind Gurdjieff's aphorism: 'To know means to know all. Not to know all means not to know. To know all it is necessary to know very little; but to know this little, it is first necessary to know pretty much'. As Professor Dingle said of his book, *The Dramatic Universe,*[2] when Volume I appeared in 1956: 'Philosophical classification and scientific principles and types of theory

---

2 London: Hodder and Stoughton, four volumes, 1956-66. Reprinted Charles Town WV, Claymont Communications, 1987.

are surveyed with a comprehensiveness and depth that can only be the product of many years of research and critical thinking'.

The very last series of talks Bennett gave he called 'The Study of Man'. He was always searching for ways to describe a total vision of man, and once he had the bit between the teeth about anything he never stopped trying. Here is what he himself said about this: 'You must understand that each time that I talk to you like this I am myself looking to see how all this can be presented in such a way that it does not take on an artificial simplicity which could give you the impression that you know something which you do not really know. Therefore, I have been experimenting with the way I have been giving these talks, and have often spoken about these things in ways that I have never done before. This is how we have to try to work at it together: by my trying to find new ways of expressing the way I see it, and by your active effort to grasp what I am saying, we can between us get this picture that is alive. Whereas if I simply tell something I had learned a long time ago, or had even written up in books before now, or you just took in what I said passively, this would not be so good. So that you must understand and approach this as if it is a joint exploration.

'Sometimes we may find that I am leading you in the wrong direction or that you are not able to make the efforts necessary to keep up with me, and we both have this responsibility to see that this does not happen, I from my side and you from yours. Because exploring does not mean that one knows where one is going, it means looking for what one has not yet found. If we did not undertake to do this together, if we were not constantly experimenting and exploring, looking for new ways of understanding, we should remain on the flat. To find a satisfactory way to present all this that does not make it over simple, and yet enables you to come, through these efforts of yours, to having some real grasp of what is being talked about, is always an exploration, an experiment; but to come to this taste of understanding means that we have to take the risk of going into the unknown. That we always have to be ready to do'.

Gurdjieff's earlier presentations, as reported by P. D. Ouspensky[3] were really sketches with no flesh. His own writings were incomprehensible to the vast majority of people. Bennett saw that the times were changing and that people had need for some realistic picture of man. Here, a 'realistic' picture includes not only the

3 *In Search of the Miraculous*, New York: Harcourt Brace, 1949 and London: Routledge and Kegan Paul, 1949.

reality of the visible worlds but of other worlds as well. He intended to take the lectures of 'The Study of Man' series and work with a young and gifted American, Brian Hartshorn, to create a book that would be comprehensible to a wide audience.

It is impossible to say whether this was only a pipe dream. Brian Hartshorn and I were left with the material of the lectures and the problem of how to make use of them. Brian undertook the forbidding task of amalgamating the various lectures given on each topic to produce a coherent whole. I set myself to put the result into as comprehensible a form as I could, without changing too much.

Bennett had assigned me the task of discussing his lectures with small groups of Academy students, and I became aware of the difficulties that people had in making sense of them. Filling in gaps and reconciling different treatments became my almost daily task, but it probably served my own development of understanding more than it did that of the students.

We are in the dilemma that neat systematic presentations of the nature of man are sterile, whereas unsystematic evocative presentations such as in Sufi stories, though more illuminating, are incomplete and partial. This is similar to the problem the seeker finds in turning to Ouspensky's *In Search of the Miraculous* and Gurdjieff's . The former is too summary and the latter is too dense. Whether this present book serves to illuminate the situation I do not know. In case it might be of use to people, the council of the Institute for Comparative Study[4], have decided to publish it.

The book is in three parts. Part One, Man, summarizes the anthropology which is to be found in Bennett's earlier books. But there is a quite remarkable step forward in understanding the three 'centers' of man: what thinking, feeling, and moving are really for. When I heard Bennett speak about this I was startled and amazed, and many things that had puzzled me in *Beelzebub's Tales* were immediately comprehensible.

In Part One, the reader will find something typical of this dynamic approach to an understanding of man. There are different schemes which do not easily match up with each other. This is something integral and is not a defect. It is only a multi-perspective approach that can get us anywhere, because this avoids the pitfalls of pigeonholing information, that is, of doing the very

---

4 The Institute for the Comparative Study of Science, History and Philosophy was set up by J. G. Bennett as a research body in 1946

thing that renders it inert. I have done what I can to enable the reader to fit things together.

In Part Two, Laws, Bennett gives some of the most important results of his researches into the meaning of Gurdjieff's scheme of seven worlds. The scheme belongs to a very ancient tradition and is often referred to, but what it actually means no one seems to consider. In *In Search of the Miraculous* it is presented in a very summary way that makes it seem to the jaundiced reader almost a childish exercise in simple mathematics. What Bennett does is to explain what it means to 'be under a greater or lesser number of laws' and how this relates to what we can do and experience. It is possibly one of the closest things to a description of genuine realization that exists.

In *The Dramatic Universe, Volume II* Bennett had outlined the theory of these worlds, but what was published was only a third of what he wrote, and he had not then come to such a vivid sense of the concrete significance of the worlds as he had just before his death. The worlds are different in the degree of conditioning of will, and Bennett is probably the only modem philosopher who has been able to deal with will adequately as a cosmic factor, and get away from the facile notion of will as a mental faculty or subjective feeling. It is here that we have the drama of waking up and becoming free. Nothing could be more important for an understanding of man than this.

In both Parts 1 and 2, Bennett speaks about very high possibilities for man. But both in his life and in his talks and writings he insisted that this was not just Gurdjieff's 'pouring from empty into void' - an exchange of useless information of no practical significance for people who are not destined to become saints, prophets, or messengers of God. All of us share in the nature of man; we are all children of a common Father. Though we may never be able to live in higher worlds, these worlds can live in us and it is important to bring this to realization. Indeed, this realization is probably what Bennett intended when he said, 'You must come to trust in the Work'. The 'Work' is the unknowable action by which higher worlds can enter into our lives. Nowhere here is it very much explained, because it can only be realized. There is nothing more hazardous than the teaching of the *Work*: it is the *Work* that teaches, and all true teachers are its instruments.

In Part Three, Worlds, there are two chapters derived from talks that Bennett gave early in 1974. They are based on the Sufi scheme of four worlds.

I do not believe that somewhere there is the absolute theory of spirituality. Spirituality is action first, experience second, and exposition third. The form of exposition must change with the times. But the reader may well be quite bewildered to read in Part 1 of three worlds, in Part 2 of seven worlds, and in Part 3 of four worlds. I can only refer to Gurdjieff himself, who said: 'If one has the requisite power and could compel a group of contemporary people, even from among those who have received so to say "a good education", to state exactly how they each understand the word "world" they would all so "beat about the bush" that involuntarily one would recall even castor oil with a certain tenderness.'[5] The difficult thing to grasp is that all of our thinking is based on things, and only works when we are in fact dealing with things. Things are without intrinsic character. They have no essence, no feeling, no nature of their own. They can be manipulated by tools for narrow, time-based purposes. Thinking in this sense is destructive of the human side of experience. Life is not a thing. Life cannot be 'thought about' without losing contact with it.

When the ideas of Gurdjieff and Bennett are 'thought about', totally mistaken conclusions are arrived at. These ideas are intended to help in the course of our own active investigation of this life of ours. They have to be seen in the light of experience, directly. They are far simpler than they seem at first.

To get to the simplicity requires a moment of insight. The words do not describe things, but the character of worlds, modes of perception, relationships, and so on. What our thinking will get out of the words is therefore not the point. We can start by seeing that whatever is accommodated easily into our thinking is not what the idea is about.

When we are in what Bennett calls the *natural world*, even words are different and speak to us differently. It is the same for everything, including the numerous 'spiritual exercises' which are proliferating in the world. The whole problem is to come into the world where things are just what they are. This is the true *starting point*. Until we are established there, we are almost condemned to feed ourselves on nonsense and imitate the poverty of things.

Anthony Blake, January 1977, Cork; November 1977, Helsinki

---

5 *Beelzebub's Tales to His Grandson*, E. P. Dutton 1950 , p. 1215

PART ONE

MAN

CHAPTER 1

The Three Worlds

"And thus, every man, if he is not just an ordinary man, that is, one who has never consciously 'worked on himself', has two worlds; and if he has worked on himself, and has become a so-to-say 'candidate for another life', he has even three worlds." This is the last sentence of the last book that Gurdjieff wrote for publication, *Life is Real Only Then When 'I Am.'*

Our thinking about different worlds is bedeviled by notions of 'this world and the next'. We think that 'me', this something or other we are aware of and know something about, is going to leave one place and go to another. But if what we do in 'this world' has a meaning for the 'next', then the worlds are connected here and now. There are also notions about a 'spiritual world' quite different from this 'material world', but all too often it is supposed that they have nothing to do with each other and are so very different that it is hardly possible to picture what this 'me' is that can pass between them.

The truth is that man can live in different worlds. He does not have to pass from the one to the other, either as stages in this life or in a succession of lives. The worlds are here and now and we live in them insofar as we are able. We do not have to go to another place or another time in order to find them. What we have to do is to establish ourselves in them; to realize them.

At first glance it might be thought that since we know a great deal about man - his behavior and social life, his history and biology and chemistry - it should be possible to find evidence for this idea of different worlds. But the point is that all this knowledge can only refer to what is knowable about man, and this leaves out of the picture what cannot be known. The information that we have about man has been gained in a certain way, and both the information and the way it has been acquired belongs to just one of the three worlds: it comes about by observation, comparison, measurement, and calculation, and these are operations which correspond to an aspect of reality, but not to the whole of reality. Outside the realm where knowledge belongs we are at a loss. If we cannot get hold of anything by means of observation and measurement, then what are we left with? Here we have partially to agree with those who try to deny the reality of an 'inner life' when they say, 'As far as we can see, all this "inner life" outside of measurement and observation is just a dream.' It is the world people have all sorts of imaginary and fantastical pictures about in their thinking and, at the same time, the world of those chaotic and unstable feelings and awareness of ours that appear insubstantial in comparison with the stability and solidity of the external things that we can touch and know. When we try to find other means to grasp hold of this world with the instruments that serve very well in the knowable world, everything is hopelessly distorted. When we try to find other means we come to a practical problem that is neither widely recognized nor adequately dealt with by more than a minority of people. It does not have to be like that. Without rejecting the techniques and findings of observation and measurement, the man who comes to some way of access to the second world is taking up what we are calling 'work on oneself'. He realizes that something more than observation is required. He also realizes that he cannot simply depend on having 'experiences' which, though they might exhibit something of the nature of the inner world, cannot amount to a life.

It is only when there is some means, some work, that enables there to be an inner life that a man can come to see the meaning of the second and of the third worlds. In the ordinary state of affairs, the worlds are there; but as we are, we cannot realize them. The inner life we have is that of a dream, and the difference between the second and third worlds cannot even be guessed at.

We shall begin our account of man and his possibilities of life with the first world. Sometimes this first or knowable world is called the 'material world', but there are such restricted ideas about what is meant by 'materiality' that we shall largely avoid using that term. Instead, we shall talk of the 'world of function'. This is the world where things happen largely subject to causal laws; that is, what we can observe. The world of function includes how this fits into that, this is here and that is over there - in other words, all the shapes and forms and arrangements that enter into the mechanics of existence, like the structure of DNA or the spiral arms of the galaxy. The point about thinking in terms of function is that then we can remember we are dealing with how things *behave* and not with what they *are.*

Function

It is commonplace to say that we know a very great deal about what electricity can do but nobody knows what electricity is. The flow of current represented in circuit diagrams does not describe anything tangible. Electrons move in the opposite direction to the flow laid down by convention. The idea of current is a picture. Then, what about the electrons? We have pictures of them also, but nobody has come up with a picture that covers everything that they do. We find ourselves left with 'something' that has a unit of 'charge' and nobody even bothers to try to make a picture of what charge is. It is simply a number used in calculations.

` Much the same is true of man. Nobody knows what a man is, but we know a very great deal about what man can do - rather, what functions man can perform or what functions the bits or parts of man can perform. In this sphere of knowledge we can include data accessible through self-observation. We can see ourselves, for example, calculating in our heads as well as we can see calculating going on by sums being worked out on paper. 'In our heads' or 'on paper' are different but they are both observable. There are problems and difficulties in making observations of any kind, and no one can pretend that it is always cut and dried. Being accurate about what goes on in our heads may be as difficult as being accurate about the composition of the soil of Mars, but we can find ways to improve the accuracy of our knowledge in any sphere.

It is in the world of function that man is said to have 'three brains'. There are the separate workings of thinking, feeling, and bodily movement. This distinguishes him from the vertebrates, or two-brained animals, which only feel and move, and from the invertebrates, or one-brained animals, which neither feel nor think. Gurdjieff is constantly describing man as a three-brained being, but it is always in the context of the world of function. It means, most simply, that man has a body and, in the spinal marrow, a brain associated with it; that he has a thinking power and, in the head, a brain associated with it, and that he has feelings and, in the nerve nodes of the sympathetic nervous system, a brain associated with them. Each of these brains allows man to be related to the world in a different manner, though it is still the same knowable world. When they are linked together in a harmonious way, man becomes a remarkable power in the world, but the brains are instruments of function and they are not what a man is.

The brains of man can be located in his physical body and are found to be tied to his physiological functioning. Yet they are an intimate part of his personal psychological experiencing. We have to understand that when we study the human body we do not find everything to be the same kind of instrument. The dry skin that is constantly being shed plays an important role in our existence, but it is outside of our awareness, like the microorganisms which live on it, whereas other parts of the organism such as the solar plexus are an inseparable part of the kind of experience we have. There is something like a continuum, with at one end more sensitive instruments and at the other less sensitive instruments. Certain organs, such as the heart and the liver, have a life of their own - this is a recognized fact in modern surgery.

The distinction of being more-or-less sensitive has a great deal to do with how we understand the word 'body'. Do we mean by it 'just flesh and blood' or do we mean also the nervous system and the capacity for different kinds of experience which are associated with it? Do we accept that our experiencing is influenced by our 'body' and therefore that our body has experiential functions? The mind-body dualism of yore is really a fake due to labeling certain functions 'mental' and others 'bodily'. As we go on investigating the human body - asking, 'What is this for? What is this little gland? What is this process for?'- we shall find all sorts of functions, and we shall invent all sorts of ways of classifying them, but the scale of more-or-less sensitive will remain a useful guide that avoids the abstract and unrealistic division into mental and physical.

The body is not simply an insensitive thing. Quite apart from the functions of thought and feeling, the body of man is distinctly human and is regulated to within much finer limits than that of any animal. Gurdjieff introduced many practical techniques aimed at awakening the various sensitivities of the human organism, for without these functions we do not have human experience. There is an enormous amount to be known about the human body. Gurdjieff's interests ranged from medicine to sacred dancing, and he made many discoveries of how the body could be used to influence our experience.

The world of function is also the world we see going on around us; the world as process. Just as every part of us has a function, so does every part of the knowable world have a function, whether it is a living body, or a tool that we use, or some kind of machine we construct, or the air we breathe, or a heavenly body. If we know something, we know it by what it does, and even such a great thing as life on this earth can be looked at in this way. We already know something about how life transforms energies and produces beings such as ourselves. We can even begin to speak in terms of what stars are for. Everything is an instrument of some kind or other and is for something. It is by concentrating our interest on the functional side of things that we are able to gain so much power over the working of this world. We are able to predict what things will do and, by combining things, produce results that we want.

If we look at things as instruments, then we are easily tempted to put the question, 'What is this for?' in human terms, and look to see how things can become instruments for man's purposes. Science could make a considerable step if it ceased to ask all the questions in human terms. When we no longer ask, 'What is life on this earth for?' in terms of what use it is to man, a very great shock will come. We will then have to look at the earth in terms of the cosmic purpose that it serves, and many new avenues of understanding will be open to us. We shall ask, 'What kind of instrument is this solar system?' and 'What part does life on the earth play in the working of the solar system?' and we shall be forced to reevaluate our place in it and ask, 'What kind of instrument is man?' and 'What purposes can man be used for?' Then we shall begin to learn anew many of the old lessons which have been forgotten.

One of Gurdjieff's common terms was 'apparatus', and for him everything was some kind of apparatus in the functioning whole of the universe. An apparatus does something and we can find out what that something is. By that we know it. We can be completely puzzled by a piece of machinery, but once we have seen it working and seen what it does, whether it is a screwdriver or a synchrotron, we know it. In a similar way, the sap of a tree, the trade winds, the ionosphere, genes, bacteria, mountains, people, thinking, and so on are all apparatuses which are known by what they do. Apparatuses are made up of other apparatuses, each of which has a function in its turn, and apparatuses are usually part of other apparatuses with greater functions. We can descend below the level of the atom or rise above the level of a galaxy, but all we shall observe is what things do. We can know about 'inner' things such as prayer only insofar as we know what it is they do, what function they perform.

However much we know in this functional way, we can never answer the question, 'What is this?'. We can give things a name and say that, 'That is a house. This is a man', but giving something a name does not tell us what it is. A name is a sign of ignorance or it points to something that cannot be known. In some cultures, names have been regarded as special and even sacred things, and when people were given names they were kept as secrets because a name was supposed to say who that person really was and expose them, and this was considered dangerous. This was at least a recognition that there was a mystery about what things were. In all probability, the sound of the words had a power to awaken a nonfunctional side of experience, a power that is now largely lost because language has become dominated by the written word. It is difficult to tell.

It may appear that we are left simply with a blank or a question mark when we venture outside of the functional world. The knowledge that we have, even the knowledge that is written in sacred books, will not help us one bit in understanding what is unknowable. But the world, ourselves, even books, also belong to other worlds, and what we have to come to see is that when observation is left aside there is still experience. It is far from empty. But the difference between the worlds is very much greater than the difference between our various senses, such as between sight and hearing. When something is created within us of the meaning of a sacred text, we find it impossible to say what it is. Our language is through-and-through functional, particularly this Indo-European language we are using, and what we can say is not what we are after.

The real means we have of access to the other worlds is the work of transformation in us. The man who 'works on himself' must be in contact with other worlds. As Gurdjieff says, he must live in at least two worlds. Transformation is at the moment just another name, but at least we can say straightaway that it cannot be understood in terms of function alone. It is not a matter of becoming taller, or even more clever, or acquiring different habits, or learning special information. It is something to do with a change in what the man is. If it is not that, then it is only a matter of tinkering with the apparatus, the sort of thing that the scholar and the athlete do.

Talking about what we cannot observe must be done with circumspection. It is in this respect that certain pictures can be helpful - as long as we remember that a picture is not knowledge, but just a way of looking at our experience. If we are not flexible in how we can look at our experience, these pictures are meaningless or misleading. To 'get the point' of them, we have to enter into them and see for ourselves what they convey.

Ouspensky produced one of the most useful pictures for helping people to come to grips with what the three worlds mean. Let us suppose, he said, that there is a room and in this room there are all sorts of instruments, such as a bed, a sewing machine, a microscope, and a telescope. If no one were in the room to use them, all their functions would cease. The sewing machine would not sew unless there were someone to set it sewing and the slide in the microscope would not reveal itself unless someone looked at it through the eyepiece. This is already something far from obvious if we take this picture as representative of how the whole world is. It is saying that every instrument must have a user; that is, someone to get it going and someone to make use of what it does. The user of the instrument is playing quite a different role to that of the instrument itself. We are used to a technological world where instruments appear to use instruments. But in these cases - like the sewing machine being set in motion and controlled by an automatic program - the using instrument is still the instrument of someone - such as the programmer - and the relationship of user to used is still there. We want to give a very special name to the role of the user: will. Will does not have to be 'someone'. It is simply the role which has the initiative. We cannot know anything about will, and that is why the chase to track down the user of an instrument leads us on an endless regress until, like Aristotle, we postulate a big 'someone' outside of the world altogether, the 'prime mover'. This mistake only happens when we try to fit into knowledge what does not belong there.

It is with the aspect of will that we shall next be concerned, but we should complete this account of Ouspensky's picture. He pointed out something very important about the conditions under which the instruments could become operative.

Imagine the room to be in darkness - then what? Immediately, we see that the only thing that can be used is the bed. Even to operate the sewing machine, some light is needed. Let us say that it needs a candle. But a candle is not enough for using the microscope and a more powerful beam is required. Finally, the only way in which the telescope can be used is if the ceiling or the wall is breached and it can reach out toward the larger world outside the room. Ouspensky's interpretation of what the 'light' meant was consciousness. We shall come back to this later under the heading of being, or what things are.

If we say that behind everything that is done there is a will to do it, we will find it hard to have a clear idea of what this could mean. In the picture that Ouspensky gives, we can think of a person as the user of the instruments and we can easily suppose that we know what a person is. It is very hard not to do this because we have been brought up to believe that people are beings who do things. It is only when we have seen for ourselves that in fact, by and large, people do not do things but are products of external factors, that the way is open to understanding will in a cosmic sense and not an anthropomorphic one. There is really little more evidence of will in most men than there is of will in insects.

Function is not just material existence or the lowest world. There are very high functions such as a star performs, but to understand what these are we would have to put ourselves in the place of the will that uses the star as an instrument. The world of function is the world of instruments of every kind -great or small, high or low, enduring or ephemeral. Everything serves for something; everything is used; everything is an instrument. Science is the study of function, but it may well be true that science has hardly begun to grasp its range and extent. Science has tended to restrict itself to those things which men can manipulate either directly or through calculation. In its manipulations, science is imitating the working of the world; but it has been caught by the absurd notion that only its own manipulations are directed by intelligence and will. Scientific activity is part of the world of function, and there is no reason to suppose that there could be any special part governed by laws that do not apply elsewhere.

When consciousness and will are minimal, the world of function reduces to a mechanism. This is the condition of a man who does not work on himself, whose inner life is nothing but a dream and whose will is blind and disconnected. He can continue to operate by inertia until there is physical death, at which point his experience begins to disintegrate until it disappears forever.

Will

Will does not do things; it is that which decides the action. The man in the room has to decide what to do and then the rest is a functional process. It is in this sense that we say that, 'the will does not do anything', in order to be quite sure that we do not think of it as something that can be observed. It is not surprising that we do not observe will in the workings of the world-in planets, in living forms-but to many it would come as a big surprise to see that we do not observe will in ourselves either. We see thoughts like, 'I will do this thing', but that is just a function, something happening, and more often than not the thought fails to be actualized. Put in another way, we can say that everything that we can observe has causes, but will never has causes and is always entirely a cause.

If we say that an insect such as an ant crawling on the ground is moved by the will to be itself, it sounds absurd. We have the feeling that when we refer to will we are referring to a 'someone' much like ourselves, and science has done a lot toward explaining the workings of nature without the use of such an animistic hypothesis. Such questions as, 'Who uses this earth?' no longer make sense, and no one can bring themselves any more to ask, 'Who uses, or could use, the instrument, man?' The difficulty lies almost entirely in the view we have of man as a being 'with will'. We have come to accept this picture in the face of all the evidence against it, and created a myth of man as he is 'ordinary man' - as a free being. Where is this freedom? How is it exercised? So much that a man does can easily be simulated by mechanical devices that it is no wonder many people have abandoned the notion of will altogether and found some incomprehensible satisfaction in thinking of themselves as will-less components of the world machine.

At the very end of *Beelzebub's Tales,* in the chapter 'From the Author', Gurdjieff says that there is no better definition of a real man, a man without quotation marks, than that he is a being who can do; which, he says, means to act consciously and from one's own initiative. He goes on to emphasize, however, that ordinary contemporary man, man as we know him, cannot do; and that for such a man the idea of 'will' is an illusion. What is called 'will' is merely the automatic functioning of the man-machine, whose actions are the results of various patterns of conditioning and the likes and dislikes of his separate parts. The naive observer is deceived into thinking that man has a will for two reasons. The first is that man's actions are related to the stimuli which set them in motion in ways which are extremely complex. The second is that man invariably claims that he has a will, largely because he is conditioned to talk about himself as the author of his acts. This leads to the most absurd difficulties in practical affairs, and when Gurdjieff arrived in Europe with his message 'man cannot do', it did not fall entirely on deaf ears.

It is pretty clear that Gurdjieff used the word 'do' in the sense of setting things in motion, deciding, rather than in the usual sense of activity. Man has a great many activities but very little 'doing' in the Gurdjieffian sense. Added to this, he is blind in the world of will and cannot make sense of his experience outside of the world of function. Will operates in him as it does in an animal, but he has overlaid everything with pictures of himself that obscure the truth of his situation. Either he assumes that he has will or he philosophizes that there is no will at all. In both cases, he is not moved to do anything about his situation.

Something peculiar operates in us. Every impulse that arises in us says 'I'. When our bodies are hungry, we say, 'I want to eat' and think that it is 'I' that is hungry. But this 'I' that wants to eat is only a state of our instrument. If anger arises in our feelings, we say, 'I am angry', with the attitude that this anger is an act of 'I', something freely chosen from within and not merely a mechanical reaction.

'I' is what we call our will and believe to be the agent of all our acts. In this sense, 'I' is an illusion, and we deceive ourselves. Every vagrant impulse, every chance desire, every passing feeling announces itself under the guise of 'I'. All the evidence points to Gurdjieff's conclusion that man has many 'I's and not one integral will. If we remember our definition of will as the role of the initiative in the use of instruments, we can also say that this means that our functions are not integrated and harmonized. As long as man is in this state where every subordinate part dignifies itself with the name of 'I', he has to all intents and purposes no will at all. He is nothing but a bundle of machines.

Gurdjieff was once asked, 'But does nobody have any will?' and he answered, 'Those that have will, have will; but you do not understand what this means. First understand that you have no will and then you can ask from knowledge, and not from ignorance as you do today.'

It is very unfortunate that Gurdjieff talked in terms of 'having will' as if it were something that could be possessed. It is better to say that will can have us, once we have surrendered our illusions. Will is the opposite pole to function. While function is altogether knowable, will is altogether unknowable, altogether out of range. It is the affirming force behind things, that which uses the instruments. As long as we identify with function in ourselves, we remain blind to will and look for who we are in the world of machines. 'I' is the will, but no one has ever seen their own 'I'. There is no answer to the question, 'But where is the 'I'?' The most realistic picture of our will is the will-o'-the wisp that can never be held.

We can say that in each one of us there is will; but also that in each part of us there is a will. There is a will in our voice. When we speak we are not speaking because we have told ourselves to speak but because there is in our vocal instrument a will to use it. Provided with the right material, our voice will go on speaking. At times, we can even see directly that what comes out of our mouths is coming out of its own accord. We do not have to make ourselves speak, there is speaking because there is a will to speak; just as our heart is moved by its will to be itself and our hand, left alone, does what is necessary. It takes very little to observe that there is no 'I' telling my voice to speak, or my heart to beat, or my hand to move. It is one thing to say that 'I have my hands and they can be used for grasping' and a quite different thing to say 'I will grasp with this hand' or 'I will look with this eye'. Every part of us has its own will and it is a great thing when all of these parts come under one law. Then we can speak of 'having 'I''.

The possibility of integration is built into the nature of the will. It relates to that which can connect the subject to the object, the unknowable to the knowable: without which it would remain ineffective. Somewhere behind the eye is the seer which, however we look, cannot be seen. Yet there is seeing. What is this? What is it that can convert the many into the one? Will is open to reconciliation with function, but this reconciliation constitutes another world, the 'world of being'.

We have tended to talk about will almost entirely in human terms, but it is as important cosmologically as it is psychologically. Will enters into everything that exists, even the most inert and passive states of matter. This does not mean, of course, that there are tiny beings inside rocks or very large super-beings inside planets and stars. Will is the dynamic of change everywhere and at all levels. When it is associated with a self-renewing body there is a living being. Even here we have fallen into the trap of talking about an 'it' as if it were an entity or object. Gurdjieff's approach was to talk about will as the 'omnipresent active element *okidanokh*'. When okidanokh enters into a new cosmic formation it divides into three independent parts or forces. It does not blend as a whole. The three separated parts then 'strive to reblend' together, and it is this striving that is the will in things. This picture is wonderfully far away from the usual pictures of will as a single kind of urge. The three forces are described as affirming, denying, and reconciling. They are the principle of every relationship. The various ways in which the three can combine give rise to different kinds of dynamism which are sometimes called laws. In Part 2 of this book we will try to understand these laws and their practical significance for us.

Gurdjieff's picture of okidanokh implies that the threefoldness of will infects everything, including the creation as a whole. There is a cosmic affirmation of creative will, a cosmic denial of mechanism, and a cosmic reconciliation of life. Life is the being of the universe through which it can be whole.

Being

In the first world, or world of function, there is man as a machine, an instrument composed of many different subordinate instruments. This is the man we can know and study. In the world of will, man is will or 'I' and he has the possibility of being master of his instruments. In the world of being, man can become a 'being in his own right'. This world has something of the nature of the other two and we can say 'being reconciles will and function'. Being is that which allows us to be a complete whole.

We can now go back to Ouspensky's picture. First of all, the light in the room is needed so that the man can use the instruments. The user needs to be aware of what the instruments are doing. But there is something else. Let us say that the sewing machine is electrical. It will not work unless it is supplied with electrical energy, and this will not happen unless there is a circuit to conduct it. Every instrument needs to be supplied with an energy appropriate to it and control of this supply of energy is a big part of control of the instrument. A car can take us from one place to another but, however strong our will to go may be, if there is no petrol in the tank we will not be able to move. The energy we need is in the petrol and it is only useful to us if it is concentrated in the tank. The principle is true for more complex machines such as living things: they need the right kind of fuel in order to work. Any old energy will not do. When we have something as complex as the human machine, each of its parts, such as body, feelings, and thought, requires for its operation a corresponding energy.

The energies of thought, feeling, and sensation can be studied, but observation is not enough; we need also to experience their transformation within us. With a car, we know how to obtain petrol and store it for use, but with the energy of thought, we neither readily recognize what it is nor do we have any idea of what sort of vessel or container should be used to store it.

When we think of light in Ouspensky's picture, this is looking at being more from the subjective side, the side of the user or will. When we think of the fuel that machines use, this is more from the side of function. The whole spectrum of light and fuel we call energy. Being can be said to be the state of concentration, or the state of availability, of energy. But energies are of different qualities and there are different levels of being corresponding to the quality of the energies that are concentrated.

It may seem strange to say this, but we cannot know energies. What we know are the results of energies being exchanged, or energies combining to change in quality. The petrol in the car is not itself the energy but the carrier of 'something' that is released through the process of combustion. The results of combustion can be observed and measured and we can make certain inferences about the quantity of energy involved, but we are only dealing in results. The archer bends his bow and releases the arrow. By the flight of the arrow, we suppose there has been a concentration of energy in the bow and that this in its turn has come about through the muscular action of the archer. It took many centuries for this picture of energy to be established and it suffered much opposition from those who were trying to do away with 'occult qualities'; things that could not be observed. Isaac Newton said, 'I do not make hypotheses,' meaning that he wanted to make quite sure that everything he spoke about was strictly observable. Now that the idea of energy has become respectable, it is all too easy to forget that energy is unseen and that all we deal in are pictures which are useful to our calculations. Energies, even of the simplest kind, do not belong to the world of function alone.

When we say that the energies concentrated in a man are on a higher level than those concentrated in a sheep we are implying that their functional organization and possibilities of will are different as well. Energies are the bridge between will and function. But man is this peculiar creature that cannot live automatically according to his nature. He has, himself, to make himself human. We can become aware of our state and realize that often we are no more than on the level of a sheep and sometimes on the level of an invertebrate. While we have three brains, each of which is designed for a work of energy concentration, we generally exist through the functioning of only one of them at a time.

Having control over oneself is far less a matter of 'keeping a stiff upper lip' than of concentrating energies in their right place. Then our instruments can work rightly. We have, for example, no real power over our bodies. Our educational systems largely neglect the development of the body, training it only for purposes of prestige, as in sport. The body must be liberated and allowed to become what it can be. Our thinking is also only an instrument, and needs to be liberated from its automatic functioning. Similarly with our feelings. Each of our instruments needs to be working with the appropriate energies and then they can work in consort together instead of at 'sixes and sevens': we can then say what we mean and mean what we say; think what we feel and feel what we think. In the properly developed man, all his instruments are subordinated to his will and do not have the illusion of 'I', which they do in the state of anarchy of ordinary man. What overcomes the anarchic isolation of the parts of a man from each other is the concentration of the right quality of energy.

Man has certain higher functions that cannot operate unless there is sufficient energy of the right quality available. In Ouspensky's picture, this is represented by the telescope. If we say that the light in the room corresponds to our state of awareness we can see that, however much of it we have in the room, however great our 'awareness of ourselves' may be, it is of no use in the operation of the telescope. The telescope needs a universal light, not the light that can be concentrated in a room. In the same way there are certain perceptions that are possible for man which, because they depend upon higher states of consciousness, cannot be awakened as long as we are only able to maintain our ordinary states of consciousness. Sometimes our ordinary state of consciousness even prevents us from realizing the possibility of higher perceptions.

The concentration of higher energies requires the formation of a suitable vessel. This means that our being must be strong enough to contain them without danger. What we call the 'transformation of being' is raising the level at which energy can be concentrated, so that experiences that at present are impossible become possible, and powers which cannot now be exercised become available to the will. Being is very often spoken about in terms of consciousness or degree of consciousness because we come to it in terms of awareness. The light in Ouspensky's room is meant to signify the awareness of the user. Sometimes he is asleep; sometimes there is a little consciousness, sometimes more. These changes determine the extent to which he is able to make use of the instruments. The disadvantage of thinking about being in terms of consciousness is that we will believe that we know what consciousness is. It is in practice quite difficult to distinguish between the different kinds of consciousness in us. We will always tend to think of more or less of the same.

Being is the very substance of things, not the bits they are made of. There are people who are more than others, not because of any functional power or possession but because of their greater being. Sometimes we can feel the presence of a person and see that what we feel is nothing that we can know and has nothing to do with any activity.

The idea of energies can help us a very great deal to understand being, though it is not the whole story. In particular, it gives us a picture of different levels and that different kinds of things exist in qualitatively different ways. Life, for example, can never be understood in functional terms alone. There is a quality of 'being alive' that we can directly experience but never observe or measure. Life is more than material existence simply because it is more. There is a danger that, in spite of all the warnings, whenever we think of energies and such things as 'living energies', we imagine a material contained in things, like water in a bottle. This is so near to how it is that it is terribly misleading. What we see is not the containment of the energy but the containment of the material within which the energy is concentrated.

But there are not material objects on the one hand and energies associated with them on the other. The difference between an object or thing and an energy is relative. When we are looking on the objective side, being is something material and tangible. When we look on the subjective side, being is spiritual and intangible, seeing rather than the seen. This relativity is what enables being to reconcile will and function.

For us men, the experience we have of the being of things is relative to our own awareness. Some things are like objects, external and knowable, and others are the opposite, more 'inside' than we ourselves are. But throughout the whole range of being there is nothing that is happening or being done or being decided; it is simply how things are. Sometimes it is right to talk about being as the existence of something, sometimes as substance, sometimes as level, and sometimes as quality. The term 'energy' relates to all of these.

We are not used to putting our attention on the aspect of our experience in which nothing is happening. In philosophy, the idea of the unchangingness of being has led to the idea of something deadly dull and inert. Nothing could be further from the truth. Being is potency; the power to organize. For us men, being is what enables us to keep ourselves together in the midst of all the activities of thought, feeling, and body. The 'more' the being, the more we are able to harmonize and hold together the various functions. Change in our being is possible because there are different energies of different levels so that our state is always a product of the combination of higher and lower actions. There is always a transformation of energy in us. The pattern of this transformation is what we are. It is our very life.

As the energies are behind the functioning of the world, will is behind the energies. There is a relationship of more-or-less active that pervades existence. Will is the active principle and function the passive. Being is both active and passive, and we find that one kind of existence is more active than another but less active than a third. If we picture a field being plowed with a horse we can see what these abstract ideas mean fairly easily. The plow breaking through the soil is active in relation to the soil, but the plow in its turn is passive toward the horse. The plowman, because of his intelligence, is more active than the horse but in his turn is passive toward the farmer who owns the land. This relative relationship permeates the whole of existence because being has these two sides of activeness akin to will and passiveness akin to function.

Will does not exist and is not a process. Since consciousness is an energy, will is also beyond consciousness. It therefore corresponds to our deepest intuitions of the unseen spiritual world that can never be known or even felt. Yet it is this unseeable world that makes us men, and it is possible for us to 'live' in the world of will.

It is particularly important to put aside ordinary notions about consciousness when we come to consider the action of will in us. Where does this enter? Through what does it take effect? If we persist in imagining that what we are in the habit of calling 'our consciousness' is the summit of ourselves, especially if we identify with this consciousness, then we can never hope to grasp how it is that will can operate within our existence.

Attention

Almost everybody knows what it is to 'pay attention' to something and also how hard it is to keep this up if we are not interested or stimulated. We can bring ourselves into a state of attention but sooner or later it goes to pieces and we have to 'bring ourselves back' again. We need to look at the act of attention as it is when there is no outside stimulus. This is quite difficult because the contemporary world is largely governed by people capturing the attention of other people, whether in education, business, politics, or religion. In all of this attention-getting activity, the subject is in a passive role, he or she is reacting to something from outside. Such attention is involuntary. What we are after is voluntary attention in which we ourselves are taking the initiative.

Voluntary attention is independent of the reactions in our instruments.

Ordinarily, our eyes follow someone attractive, our nose is enticed by a delicious smell, or our feelings are stimulated by a compliment; all of it is only the stimulation from outside of one or another of our instruments. We are controlled by whatever happens to attract us. If it is in our feelings, then it is what interests and concerns us. If it is something in the environment, then that is where we are. Involuntary attention is when we operate from the mechanics of function.

'To act from oneself' - what can this mean? It cannot mean to act from this part or that part because all the parts are simply instruments. It really means to act from the will. But how can the will have an effect in the world of our instruments? It is not enough to say that it is through the energies. Not all the energies will respond directly to the will, and for the world of function, will is nonexistent. To be effective, the will needs an energy that is like itself. Man has been given such an energy and with this he can set himself free.

Many people believe this energy to be thought or consciousness; but it takes very little to realize that something deeper stimulates thought and that consciousness does not initiate anything.

Neither thought nor consciousness is a true beginning. In every act of will there is a beginning of something new, and the only thing that corresponds to an act of will is creative energy.

But how does the creative act end up by, so to say, coming out of our eyes or out of our ears? There is a transmission between energies of different qualities so that an operation at a higher level has corresponding consequences at a lower one. It is terribly hard not to picture this as some sort of cause and effect, which might belong to the world of function.

The majority of people persist in picturing the will as if it were a function only because they cannot picture anything else. Yet we all have some experience of real attention, and it is not impossibly difficult to see that it is not a process. At the moment of bringing attention to something there is no effort; effort only comes in when we try to sustain our attention. This experience, which we can verify for ourselves, shows us that the act of will and the creative action that goes with it are timeless, but when the action enters the range of energies of which our minds are made, it comes under temporal conditions. The higher energies of mind are able to organize the lower ones, 'lend' them a coherence that in themselves they lack but, reciprocally, the lower energies are able to disorganize the higher ones and introduce into them something of the incoherence of the lower levels. This relativity of organization and disorganization is what we experience in the struggle to keep our attention on something. If for some reason there is an increase in the concentration of the higher energies, the struggle fades and everything becomes easy.

Work with attention enters into all work on oneself. It is the ground on which a great deal is based. If we cannot tell the difference between voluntary and involuntary attention, we are living in a dream world. The science of attention is hardly known in the contemporary world, and to come to a real understanding of this takes a very long time once we have been conditioned by contemporary culture.

The Image of God

In the chapter 'Purgatory' of *Beelzebub's Tales,* Gurdjieff says that the only true saying that has come down to man from the past is that 'man is made in the image of God'. And then he says that this does not mean that God is to be understood in the image of man, especially not as an elderly Jewish gentleman with a beard and a comb sticking out of his pocket. It means that man is made according to the same pattern as the great whole, the Megalocosmos. The man that is so made is real man, not man in quotation marks; he is one in whom all three centers are awakened so that in himself he can have his own 'law of three'.

What are these centers? If we simply say they are to do with thought, feeling, and physical movement, they will appear to be entirely functional. It is better to say that each of them represents the presence of one of the three worlds. The body is obviously the functional part.

It is feeling that can be transformed into being. Our feelings are capable of going beyond anything that knowledge can give us. Feelings reach the world of being, and the state of our feelings can be taken as an indication of our state of being. For the most part the ordinary tumult of our feelings is testimony only to the incoherence of our being. Gurdjieff described these ordinary emotional states as 'negative' in contrast to the 'positive emotions' such as faith, wish, and hope, which can bring us toward wholeness.

The center of thinking is the seat of the will. There should be no difficulty in seeing that this represents a very great transformation from the ordinary state. If we call our will 'I', or the 'Master', then we can fairly say that our head brains have exiled their Master, for morning, noon and night they are filled with dreams. We can hardly use our thinking for anything but dealing with the world of function, but its real purpose is much higher, that it should be the seat of the creative vision through which will can enter.

The threefold man of Gurdjieff is probably the same as the man of body, soul, and spirit. What we need to keep clearly before us is that whatever the terminology, this is man living in three worlds, the man who is a machine and yet free, is a soul and yet has instruments, is a will and yet exists. This man is the 'image of God'.

Many years ago, shortly before I met Gurdjieff in 1920, I was a young officer in the army stationed in Constantinople and I had a vision which had a very profound effect upon my life. At that time I was almost obsessively interested in the notion of higher dimensions, and in trying to find ways in which it would be possible to explore them. It was while I was so concerned with all this that I had a vision in which I saw the whole of the existing universe as one sphere, and not an ordinary sphere in three dimensions but one which had all space and time in it. I saw how everything existed in this which I later came to understand is what we refer to as the world of function. It contained the whole knowable world, what we call the knowable universe, and it was swelling and expanding like a soap bubble and everything existing was on its surface. But outside of it, beyond it in the light were free beings who were not confined to the surface of the sphere. They were flying in the future which the sphere hadn't reached, and I saw that this was the freedom which all of life was trying to reach. But I also saw that there was a dark region inside where one could be left behind. I have no doubt that this picture I saw in my mind is how it is. One's consciousness changes and then one sees things.

I suppose I saw it in that particular way because I was trying to understand where freedom is in the world. In the vision I saw that freedom is only outside the world. But I could also see something connected with the free world and with the state of affairs on the sphere. There was a kind of atmosphere around the sphere which was half bound and half free, which I later came to realize is what is meant by being. When I met Gurdjieff not long afterward, he confirmed the accuracy of the vision and I understood that we have to be able to get free, to get into the world where one is free.

When there is one vessel in us for the concentration of energy, there can be one will and we can be whole. The unification of our being is a practical undertaking, consisting of struggle with ourselves and sacrifice. Struggle is possible because of the relativity of being. Being is both subjective and objective, to some degree knowable and externalizable, like function, and to some degree unknowable and internal, like will. A higher state of being is subjective in relation to a lower state of being; and we can also say that it is more active. From a higher state of being we can look at and know a lower state as if it were of the functional world.

Because of the subjective side of being there is always some sense of 'I-ness' in us, and we can be deceived into thinking that we do become aware of 'I' or our will. We are filled with an awareness of our own presence and we call this 'I' – 'I am really here'. In reality what we are aware of is the bodily instrument ('am') and at the same time our feelings have been awakened ('I'). Even when our feelings are connected to a higher state of being and the feeling of 'I' is very strong, what we are actually experiencing is the altered state of being, and not the will.

It seems a very hard thing to say that not only is will unknowable but it cannot even be experienced, but freedom can never be known or observed if it is authentic. We said that the head-brain is the seat of creative vision and by this will can enter into us. We do know that the thinking center is designed for working with mental images. It is possible for us to produce a mental image of something that we want to bring about and carry this through 'as if' it were directed by the will. There will come a time when the connection between ourselves and will is made and it really is the will that directs.

The will side is strengthened in us whenever we work from our own initiative, uninfluenced by the likes and dislikes, pleasures or pains, associations, and so on of our machines; and regardless of the reactions we have toward other people. Until we have learned to work in this manner, whatever exercises we know and whatever results we seem to be achieving, we have not actually crossed the threshold of work on the will.

Each of the three sides of man needs to be developed. When they are developed in harmony together, something emerges that is the very wholeness of the man. According to Gurdjieff, there are traditions to do with developing man through function, others through being, and others through will. The way he wished to bring people to was the Fourth Way, the way of balanced development.

Liberation in This Life

There is a meaning in the words 'individual will', and the transformation of man is toward his individuality. Man as a 'being who can do' can play a very important role in the cosmos. Gurdjieff says that such relatively liberated beings are necessary because they are able to help the Creator in the governing of the 'expanding world'. Thus it is provided for that there should be the possibility of transformation in this life, to produce, as he put it, 'accelerated results'. In the words of the Buddha, 'liberation here in this very life' is possible. Again, there is an Upanishad which says, 'To him that makes it his sole and only aim, this Self reveals its own true nature.' This is such a great thing to set before man. We see that so few take hold of the possibility that is offered.

When I was with Gurdjieff toward the end of his life, I was in dire trouble, in real despair over what was happening. One day I was talking with him and he said, "Now look, so many years ago you came to me and talked of freedom. If you had seen where this would lead to would you have started on this path?" I said that I could not have done otherwise.

Those who do not follow this path fulfill their destiny by another way. The whole of life on this earth comes eventually to completion. It is possible for people to go with this and be transformed with life as a whole. That is the way of natural evolution, but in it there is no possibility of a personal transformation. It is an impersonal process, and in Gurdjieff's phrase those who go by that way themselves 'perish like dirty dog'. But there is more than an either-or before us; there is an intermediate possibility. If once in this life we have entered the region where being is changed, then death will not stop the action and we have the possibility to enter the creative world, the world of doing. But if it is really freedom that we aspire to, then we must be prepared to put it before everything else.

The choice is essentially that given in Deuteronomy, 'Today I have set before you light and darkness, life and death: Choose ye therefore life that you and your seed might live.' This is the choice that is always with us; that is with us here and now.

CHAPTER 2

Energies

All teachings concerned with the possible transformation of man refer to different worlds and, indeed, transformation would not mean anything unless there were quite different kinds of identity belonging to different modes of experience. Transformation in man is a change in nature. Some people, however, take the transformation of man to mean liberation altogether from this visible world in order to be able to live in a totally different world. This literally escapist view, as we shall see, is simply substituting for a life of mechanism a life of dreaming. The real man lives in the three worlds here and now, not in one world now and another in future time.

The first world of function is what we can see and know through our senses. It is also the world we can think about and calculate with because the function of our thinking is ideally suited to engage with the functioning of the external world. It is the world of things, objects, or bodies, from submicroscopic particles to galaxies millions of light-years away. The bodies can be solid, liquid, gaseous, dispersed, living, or whatever; all that is ever observed and measured is the movement and activity of bodies. In the language of Sufism, this is the *ālam-i ajsām,* literally the 'world of bodies'; *ālam* means world and *ajsām* is the plural of the word *jasm,* body. Even the most superficial study shows that not everything in the world of bodies is the same, and that is why we have the different branches of science. There are inert, non-living bodies and there are living bodies. There are sentient bodies and bodies of beings who are masters of themselves. There are cosmic bodies whose purpose we know very little about. All that we know about them is bodily, their existence in the *ālam-i ajsām.*

If we study things entirely in terms of the world of bodies we cannot understand very much of their possibilities. This is especially true of man. We can observe men doing this or that, behaving in all sorts of ways, but none of this will lead us to see what it is that man should be undertaking, what it is that man should be responsible for. In the visible world, men live and die like animals, or worse. But what can the life of man be when he wakes up to the reality of other worlds? What part can man play in the life of the earth when he consciously lives his life? These kinds of questions cannot be answered in terms of the *ālam-i ajsām*. They have to do with what is going on behind the scenario of the visible visible world. The world of bodies is working in such-and-such a way. Can it work in any other way? Why is it working in this sort of way?

An important step toward answering these questions comes with the realization that if we can control energies, we can control the behavior of bodies. This is easy enough to understand with our machines. If we cannot control the supply of petrol to our car, we are not in control of it. We are not so used to thinking in these terms when it comes to more complex instruments; but it is fairly clear that if we control the supply of food and air to living things they are more firmly under our control than if we try to give them orders or push them around. In the same way, the control of stimulation which releases energy in people is one of the ways in which people can be manipulated. Unfortunately, very few of those who are able to manipulate others in this way see the possibilities and importance of control over themselves.

By learning about the control of energies we can do things that are very difficult to do just by wanting to do them, or 'trying' to do them, or by feeling that we 'ought' to do them. Self-control by attempting to change and regulate behavior is very much more cumbersome and ineffective. For example, if we find in ourselves some negative form of behavior, some anger or distress that is serving for nothing, then the thing to realize is how to cut off the supply of energy that is keeping it going. Inhibition in the world of function only serves to produce the now very famous 'repression' with all sorts of unwished for consequences. Or we may wish to perform a certain task which requires us to be in a particular state. We have to learn to generate the energy that that state needs; otherwise, we have to wait about until it 'happens'. Gurdjieff has a lot to say about this from practical experience in *Life Is Real Only Then When "I Am."* Such work can only be safely attempted when our 'I' has taken its rightful place in us and is no longer usurped by egoism.

One of the many and one of the most powerful practical techniques that Gurdjieff introduced was his 'movements'. These make very complex demands on the attention, and it is very easy to come to see that, no matter how much we may wish to keep our attention on some sequence or other, the contact we have will last only for a time. Our capacity for attention depends upon something of which we have only a limited supply. When this something is exhausted, our attention goes, but after a while it returns again because there is a constant replenishing of the supply. Although there is always something going into our reservoirs, it is not enough for us to work in an uninterrupted fashion. The movements of Gurdjieff are a very good way of learning about the reality of energies. It is another step to come to be able to concentrate the energies that are needed.

We can say that in order to do something we must have the right kind of energy and it must be available in the right form, but this does not mean that we know what these energies are. In the world of energies we do not know what we are dealing with. Many people make the mistake of trying to 'know' the various energies. All that we can observe are different kinds of function, from which we know that there are different kinds of energies which cannot be observed. This is understood in contemporary science. It is only in the last two hundred years or less that science has used the word 'energy'. The word was introduced in the first half of the nineteenth century, not because anyone observed energy but because it was convenient to have a word to describe the way in which things behaved when they changed their composition; for example, when coal was being burned. It was discovered that there was a constant relation between a moving kind of energy and a hot kind of energy. It was a useful thing to have a word to describe what was present and measurable in a hot body and what was present and measurable in a moving body. Then it was discovered that electrical energy could also be measured and converted, which changed the meaning of 'electricity'. The standard of measurement of energy was made the 'amount of work' that could be done. That is something entirely functional, so that all measurements of energy came down to a matter of observables, though the energies themselves were never observed.

The saying in the Gospels, 'By their fruits you shall know them', can well be applied to the energies. We do not know what the energies are as we know what bodies are. We can say, 'There is a chair; there is a cushion; that is a window', and we are able to recognize what we are talking about. But if we say, 'This is heat', it is not the same. We are referring, through our experience of something hot, to what we believe to be there. It is the same with light. We never see the energy of light itself; all we see are things and surfaces or dust motes in the air. We never see or touch the energy of gravitation, and it took men of great genius to point beyond the observable falling of bodies and circling of planets to this energy.

If we speak with each other we know that there is some energy by which we are speaking, but that is all we know. It is the same when we are thinking in ourselves. We can see the thoughts going on, but it is quite another thing to be aware of the energy involved.

There is no experiment that we can devise which would reveal energies to us directly. They are altogether out of reach by the senses and any kind of observation. But this does not entirely mean that they are altogether outside of experience. In the Sufi terminology, the world of energies is called the *ālam-i arvāh*. *Arvah* is the plural of the word *rub,* which, like the Hebrew word *rob,* means 'spirit'. But when people discovered that there were powers working in the world and called these spirits, they were really discovering the same thing that science was to discover through its study of material changes and which it calls energies. We can therefore correctly translate *ālam-i arvāh* as the 'world of energies'. What this term signifies was discovered a long time ago: that there is something invisible behind all that we are able to see which yet acts in the visible world.

There is a constant intercourse between the worlds of bodies and energies. Everything existing has a place in both these worlds. There is no sharp impenetrable barrier between the two worlds, and it is possible for energy to be converted into the material from which bodies are made, just as such material can be converted into energy. And yet the two worlds are very different, as land and water are very different, although there is the shore in which they touch each other. Something is constantly happening between the two. The land is given life by the rains, which have their source in the sea, just as the world of energies makes possible all the actions which take place in the world of bodies. And reciprocally, the sea is fed by nutrients which wash off the land, just as the world of bodies provides the apparatuses in which energies are transformed. Energies themselves do not have any place, and if they are to be localized so that they can interact with each other, they must be contained in some body.

A body that contains energy for one set of transformations is itself an energy contained in some other kind of body for other transformations. There is not one set of things that is bodies and another set of things that is energies. The relativity of existence has to do with transformations on different levels. This makes it possible to talk about bodies which man can acquire and which are quite different from his physical or planetary apparatus.

We can say that everything that exists in the universe is as it is in order that various qualities of energy can be stored and the various energy transformations that make up the cosmic economy can take place. This is fairly easy to see in the mechanical world. We know how it is possible to convert chemical energy into heat, heat into motion, motion into electrical energy, and so on, as in a power station. The way we live depends more and more on such transformations, and only a small part of our energy needs is supplied through metabolizing the foods we eat, as the animals produce their energy. This has made us peculiarly dependent upon the external world, as we are always having to borrow energy from it. We should realize that the energies of life are transformed just as the lower energies are. There are specific energies connected with the physiological functions of all living creatures, endowing them with the peculiar qualities characteristic of life. All of these are constantly being transformed. There are also energies connected with our psychological functions which undergo transformation; and there are even higher energies than these which must be transformed. Everything, from rocks and stones and soil, up through plants, invertebrates, and vertebrates, up to man and beyond him, has a role to play in the cosmic process of energy transformation.

Transformation Up and Transformation Down

There are two ways in which energies are transformed, and for each of them there has to be a certain kind of apparatus so that the energies can be brought together in an appropriate manner. There is first the transformation of a lower grade of energy into a higher one. This requires what we call a 'generator'. In the electrical generator, kinetic energy of motion is converted into electrical energy which can be used for high-grade work. We can also call this a transformation from the world of function into the world of energies. The opposite way, from the world of energies into the world of function, is the kind in which energy of a higher grade is downgraded to a lower level in order to produce external results. Here what we have is an 'engine'. An electrical engine uses electrical energy to produce motions. The sewing machine we mentioned in Chapter 1 is an example.

One way is upgrading energy and is called 'anabolic', meaning 'going upward' and the other way is downgrading energy and this is called 'catabolic', that is, 'going downward'. We speak about them separately, but in fact every transformation of energy involves both anabolic and catabolic changes at the same time. We must also bear in mind that a single body may be the carrier of a number of different kinds of energies and that a large number of these may be transformed at the same time under certain conditions. This is obviously the case with the food we eat. In digestion, our bodies undertake a very complex work of transformation, as a result of which we have available a whole range of energies, corresponding to the different tasks that have to be accomplished to maintain our lives. Thus we have energies for maintaining the heat of our bodies, fuel for the various energies of our organism, energies for renewing our tissues, energies for the digestive process itself, energies for our nervous system, as well as energies for our thinking and feeling. All of these are derived from food, with some assistance from the air.

Our role in the world is connected with the conscious transformation of energies. It is an easy thing to say but not so easy to realize what it means in practice. It is likely that we can feel what this means without having any clear idea to go with our feeling. But our feelings may be more true than we know. Man has a potential for bringing about the transformation of energies that other forms of life and nonliving things are unable to transform. Learning how such energy transformations are to be accomplished is the same work as learning how our own transformation, our own self-creation, is to be achieved. The way to do it is in this elusive 'working from oneself', not from external stimulation. It requires of us that we work with energies of a higher grade than those which engage the attention of ordinary man, including the 'ordinary man' who is a very big part of every man without exception. As it is, we transform energies, so to say, 'willy-nilly' and often to our personal detriment because all the initiative for these transformations comes from outside us. When we eat, we breathe, we see, we touch, and so on, we are taking in energies, and unless we are trying to work on ourselves, these energies transform automatically in us with automatic consequences. When it is like that, we are helpless. As Gurdjieff put it, we are just waiting about 'for roast pigeon to fly into our mouths'.

These sorts of ideas can easily be verified even by such a simple thing as reading. If we read passively, from time to time we may be sensitive to the meaning of the words but the net result is only a stimulation of chance associations. What is written may even be completely misread. But when we try to bring ourselves into contact with the process of reading, so that we are able to distinguish between our associations and what is being said in the book, an energy is accredited to our account. Through this, we may be able to understand something in a completely different way.

Using our picture of the land and the sea, we can say that in the automatic life we are completely dependent on whatever rainfall there might be. If there is rain, something can happen, otherwise we are inoperative. But in the conscious life we can swim into the water and we can even learn to set sail and travel over the ocean. We can pass over from the world of function into the world of energies and learn how to move 'as a spirit'.

The energies of our psyche, that we ordinarily experience as the stuff of ourselves, are those of sensation, thought, and feeling. If we are to learn to work with our own initiative, independent of outside direction, we have to learn how to localize these energies, move them about, combine them, and transform them. In other words, we have to learn how to get our generators and engines under our own control. Then, in eating, breathing, and taking in impressions we will no longer be merely sustaining our functional activity; we shall also be making something that belongs to the world of being, something able to move in the world of energies.

The transformation which can give us being is also required for the working of the world. It is an obligation that man has, and is not required of any other form of life. As we shall see later, it has very much to do with how a man brings himself into contact with the energies in himself and how he is able to transform negative impulses and states in himself into positive results.

The Scale of Energies

There is an ancient system of classification, which is really quite simple, in which all the energies find their place in one of twelve different categories. I learned the basis of it through Gurdjieff, when I heard him give a lecture on it at the Prieuré many years ago. Afterward, when I was with Ouspensky, I took part in a great deal of research on this system and discovered that it belongs to a very ancient tradition that comes from Asia, and appears in a number of teachings - in Buddhism, in Sufism, in the Qabala, and even in Christianity as, for example, in Dionysius' *Celestial Hierarchy*. Again and again it has been lost and then found again. People have even come to discover it who had no idea that they had found something which had been known in the past, as when, as recently as the last twenty years, a scientist proposed in a book that we should look at existence in terms of twelve different levels, each one with a corresponding energy.

In this classification of energy into twelve categories or twelve grades, it is this 'twelveness' that is ancient and very remarkable, as one finds this number twelve in connection with levels and transformation in all traditions. My own experience from many, many years of work with this system is that through understanding this, getting accustomed to using this terminology, it is possible to speak very explicitly and very clearly about things that would otherwise be very subtle and hard to convey. This is because this classification takes in all the different kinds of energies that there are, which underlie all the facets of our experience, ranging from the kinds of energies that physical science studies, through those which produce the phenomena that the science of life studies, through those responsible for the phenomena psychological science studies, and includes the energies which we can call spiritual, and which transcend ordinary study.

We are differently related to the different energies. We can know certain energies, such as electricity, only by what they do. Their working is outside of us, and in this sense they are 'objective'. However, there are certain energies such as consciousness in which we become aware, and these can be called 'subjective'. These energies directly enter our experience, but it is not true to say that in all cases we can become aware of them.

When we think, it is the energy of thought which is working and, although we do not observe this energy any more than we can observe electricity, there is a great difference in the way that we experience them. What we think, and the energy of thought, are not separate from each other, as electricity and the results of electricity are. We are *inside* the workings of thought. But an energy which is internal for one perspective can be external for another; the difference is relative. This is easy to see in a material sense: if we are sitting inside a room, the room is external for us, but for the house it is internal. It takes practice to recognize that the same principle applies to our energies. If 'conscious energy' is in operation, then although our ordinary feelings, sensations, and thoughts may continue unabated, we are no longer inside them in the same way, but we are removed from them as if they were objective or 'outside'. Similarly, when we snap out of a reverie; suddenly we notice that this daydream has been going on, whereas a moment before we *were* that dreaming. It is this relativity that gives us the chance to see the content of ourselves objectively.

There is a threshold for us between the energies that belong to the 'within' and the energies that belong to the 'without'. Below a certain point, what is going on can no longer be a direct part of our experience. In the scheme of energies, therefore, we divide the spectrum into two halves and we speak of six energies that are objective and six that are subjective.

We also take account of the special character of life. In life there is both sentience and mechanism. Life is between the subjective and the objective and has something of them both. If we make the energies of life the middle region of the scale, then we will have also energies 'above life' and energies 'below life'. We are going to make each region consist of four energies so that there are twelve in all. In the first we have the four energies that are below life, or Material; in the second the four energies of life itself; and in the third the four energies that are above life, or Cosmic.

If we look at the two divisions we have made, we can see that some of the life energies are external, below the threshold of awareness, and some are internal, above the threshold of awareness.

The peculiar property of a living being is that it is in between. In our own living bodies there are life processes of which we cannot be aware, or physiological processes which have nothing subjective in them because they are so very much closer to chemical processes than to conscious ones. Our body manages to repair its tissues in a way of which we are totally unaware. There are also processes where there is awareness: our experience is full of the workings of the energies of thought and feeling generated in our bodies. Life, no matter how primitive, is both mechanical process and 'experience'.

In looking at this scheme we have to be careful not to think that we have twelve distinct things described in it. Energies are not like bodies and they are not separated and distinguished as bodies are. It is better to think of the scale as a series of gradations so that each energy merges into the next. Every level of energy is organized by the level above and disorganized by the level below. This is how we can recognize their difference.

Within any one level of energy there can be many different kinds. For example, thought, feeling, and sensation are all on the same level of energy but they operate from different centers and produce different results in us. The energies we meet with in practical situations are always a blend of different energies, and we can never deal with any one energy in a pure, isolated form.

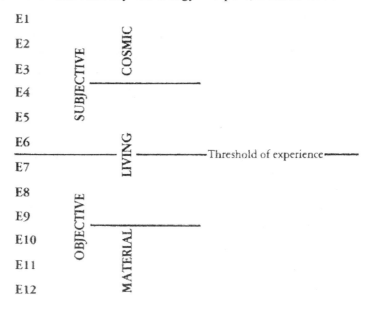

SCALE OF ENERGIES AND THRESHOLD OF EXPERIENCE FIG. 2.1

The Material Energies

Even within the domain of the material energies we can distinguish between crude, low-grade energies and energies which allow bodies to have all their very different, subtle properties. It seems pretty clear, for example, that there is a difference between 'hotness' and 'pliability'. Though it is something of a simplification, we can say that pliability has to do with the intrinsic properties of bodies while hotness is in only something that can be added and taken away without making fundamental changes. That pliability can be affected by heat is only an example of how energies on different levels can influence each other.

We can say that the level of an energy depends on how far it is in itself organized and how versatile it is, how many different things it can do. In this sense, it is pretty clear that we can take as our lowest energy that which has no intrinsic power of organization, something that is the very epitome of disorganization.

E12 - Dispersed Energy

We call this lowest form of energy 'dispersed' because its tendency is to spread out and reduce the level of organization. It is, of course, the 'heat energy' studied in thermodynamics. Associated with it are laws, such as the second law of thermodynamics, which says that disorder increases with every exchange of energy. Heat is the energy of all random motions, or we can say that it is the energy of 'motion without direction'. Of course, every moving body has a direction in its path or flow, but when there are a great number of such bodies moving about one another, like the particles of air in a room, they move, as we say, 'at random', with no consistent direction. This dispersed motion of the particles is what we call the 'heat' of the air, and it is a real and measurable energy. But we are not directly aware of it. We are aware simply of differentials in degrees of 'hotness', which are not at all the same thing. Sometimes, when a shaft of sunlight falls into a room, we can see the motes of dust dancing about under the bombardment of the particles of air. This is a result of the heat energy in the air, but it is not the energy itself.

The energy is called 'dispersed' because it has no place of its own and no form or structure of its own and, while everything that exists is hot in one degree or another, heat flows equally passively through everything from where it is hotter to where it is cooler. While heat is necessary in some ways and many objects can only exist within a certain range of temperatures, it cannot do anything by itself.

According to the Hindu cosmology of the *Vedas*, warmth or *tapas* is the starting point of the creation. The dispersive nature of heat that we discover within the world is what we can understand of the primal chaos out of which the world was evolved. It is the antithesis of the transcendental power that ordained that the world should be brought into being. In heat is the beginning of motion, in motion the beginning of change, in change the beginning of growth, in growth the beginning of transformation, and in transformation the beginning of unity. It is no easy thing to understand what it is that heat contributes to the world process of transformation.

E11 – Directed Energy

The second kind of energy comes from separation, and arises when motion has a consistent direction. This can be made to happen even with a flow of heat. If we heat one end of a metal bar or wire and keep the other end cool, then there will be a constant flow of energy from one end to the other. The heat energy has been given a direction because it has been organized through the physical properties of the bar. In the same way, if we lift something up there is then a direction from it to the earth along which it will fall. The gravitational field of the earth is inherently directed, and whenever something is raised up, it acquires a gravitational potential energy by virtue of its separation. This energy is directed. Similarly, when we connect the poles of a battery, there is a flow of energy which also has a direction.

'Up and down' and 'positive and negative' represent the polar character of the directed energies - such as gravitation, electricity, and magnetism. With each of them is associated a 'field of force', and this field is really the direction in which things will move that are affected by the particular energy. Examples of this are very easy to see. If we shake iron filings onto a piece of paper held over a magnet, they will form a pattern which displays the magnetic field in which they rest. If we throw a ball, we give it a certain directed energy, but it also acquires energy from its movement in the earth's gravitational field and the exchange between these energies gives its trajectory. It is largely these energies that are studied by physical science.

E10 - Cohesive Energy

The third energy we will talk about includes what is called the 'chemical energies', and comprises all the energies by which things are held together. There are 'binding energies' which hold atomic nuclei, atoms, and molecules together, and it is through these that chemical elements and chemical compounds can exist. These energies are at the very basis of the structure of matter as we know it, for they give solids and liquids their cohesion. There are energies on the surface of bodies by which they are maintained, and which exert an attraction when they are brought together so that bodies can be coalesced. In liquids this surface energy produces the properties of surface tension. What we experience through our senses is largely the forms that are produced through the cohesive energies. They give a pattern to matter. We can see this very clearly in the crystal, where the 'lattice energies' establish a very definite three-dimensional form. The cohesive energies are really responsible for producing the familiar world of surfaces and volumes, of solids and liquids. They are very much better understood than they were a hundred years ago, but there is still a great deal to be discovered about them. In particular, it is not really understood that it is these energies that actually 'make bodies'. Every one of the things that we deal with, including ourselves, is held together by cohesive energy in some form or other.

This kind of energy can be said to be the very stuff of the *ālam-i ajsām,* the world of bodies. Without it, there could be no solid bodies. A great deal of the universe is like that. There are vast regions which we loosely call 'outer space', in which there are no solid bodies, but only fields of force and the dispersed energies of very attenuated gases. Our Earth is very exceptional in that it has solids, liquids, and gases in innumerable varieties. Because of this, certain transformations are possible that cannot occur in other parts of the universe. Due to this concentration of cohesive energy, the Earth has very important possibilities.

E9 - Plastic Energy

The cohesive energies cannot account for all that we find in material objects. Bodies have to do more than cohere. They have to be able to adapt themselves so as to respond to each other. This is clearly very important for living things because they would be fixed and frozen and dead if there were no energy higher than cohesive. It is necessary that things should be able to alter their shape to some degree and yet remain what they are. We ascribe this property to what we call 'plastic' energy.

Our bodies are wonderfully plastic. How is it that we are able to move our hands about? How is it that our vocal cords can vibrate so that we can produce sounds without our throat breaking into pieces? These things are possible because the hands and the larynx are elastic. Every muscle and artery is a beautiful example of how the plastic energy can work, and every organ of the body relies on this energy. That things can change their shape and yet remain what they are is one of the highest properties that we can associate with a thing. It ought to be familiar enough to us through technology, where we work with materials: bending, stretching, flattening, twisting, compressing, and so on. But we do these things without noticing what a marvel it is that they are possible. The plastic energy is the most free, the most versatile, and the most active of all the material energies. It is through discovering its powers that we have been able to make such an impact upon our environment.

The plastic energy comes into play because nothing is continuous. There are *holes* in things. This means that the inside of things can be rearranged to accommodate to external forces. This is how a liquid flows, constantly rearranging itself internally. It is also because there are holes in things that they can be cut and divided in a relatively easy way. If, for example, a crystal was perfect with no gaps in its lattice structure, it would take an enormous energy to divide it or change its shape and then the whole crystal would probably shatter. The 'imperfections' of materials give them their power of response to the environment. These are 'imperfections' only from a cohesive point of view.

It is possible to transform some of the cohesive energy into plastic energy. This happens with certain materials, such as clay, which 'come to life' when we handle them, mold them, manipulate them. It comes about in the soil through plowing and digging - and, of course, through the action of myriads of micro-organisms and invertebrates - and what is looked for in soil is really a plastic quality. Soil, above everything else, demonstrates the importance of discontinuities in the cohesive properties of things. It is the plasticity in our own hands that enables us to recognize the workings of this energy in the soil we rub between our fingers. The plastic energy is the highest kind that is possible without life, and if we want to find an extra degree of freedom in things, we have to look to the living energies.

The Living Energies

The living energies are of direct concern to us not only because they bring with them life but also because they include energies that cross the threshold of awareness. Life is a state of affairs that is connected with bodies and every form of life that we know is the life of some living body. If there is something or other that has experience which is not connected with bodies, we can say straightaway that it is beyond life. Every living body, even the very simplest, has an immensely complex organization, far beyond that of anything that is not living. We now know from biochemistry that even the simplest cells, such as a tiny bacillus five-hundredths of an inch in length, have a structure that contains thousands upon thousands of atoms arranged in the most complex way. More importantly, it has a central molecular complex that determines its form and structure and directs its growth. It is able to grow according to the pattern that is in it, and, unlike the crystal, it is able to grow by using materials that are different from its own, converting them into its own nature.

E8 - Constructive Energy

The first property of living things is that they can feed on their environment. They are active in relation to the non-living world. The real transition from the merely material to the living form is in the power to maintain a body at a higher level than that of its environment. This power of constructing a body we attribute to the 'constructive' energy. Studies in the field of genetics are showing how every living thing has an organizing pattern which directs its growth and determines its particular structure. DNA, deoxyribonucleic acid, is a carrier of constructive energy and it is the basic genetic material.

It is likely that life began with the emergence of forms that were just able to reproduce themselves. The appearance of very complex molecular substances was an actualization of the potential of the constructive energy which, before that stage, could not be concentrated. We also see examples of the constructive energy in biologically potent substances such as enzymes, which are able to act on the non-living world in order to break things down or build them up. Chlorophyll is another example, and one that is important for the whole economy of life on the Earth. We can see this energy at work in the activity of viruses, which are inert in themselves but take on the characteristics of life when introduced into living things. The constructive energy stands at the very threshold of life.

E7 - Vital Energy

The second living energy can be called the 'directed energy of life'. There is a certain similarity between each of the three groups of energies, and the vital energy gives to living things their characteristic outward-directed, goal-seeking quality. We can call it the 'urge to live', but it has nothing to do with a state of awareness, and pervades all of life, from the simplest unicellular creature, up through the plants and animals, to man himself. Whereas the constructive energy allows living things to live, the vital energy drives them to live. We can say that the vital energy is life itself. Ordinarily, we look at living things and say that they have life, but in reality it is the reverse: life, the vital energy, has living things and they are its instruments.

It is the vital energy which gives all the functions of living things, such as nutrition and reproduction, their assertive character. When an organism is no longer able to maintain its hold on the vital energy, then it dies. At death, when the functions cease, this energy actually leaves the body and it is then free to be absorbed into other living bodies. It is possible to transfer the vital energy from one body to another, and this is what is done in a certain sort of healing. But unless we understand the consequences of such an act, we may be doing harm and only disrupting the regulative mechanism of the organism. So long as the body cannot maintain the organization necessary for the concentration of vital energy, no addition from outside will be of help.

The vital energy stands at the threshold of awareness. From this energy downward all the energies have the objective quality, so that we only experience them from outside. But this energy in its upper limit reaches to the next level of the automatic energy, and through this we have the possibility of becoming aware of the vitality of our organism from inside, an awareness of ourselves as living animals.

E6 - Automatic Energy

The drives of sex and food come out of the vital energy, but the organization of these functions comes from the automatic energy. For the most part, the automatic energy is the energy of habit. Through it, patterns of behavior are transmitted from generation to generation so that, for example, birds know how to build their nests and where to migrate. We see it working in the dog that curls around and around as it settles, acting from the pattern that belonged to the time when its ancestors slept in grasslands. It is evident to an extraordinary degree in the social life of insects. When we look at a termite colony, able to act on the nonliving world in order to break things down or build them up. Chlorophyll is another example and one that is important for the whole economy of life on the earth. We can see this energy at work in the activity of viruses, which are inert in themselves but take on the characteristics of life when introduced into living things. The constructive energy stands at the very threshold of life.

E5 - Sensitive Energy

Sensitivity is the limit of our ordinary awareness and the highest energy that we can have under our control. The sensitive energy needs a very complex apparatus in order to function in a living thing. For this reason, it finds its greatest scope in man, each of whose three brains give it the possibility of a different quality of operation. All living things share in the working of the sensitive energy to one degree or another, though it first begins to flower in the vertebrates, each of whose separate species exists for the purpose of transforming particular gradations of sensitive energy. We need to understand the importance of these transformations if we are to understand the significance of the variety of living species. Every one of them has a special role to play in the transformation of the sensitive energy. We cannot doubt that animals, especially warm-blooded ones, have just as much or even more sensitivity in their feelings than most men and women, and it is this sensitivity that gives them their particular characters. We exterminate species only at a great risk to ourselves because we ourselves will have to take on the role of transforming those energies for which they existed. There are enormous forces to which all life, including man, is subject, which regulate the transformation of energies on the Earth.

The sensitive energy gives the possibility of choosing, but in animals this is largely a matter of being sensitive to what is good to eat or harmful. It enables a contact between the living body and its environment that is more than a contact of bodies. Through it, animals and men are aware of the world about them.

It plays the same part with living things that the plastic energy plays with material objects. It gives them the possibility of transformation and change. Only man is able to take full advantage of this possibility. But so long as we spend most of our time in

an automatic state, our sensitivity remains in a dream in which
we take in impressions in a vague way while remaining out of
touch with our behavior. Gurdjieff described the state of this energy in ordinary man as like that of a 'cloud' drifting along with
the body, lacking in any kind of organization. When we are interested in something, this energy concentrates in that direction.
When we eat something delicious, it becomes a temporary 'soul'
in the shape of a mouth. It is attracted and repelled by the things
about us. If we are to become as we ought to be, we have to learn
how to arouse and sustain the working of the sensitive energy in
our bodies, in our feelings, and in our thought. Until we can do
this we have not come even to the threshold of transformation.
Learning how to bring our centers into the sensitive state is the
only manner in which we can prepare them for the action of the
higher energies.

The sensitive energy enables us to be aware of our thoughts,
our feelings, and our bodily states; that is, the associations, reactions and sensations of our mechanical life. The condition of the
man-machine is to exist as thoughts, feelings, and bodily states so
that he is a slave to every fleeting impulse. It is only when we are
aware of alternatives that we can choose. When we are sensitive
we can accept or reject what is before us, but we must be careful
not to confuse this possibility with automatic reaction. To avoid
this confusion, we have to know what it is to hold together opposites. When we like something, it is useful to see how we can dislike it and vice versa. If we find ourselves saying 'no' to an idea, it
is useful to see ourselves in agreement with it also. It is only when
we are able to come under the combined action of 'yes' and 'no'
that we really have the possibility of choice.

Sensitive energy gives us contact with our functions and with
the world around us. Ordinarily we are not often aware of the
meaning of the words that occur in our thought and speech. Words
are simply strung together by the automatic machine that Gurdjieff called the 'formatory apparatus': there is no one speaking
and no one thinking. It is therefore very important that we should
practice asking ourselves, "What do these words proceeding in me
mean?" This in itself can bring about at least a temporary contact
with their meaning. Of course, 'asking ourselves' in this sense
is more than forming another string of words in our minds; it is
a concentration of sensitive energy. Everyone assumes that they
have feelings, but in reality most people have little sensitivity in
their feeling life. It is all closed in to a narrow circle of reac-

tions. If we begin seriously to study our emotional life, especially if we can do this with others who have the same aim, we will soon see how much imagination we have about it and how emotionally insensitive we are to people. Gurdjieff, in the final chapter of *Beelzebub's Tales,* has a great deal to say about the impoverishment of our emotional life. In the ancient analogy in which the body of man is represented by a carriage, in Gurdjieff's version a 'hackney carriage', the mind is represented by the driver and the feelings by the horse. Gurdjieff gives us a picture of the horse as a broken-down, maltreated nag who is the slave of anyone who shows it the least bit of affection. And he goes on to describe how, whenever there really is experience of feeling, we are incapable of giving it expression and as a result become more and more cut off from other people and 'driven back inside' ourselves. The feelings should really be the way of opening ourselves.

It is very difficult to work directly on the feelings; the body is much easier. By simply bringing our attention into the body, it becomes sensitive. This we properly call 'sensing' and the energy involved, 'sensation'. Work with the head brain is also much easier than with the feeling brain. It is possible to some degree to keep our attention on an idea or a pattern. By combining sensitive thought with sensitive bodily presence, something can be evoked in the feelings. The most practical way of overcoming automatisms in any brain is by combining the action of the other two.

It is not true to say that with the sensitive energy we are able to initiate an action. Sensitive operations depend on what has gone before. It enables us to choose within an existing situation but not to change the situation itself. To go beyond what actually exists and to become free from 'yes' and 'no' we require the cosmic energies.

The Cosmic Energies

With the cosmic energies, we go within our awareness, to regions where our ordinary experience is 'outside'. It is in these regions, and with these energies, that we have the possibility of becoming free. They are the energies beyond life. With them our identity goes beyond that of a living body.

E4 - Conscious Energy

In ordinary speech, 'consciousness' means the state of being aware of things going on, produced by the sensitive energy. What we mean by consciousness is something of a higher order that can be described crudely as an 'awareness of our ordinary awareness'. If we want to understand transformation in man, it is necessary to understand the distinction between sensitivity and consciousness. It is easy to believe that we can 'observe ourselves'. Most people even take it for granted that they know what is going on in themselves and what their states are, but most so-called self-observation is simply the observation by one center of another. For example, we can think of our body and the way in which it is moving or feel the thoughts that are coursing through our minds. All this is just the observation by one center of the functioning of another center. In it we do not see ourselves; it is the parts of ourselves that are seeing each other. Real self-observation requires what is called the 'separation of oneself from oneself'. This means a separation from all the functioning of thought, feeling, and body. Our functioning is then still part of 'us' but 'we' are no longer just a part of it. Once we have had this experience, the taste is unmistakable when it comes to us again. But when it is not there, we can very easily deceive ourselves that it is.

It is because conscious energy is a cosmic energy that we cannot make ourselves conscious. It does not come directly from efforts, as sensitivity does. As we learn more about the transformation of energies, we will come to understand that there is always a spontaneous component in the arising of consciousness. That is why the act of voluntary attention, which awakens consciousness, is essentially creative.

Consciousness can also be liberated in us by shocks, such as intense emotional impacts. This makes possible a whole series of transformations. The conscious energy can blend with the automatic energy in us, and the result is energy of an intermediate level, that is, sensitivity. Gurdjieff formulated this kind of transformation as 'the higher blends with the lower to actualize the middle, which is higher for the preceding lower and lower for the succeeding higher'. This spells out what happens very exactly. The sensitive energy that is liberated is then available for blending with the energy above consciousness, the creative energy. The result is more consciousness. It is possible for us to look at things in a new way, to think and feel in a new way. But we are at risk because of the conditioning inherent in our sensitivity, where we keep our self-image, our assumptions, our attitudes, and our dreams. These bring into play a disorganizing force. We 'cannot bear' the contradictions in us, the combination of yes and no that is made possible by the concentration of conscious energy. Very quickly, we 'go back to sleep'. The world looks too different from how we have assumed it to be.

So, although it is not right to say that we can make ourselves conscious, we can prepare for consciousness by giving our sensitivity experience of the combination of 'yes' and 'no', and also of 'inner' and 'outer'. This was Ouspensky's way of preparing people for the experience of 'self-remembering', which he said we could only pretend to bring about in ourselves, because we are not able to summon up enough emotional energy. To bring about a 'shock' in oneself is a very great thing and a rare ability. We should also add that bringing about shocks in other people, even with the intention of 'doing them good', is highly undesirable because the result of this is dependence and lack of spontaneity.

When consciousness is in us, we see that our ordinary state of awareness is like sleep, or like 'flatland'. We see that in this ordinary state we believe ourselves to be some being that is there, whereas in reality there is no such being. What is revealed is not a being but the image of a being. Only with a sufficient concentration of conscious energy is this clear. In our ordinary state, there is usually so little that at best all we can have is some nagging suspicion that 'things are not as they seem to be'. Even this little gives us some freedom to work. It is said that it is always possible for us to 'remember ourselves' even if it is only for a fraction of a second. It is very important that we do what we can do with the amount of conscious energy that we have. People working together under certain conditions can concentrate enough conscious energy for at least some of them to 'wake up' and see something, and this will be of benefit to all of them.

It takes a long time for us to become accustomed to the separation of consciousness and sensitivity in us. Nothing of this is cultivated through the ordinary processes of education. We have to learn how to recognize perceptions and actions of a higher order, and we have to train ourselves in the way of 'struggle with ourselves', the bringing about of the struggle between 'yes' and 'no', by which the soil is prepared for the sowing of conscious seeds.

When consciousness comes, it is more true to say that it has us than that we have it. We have the ridiculous phrase, 'I am conscious', which we use in the same way as 'I am hot'. It would be better to say, 'I am conscioused'. It is our sensitivity which persuades us that we 'have' consciousness or that we 'have' an 'I'. Consciousness is not personalized and it is not localized. It is everywhere. When we claim it as our own, this is as silly as claiming that the atmosphere is ours because we can take a breath. We are so concerned with external things that we are not aware that consciousness is inside everything. It is differently concentrated in different things, and has very different effects. When we catch a glimpse of the reality of consciousness in nature, it is a great and wonderful thing. Then we really begin to understand that consciousness is not a human prerogative.

One of the most striking effects of consciousness in us is that kind of experience in which we are aware that as we look at something, we are being seen. This is such a reversal to our ordinary way of experiencing that it is quite unmistakably something of a higher order.

Though consciousness is not something we can control, as we can switch on or off a light, we can learn to put ourselves in the way of conscious experience. It is consciousness that makes us aware of what we are and *it* enables us to think what we wish to think, feel what we wish to feel, and move our bodies as we intend. It is consciousness that enables us to experience all of our centers simultaneously.

If we go back to our picture of the land and the sea, entering into conscious experience is like plunging into the water. We need to learn how to swim. We cannot act upon the world of consciousness but we can learn to participate in it, and take part in the energy transformations which sustain it. Man has the role of linking together the world of life and the world of the cosmic energies. The liberation of consciousness in us is a cosmic obligation.

Many practices which have come down to us from ancient times are to do with the liberation of consciousness. One that is especially informative is the 'stilling of the mind' or, in yogic terms, 'constraint on the fluctuations of the mind-stuff'. Through this we do become an 'object of consciousness', but we do not become by this alone a 'being in our own right'. For this, higher orders of energy are needed, for consciousness itself must be transformed.

E3 - Creative Energy

The second of the cosmic energies is beyond consciousness and for this reason has a hidden quality. This does not mean that it is a rare thing for this energy to work in us. The creative energy is in the sexual act, but what we experience of it are its results in the sensitive energy. We are not aware of the action in which the child is conceived or the man and woman joined together. The creative energy is beyond 'our' reach, but we are not beyond the reach of it. We can be the instrument through which the creative energy acts in the world. It is the highest energy which can work in man. Perhaps the decisive difference between man and any animal is that man is endowed with the possibility of being a conscious instrument of creativity.

There is a special sense in which to use the word 'seeing'. We want to use this word in a way that does not signify the action of our organs of sight nor even our awareness in general. Seeing is a much higher thing than knowing or feeling or sensing because it is a direct perception of how things are. Then we are able to know everything that is necessary for us to know, whether of ourselves or of the world. The conscious energy by which we can observe ourselves is under the control of the creative energy. It is the creative power which gives us access to what is beyond ourselves, the cosmic process. It bypasses the ordinary centers, and operates through what Gurdjieff calls the 'higher centers'.

The creative energy is the energy which gives us freedom, and enables us to create ourselves. It is the energy through which we are able to exercise voluntary attention. When we try to attend, we find we have very little power to do it. It all slips away, no matter how hard we try. This gives us a measure of our effective freedom. The creative energy is the energy of 'I', and it is only when the will and this energy are united that we have power. A man is only a free individual when he can have the working of the creative energy united with his everyday life.

Creative energy is released in the transformation of our consciousness. This transformation we can know in terms of the diminishing power that 'negative emotions' have over us, and the increasing power that 'positive emotions' have in us. These terms are the ones used by Gurdjieff. The 'negative emotions' are the ordinary emotions which are under the law that they must produce their opposites, so that pity turns to disgust and love to hate. The 'positive emotions' have no opposites, though they may have the same names as negative ones, such as 'joy', 'hope' or 'love'. The positive emotions are not reactions, but something evoked in our consciousness by the creative energy. To transform consciousness, the unitive energy which is of a higher order than the creative energy must take part. While the unitive energy is present everywhere, we men are hardly open to it. The reason for this is very important to understand. The energy of consciousness always produces in us the feeling of 'I'. The possibility of the transformation of consciousness in us is something we are most afraid of because it appears to us that this will result in the loss of our 'I'. Here we have the mystical experience of the 'dark night of the soul', in which comes the fear of losing who we are.

But it is only when we can allow this emptying in ourselves that the unitive energy can enter and, in transforming the consciousness, produce the creative energy, which is the energy of our real 'I', not the one that we feel.Then we are a man 'who can do', according to Gurdjieff's definition. That means that we become creators in our own right, truly 'like God'.

In the first kind of transformation we spoke of - that is, the action of consciousness upon automatism, which produces sensitivity - it would be quite right to say that 'we ourselves' have to do the work, as long as we realize that what we mean by 'we' is consciousness. But in this second kind of transformation, we draw on the unitive energy, and such a way of talking would be utterly wrong. Our role is one of submission.

It is always the case that, even with the very highest things, it is possible for us yet very ordinary men to get a taste. One of the ways in which the creative energy works in us is in the revelation of our own nothingness. If consciousness shows us that we are asleep, creativity shows us that we are nothing at all. The conscious energy can produce in us the feeling that 'I' am seeing my sleep. Before the creative energy, the 'I' vanishes altogether and nothing at all is left. This is not the same as even acute depression, which is only a sensitive state. It is what in Sufism is called *fanā*, which means 'annihilation', and in this form of it, even if only for a moment, we are dead to ourselves and to the world. It is said that 'to "do" we must give up the illusion of doing'.

E₂ - Unitive Energy

The world is constantly under the action of the unitive energy, which we can also call the energy of cosmic love, though we must realize that it rarely reaches man directly. Man, as he is, is not a being of love, not even in the way that he is creative. Love is the redemptive power by which the lower orders of creation are enabled to return to the Source. We can hardly guess at its nature;

but we believe that it is the power which makes us all one and undivided, in which there are not many wills but only One Will. It is beyond our understanding, but we feel that it can only enter us when our own will is surrendered.

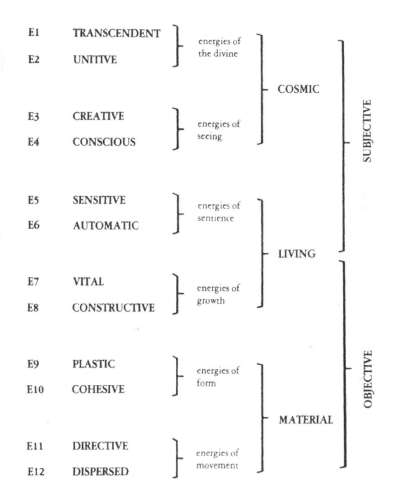

SCHEME OF ENERGIES
FIG. 2.2

El - Transcendental Energy

All we can say is that this energy transcends the bounds of the creation, and we postulate it as the master of all energies.

The whole of the creation is engaged in a universal transformation, which Gurdjieff referred to as the *trogoautoegocrat.* All the energies are necessary for this purpose. And all the energies concern us, even though the top two are quite beyond our reach and the lower energies are common to everything that exists, and are not specific for life, this Earth, or even for material bodies as we know them. We people are made so that we are able to transform a whole range of energies, from the material energies through the life energies - two of which, the automatic and the sensitive, we can experience more or less directly - to the cosmic energies of consciousness and creativity. The higher energies cannot be transformed in us, however, unless there is conscious work. Freedom is not a property of man; he has to create it in himself. This is the goal of 'work on oneself'. We say, with Gurdjieff, that man is a cosmic apparatus for the transformation of energies; that is, a special container or vessel in which energies, even energies of a very high order, can be brought together. Yet man is a very peculiar apparatus because he has the possibility to choose how he will be used. Either he can live in a dream world of his hopes and fears, desires and ambitions, and the pursuit of some phantom of 'happiness', unconscious and uncaring of the transformations that are brought about in the energies of which he is made, or he can become a conscious instrument of transformation and then no longer live, as the former is bound to do, only as an animal. It is by conscious work that man fulfills his cosmic obligations. It is by this very same work that he can attain an imperishable reality.

CHAPTER 3

Three-Centered Being

At the end of *Beelzebub's Tales,* Gurdjieff appends an extract from a lecture of his that was read in New York in 1924. The lecture was called 'The Variety, according to Law, of the Manifestations of Human Individuality', and in this he asserts that it is in the very nature of man, by the time he has reached 'responsible age', to consist of 'four distinct personalities'. Three of these 'personalities' are what we know as the automatisms of thinking, feeling, and moving; and the fourth is the master of these automatisms, the real 'I'. For there to be this master, each of the three component personalities requires its own particular form of education in order to be 'spiritualized'.

The beginning of the study of centers is in observing the differences between different kinds of perceptions, different needs and desires, and different functionings. We begin to realize that the various instinctive processes of the body, such as the circulation of the blood, respiration, digestion, and so on, enter into our activity and shape our behavior in a way we are not ordinarily even aware of. Gurdjieff, as Beelzebub, sarcastically remarks on the way our mentation is influenced by the 'organs of digestion and sex'. The instinctive processes go by themselves and are organized by themselves apart from the rest of us. Then there are instruments such as our hands, which carry with them the inclination to be doing things, whether we are active or indolent. Our hands have this 'doing' nature in their own right. Every part of the body that can manifest in the external world has this nature. All of this, internal and outer directed, is one complex with its own organization. It is exactly as if there is an 'instinctive-moving' person who is breathing, digesting, looking, walking, handling, and making.

We can begin to recognize an emotional life in the states, interests, reactions, moods, desires, and all the things which give our experience its color and its direction. There are also states which are, so to say, grafted on to the emotional life by disfunctions of. the body, so that from illness there comes depression and from injuries negativity. However it arises, this emotional life is not 'ours' but has a logic or an automatism of its own. There is in us a personality of emotion which is not the same as the 'moving-instinctive' personality. It is also not the same as the personality of thinking. Thoughts go on continuously in our minds: words, pictures, and dreams. They come and they go; they are coherent and incoherent. There is analysis and association. All of this goes by itself and thinking is also a personality in itself.

According to Gurdjieff, man without the fourth personality, his own principle of wholeness, is just like three people living in one organism. In the ordinary state, the three components of thinking, feeling, and moving are not in communication and only act on each other mechanically, being 'outside' each other. This is inevitably what the study of our functions leads us to see, but it does not come easily. It is straightforward enough to learn how to group the functions in us into three parts, but it is a bigger thing really to see for ourselves that each of these parts has its own principle of organization. For the greater part of our lives, 'we' are living in only one of the three. Our center of gravity passes from thinking to feeling to moving from moment to moment, and we are nearly always identified with the function 'we' happen to be in. But we can make use, when it happens, of the observation by one 'brain' of another, to learn that there are such things as 'brains' associated with the feeling and moving functions as well as with the thinking (where we tend to take it for granted).

What we mean by the word 'brain' is not simply part of our physiological organization, to be associated with an aspect of the nervous system. The moving part, for example, can exhibit the most extraordinary skills that show without doubt that it is organized on the sensitive level and not only on the automatic level of the nerves and blood. Indeed, what we intend to mean by 'brain' is the organization of a function on all levels, and in this sense, a brain can even be creative. As the level of organization of a brain is raised, it becomes more subjective. When this passes into the levels of cosmic energy, we say that the brain is becoming spiritualized.

This brings us to will, and why Gurdjieff used the three different terms 'brain', 'spiritualization' and 'center'. A brain is a specific way in which the will can be related to the world of bodies. When a brain is spiritualized, it acts from the will and it is the will that is the center. So, when we used this word 'center' we are talking about thinking, feeling and moving from the side of will rather than from the side of function. When a man is truly a 'three-centered being' he has real 'I', or his own will.

A three-centered being has all the same possibilities as the 'Actualizer of Everything Existing'. It is therefore the most extraordinary thing, very far away from the ordinary state of man. As we are, we are not only not free but we are also unbalanced. Generally speaking, everyone tends to have one of their brains of body, feeling and mind more active than the others. This gives us a very lopsided kind of experience and life. Gurdjieff called a man dominated by his body Man Number 1; by his feelings Man Number 2 and by his intellectual apparatus, Man Number 3. None of them is able to act freely and none of them is able to come to the threshold of transformation, or even an understanding of it, because this requires the coordinated and balanced working of all three brains.

In one of Gurdjieff's most famous aphorisms, he says that 'Understanding with one brain is hallucination; understanding with two brains is semi-hallucination; only understanding with three brains is really understanding'. It is a common illusion to believe that we can do something to begin our transformation if we subject ourselves to certain kinds of influences or practice certain kinds of exercises, but none of these is any use unless we have reached the starting point.

It is only the man who is balanced, called by Gurdjieff Man Number 4, who is able to have a real purpose in life, who can understand what he wants, and who can begin to work toward his own transformation. He is the first kind of man that we can call normal, a man in the true sense of the word. He is able to function through his own initiative and his efforts will be productive. In contrast to this, men of the first three kinds are always handicapped. Their knowledge of things is incomplete and distorted, biased toward what they can think about, or react to, or sense. Their attempts at action are lopsided and even counterproductive. For real, and not imaginary, work of transformation, we have to reach the starting point. It is this that can take quite a long time. Sometimes it is said that 'the first step is the hardest of all'.

The Three Worlds in Man

The three worlds that we spoke about in the first chapter were those of function, being, and will. Everything that exists, including man, has a place in each of these worlds. We can also say that each of the three worlds is in everything.

Will does not always mean freedom and being does not always mean self-consciousness. As ordinary men we are still subject to will, but we do not have our own 'I', and our level of being may be no more than that of an automatism. When something exists entirely through exchanges of energy that are contained in material bodies, there is nothing in it which can survive physical destruction. And when something has no individualized will, it can operate only as part of the world process. Man has the possibility of attaining imperishable being and having a real 'I', but it is only a possibility.

If man is to transform himself, the three worlds of will, being, and function must combine in him. It is only in a work that realizes an individual will, produces a coherent being, and coordinates a variety of functions that he can become as he ought to be. This is the real meaning of the phrase "three-centered being": the wholeness of a man derives from each of the three worlds, and in the man who is transformed they are no longer separate but work synergically 'as one'. We can form some picture of this by trying to imagine what each of the worlds would be like in complete isolation from the other two.

Function alone is meaningless mechanism. It is for nothing and it is nothing. We can go back to Ouspensky's room and picture it totally in darkness with no one to sleep on the bed, no one to look through the microscope, and no one to sew with the sewing machine. It is a world without depth, in which nothing has any identity of its own. There is only a 'going-on', a movement that changes nothing. It corresponds to the 'mechanical view' of the universe, in which it is supposed that there is nothing but mechanism and that identity and purpose are illusory. We can try to project ourselves into the world of a one-brained animal, say a worm. The experience of a worm such as it is must closely correspond to what we mean by the world of function, lacking in the depth of being and the purposefulness of will. The totally functional condition is not beyond our experience. Traditionally, this is referred to by such names as the 'outer darkness', where men live as mechanisms among mechanisms and nothing has any meaning.

Pure will alone is the state before the creation of the world, an affirmation lacking in the means of its realization. Very probably, it was an intuition of this state that came to Schopenhauer and led him to consider will to be a blind urge, in itself incapable of vision. The 'man' in Ouspensky's room reaches out in the darkness; not only can he not see the instruments but neither can he recognize them if he could, nor are there any instruments at all. He is in a void; he reaches out in nothingness, blindly. Something of this condition is communicated to us by the will, when we feel an urge that has nothing to do with what exists or can be known. It is a longing that has no words, form, or comprehensible objective. What is lacking is the creative power 'to do', and a field of action.

The state of pure being is 'light' in the room with nothing to be seen and no one to see; a blank state of awareness where dream and reality cannot be distinguished because there is nothing by which to distinguish them. Nothing is happening and there is no aim or purpose. There are times when something akin to this state comes over us, creating a hiatus or totally blank condition very different from sleep.

Everything that belongs to the real world is a combination of function, being, and will. To man is given the possibility of transforming this combination in him, that is, of becoming a 'self-creator', a being of 'three centers'. It is in the brains that this work begins, but we must be careful not to fall back into the delusion that we 'are something' apart from them and that it is 'we' who work upon them. At the beginning of the work there has to come a re-education of the three brains so that each of them in its own particular domain comes to operate in a normal fashion. Such as we are, we do not have a normal intellectual, emotional, or physical life. Instead of the normal urges we are filled with abnormal needs and desires, urges which are unrelated to our true well-being. We have imaginary pictures of what is needed for our bodies, we cultivate negative emotions, and we allow our heads to be stuffed with nonsense. Little by little we have to develop an understanding of what thinking, feeling, and action are and what they are for.

Each of the three brains is an organization of functions, which can operate with greater or lesser degrees of awareness. An ancient picture of the thinking apparatus is that of a lamp. When a lamp is filled with a heavy oil it smokes and smells; but when it is filled with a light, clear oil that has been filtered and purified the flame is bright and clear and the light it gives is strong and steady.

The grades of fuel correspond to the levels of energy, as these in their turn correspond to levels of awareness. The higher energies in us have very much to do with our possibilities of functioning beyond the boundaries of what we have become conditioned to do. Everybody knows how a challenge can evoke the most extraordinary response from people. Countless people have reported on the feats of ingenuity they have performed, often in a fraction of a second, when in danger. But waiting for shocks or challenges from outside is no way to undertake the work of transformation. We can begin to work with the exercise of our own initiative in our functions so that instead of moving, thinking, or feeling in reaction to a stimulus, we move, think, or feel from we ourselves. Our power to do this is limited, but we need to learn to use the power that we have.

Man as a three-brained being has three kinds of intelligence, because each of the brains is intelligent in its own way. The brain is the being of the given center and brings into operation the will that in itself we can never know. Each brain perceives, functions, and experiences in a different way, and it is that which produces the experience or taste of three fundamental urges. These urges are not themselves the will; they are the threefold 'face' of it that we can see. Each center is an urge in us. There is the 'will-to-see' of the thinking center: the urge to grasp and understand reality which has its distant echoes in the naggings of curiosity. There is the 'will-to-be' of the feeling center; the urge to become whole with oneself and the world that can turn into its opposite of vanity. There is the 'will-to-live' of the moving center; the urge to do and to retain a hold on life. By these urges we can be spiritualized. It is through them that the worlds of function, being, and will can become a whole reality: the world of function through the moving center, the world of being through the feeling center and the world of will through the thinking center: and the three of them as one.

The Moving Center

It is not immediately clear what form bodily or moving intelligence might take. Our difficulty in visualizing the intelligence of the body brain arises because we think that it must somehow be similar to the intelligence that we are aware of in the thinking brain. But it is not at all the same. The moving brain is associated with parts of the nervous system, in the spinal cord and parts of the head brain, that do not work in the same way as those parts which operate in mental association. Our thinking intelligence is very much engaged in connecting past and future, but this does not enter the experience of the moving part. The intelligence of the body is almost wholly concerned with the immediate present. It does not make plans. It is not concerned with results in the future or correcting something that has happened in the past. Things are registered by the body, but not as the memories the mind knows. They are either active or latent, but not yesterday or last year.

Most people realize that the moving part of us works very much faster than the thinking part. Something falls off the table and our hands have reached out, saved it, and returned it before our 'minds' have begun to notice what has happened. In spite of such common experiences, we are always making the mistake of treating everything that the body does as 'automatic,' associating purpose and awareness only with our minds. The moving intelligence of the body brain gives us the power to perform very complex tasks. It is essential in the learning of languages, where we have to acquire a skill by imitation and be able to make a response quicker than we can think. If we had to rely on the thinking brain for the carrying out of actions we would never be able to live as human beings. Our minds may say 'I will go to such and such a place' but it is the intelligence of the body which will get us there, will drive the car, respond to road conditions, adjust to the environment and the machine which is transporting us. The absurdity is that because the moving center does not daydream most people regard it as unconscious.

The brain we are talking about has two aspects to it, and sometimes Gurdjieff distinguished these two by giving them different names. There is both an instinctive function, which deals with the regulation of our physiological activities, and a moving function, which deals with our outward activities. The instinctive brain gives us the extraordinary power of inner regulation that is proper to a human organism. Whereas our thinking brains can deal, at most, with only two or three ideas at a time, the digestive process alone involves the balance and coordination of hundreds of different functions, all of which affect each other. The instinctive processes of the body are ready to function at birth. Some of them, such as growth and the circulation of the blood, are at work even long before we are born. From the moment of birth, food can no longer be taken in a prepared form through the umbilical cord, but within hours or days, at the most, the child is able to take it in through the mouth and digest it by itself.

Breathing is a remarkable power. Before birth, we breathe through our mother. After birth, we ourselves breathe. Breathing is, perhaps, the most powerful urge that we can know. If something interferes with our breathing, everything else disappears except the will to breathe: thoughts, feelings, and all other bodily forces are as nothing. We do not breathe because we know that we have to breathe; we simply breathe because we have to. We cannot put our finger on this urge and say, 'Here it is; it is this'. The urge has the hidden character of the will, and, although it can dominate our experience, it is not possible for us to experience it as something of which we can be aware. It is never objective. In comparison, our so-called decisions and choices are in reality very far away from will. It represents a total commitment that our minds are incapable of understanding.

In breathing, we see the urge to live. This urge is apparent in all those cases where people cling on to life, even though their bodies are damaged or diseased, and no matter how severe their agony. What is working in them is the will of the instinctive center to preserve life at all costs. It has nothing to do with the mind or the feelings or any external action. So it is possible to go through life without once being aware that there is a mystery in the preservation of our existence.

The activities of our moving center are not already prepared, as are those of instinct. It is the moving center which gives us the power of dealing with the world, but the human being is far less prepared for external action at the moment of birth than any other animal. A newborn reindeer is able to run with the herd. A moment after birth, a monkey can grasp and hold on to things and stop itself from falling. It is very extraordinary how helpless the human infant is. So many things that are instinctive for the animals have to be learned by humans. This is so because there is a creative potential in the moving center of man. And this power of creative action is most closely associated with our hands. Our hands are very extraordinary instruments. No other animal has anything which is nearly as versatile. It is through this instrument that nearly all our powers of 'making' come. It is also striking that the fundamental difference between *Homo erectus,* such as the Neanderthal man, and *Homo sapiens sapiens,* that is, men such as we are, is not in brain capacity but in the anatomical power of speech.

We are able to move in most of the ways that animals can, apart from flying. We can climb, we can crawl, we can walk and lope and run and jump and dance; we can tumble and toss and turn. But it takes time to acquire these skills. Much of a child's learning consists of the recognition of objects and how to handle them; how to produce sounds, these things are learned by imitation, which is a power of the moving center. But this imitation is not the copying that turns adults into slaves, because it is stimulated by a creative power. It is a very unfortunate thing that the development of the moving intelligence so often comes to a stop even during childhood. The human body has an enormous potential and contemporary education develops very little of it.

It is in the nature of the moving brain to do things, that is, produce changes in the external environment. This we have to a far greater extent than any animal because so much of their external activity is connected with the preservation of life. We have the urge to adapt the world to ourselves rather than adapt ourselves to the world. We are *Homo faber,* man the maker. Of course, our thinking is very much drawn into our activity in the world of bodies, but it is from the urge of the body that this comes. So much human effort is devoted, through the artifacts we have created as well as through our natural instruments, to extending our powers to act upon the world. It is this urge which makes us go out over the earth, exploring, changing, experimenting. This urge is not the urge to understand or to know, but to produce results that we can see. Its place is the world of bodies, the *ālam-i ajsām.*

There is another powerful urge connected with the body and that is the urge which drives us to sex. This is very powerful because it is intimately connected with the working of the creative energy. We can treat it as something in its own right, apart from both the urge-to-live of the instinctive brain and the urge-to-act of the moving brain. Yet it is still a power in our bodies rather than in our minds or feelings. It should not be thought of in terms of desires or wishes. Certainly these things arise, but they are not at the center of sex. The feelings, thoughts, and tensions that arise in us in association with sex are nothing but a reflection of the confusion that exists in us. It may seem strange to say that the true sexual urge is beyond our experience, but that is how it is. Many people say that the secret of our transformation lies in sex; but this is not the 'sex' that we know: it is the creative urge that lies beyond the scope of our awareness.

We now begin to see that in this one region of the functions of the body, we have to take account of three urges: to live, to 'do', and to sex. These are the normal urges, not those habits into which we have become conditioned. To realize them, to become 'spiritualized' in the world of bodies or the world of function, we have to accustom ourselves to the working of higher levels of energy in the body brain. Gurdjieff also devoted an enormous effort to finding ways in which the intelligence of movement could be actualized in people. We have a marvelous capacity for doing things with our bodies, but most of the time is spent in stereotyped postures, gestures, and motions. We have the possibility denied the other animals of acting on this world in a creative manner and yet an honest appraisal of what we do with the earth shows that most of our 'creations' are not only lacking in creativity but deny it entry into our lives. As for the normal sexual urge which should be in man, its effects are nowhere to be found, so overlaid with all kinds of rubbish is our sexuality. And, despite the fact that our instinctive workings are largely 'out of sight', we nevertheless manage to disrupt many of them as well, through what Gurdjieff called our 'way of life, unbecoming to three brained beings': ulcers, heart disease, cancers of various kinds, the troubles we cause for our bodies are endless. First, we have to become aware of the senseless habits that we have. Second, we have to explore the potentials of our bodies and become familiar with how they work. No work of transformation is possible without knowledge of our own body. Third, we have to accustom the body to entirely new usages, and for this purpose the ability to concentrate the sensitive energy in the form of sensation is indispensable. As we said before, if the operation of one brain is to be changed, it is necessary to bring to bear the other two. In the system of movements created by Gurdjieff, all three brains are educated to work together.

The Feeling Center

In all his writings, Gurdjieff emphasizes again and again that our modern system of education completely neglects our feeling nature, which is, for that reason, our most immature function. Our feelings tend to be very unreliable, very unstable, and we cannot think as we want largely because our feelings are in control. For most of the time, we have automatic emotions of like and dislike. We also spend a great deal of our time in states of emotion that are unmistakably negative, such as anger, pity, and fear. We can realize through this how far we are away from what we ought to be as human beings, for these negative emotions serve no useful purpose and are quite unnecessary. They have been grafted onto us by our environment, arising in the first place as an emotional counterpart to the instinctive reactions we have to pain and bodily discomfort. It can even be to some extent that these are hereditary, and now part and parcel of our lives. What it all means is that our feelings are in a state of slavery. It is only when we have worked so as not to express negative emotions, and then so as to be able to neutralize them when they arise, that we can begin to understand the potential of our feeling nature and what purpose it should serve.

The true power of the feelings is to be able to perceive directly how things are. This is not done through knowing, sight, or hearing but through participation, by entering into things. The feeling nature of the normal man can penetrate into the depth of the world, beyond the world of bodies, which we can reach with our senses, and beyond what can be grasped by conceptual thinking. The real nature of feeling is not in time and space but in 'eternity'. Eternity is the zone of experience in which things do not go on as processes but are what they are.[6]

According to Gurdjieff, the disorganization of our feeling nature extends even to its physiological base. Whereas the moving and thinking brains can be associated with definite places, the feeling brain is scattered in the 'nerve nodes', the majority of which are concentrated in the solar plexus. The unification of the feelings is a very great thing.

Very often it is the feeling nature in us that first starts us on the path of transformation. We feel our own emptiness and have a longing to have some substance for ourselves or to have an assurance that we have a place in the world. These feelings are genuine and an expression of the normal urge that can move our feelings: the urge-to-be. This is not the same as the urge that is proper to our bodies. The worm, for example, lived and fulfilled its function better than we do long before we appeared, and probably long after we will have disappeared the worm will go on playing its

---

6 Bennett used eternity in a technical sense as one of six fundamental dimensions of existence. These are the three dimensions which are space-like, plus the three that are time-like: successive time, eternity or potential, and hyparxis, the dimension of interaction between potential and actual. In eternity there is the pattern of things, as in successive time there is their behavior. If time has to do with function, eternity has to do with being.

part in maintaining this planet, but it is satisfied with merely living. We are not always satisfied with this, and in reality we need something more. We can try to fill our feelings by acting on the world, doing things, possessing things, or we can try to come to some mental mastery of the world by knowing. Yet however much we bring our powers of thought and our powers of action to the front of our life, this never satisfies what is in our feelings. Something is lacking in us and we have an inner hunger that drives us on, an urge to come closer to other people, to overcome our inner emptiness, and to find our place in the scheme of things. It is only when we stop trying to use the world to fill this hunger that things can begin to come right for us. Then we can begin to feel how great a contradiction there is between the state in which we are and what is destined for us. We cannot come to this by thought. We have to feel how big a task there is in front of man - if only he can take it on.

It is almost impossible to arrive at what man truly is by thinking. But when our feelings are open to something deeper and the ordinary emotional uproar is abated in us, then it is possible to feel what this human nature is, feel that it has been present on the earth for many thousand years, and feel the greatness of the destiny that belongs to it. This is how it is when our feeling nature becomes open to the working of the higher energies. So essential is the right working of our feelings that we can say that the transformation of man is the same as the transformation of his feeling nature. Until this has begun, transformation has not begun at all in any way.

The sense of inner emptiness can give us, under the right conditions, a drive for unity and completeness not only within ourselves but with others. We seek the feeling that we belong together. This need for other people is quite different from the need to know about them or to do things with them. It is also very different, though this is hard for us to understand in the ordinary state, from the desire to be with people who like us or are good to us. That sort of desire can do nothing for us. Neither can the almost universal habit among people of talking, which is thought to be 'communicating', help us to *be* together. This kind of 'communication' keeps us separate. It is trying to do with function what belongs to being. When we can be with other people and not be altogether wrapped up in our own associations, it is a very big thing. It enables us to be with other people in silence and feel ourselves at one with them. If we are able to share in this way, a connection is made which does not depend on knowing, but is a direct awareness. Only when this sort of experience begins to play a significant part in our lives can we begin to be what we are.

Beyond this awareness we can come to the highest level in being, which is love. Then we are led entirely beyond ourselves to the unity of everything. It is a rare thing for men.

The urge to be, which has as its culmination love, takes root in us through the feeling of our own emptiness. It is clouded by our 'lust for existence', the drive to fill ourselves from things outside. We need to be disillusioned with the world and what it can give us; we need to see that our feelings should not be dependent on what comes to us from the external world. The feeling nature is not designed for the world of bodies but for the *ālam-i arvāh,* which we described as the 'world of energies'. It does not work from the outside of things. The *ālam-i arvāh* in its original meaning was the world of 'spirits', which we can understand as the 'essence of things', or what they are.

It is only when we begin to get a clear picture of the privation of our feeling lives that we can begin to see the urgency of the need for work upon ourselves. We are hardly able to feel more than one thing at the same time: we are happy or we are sad, but rarely both. We have to understand that this is slavery. Struggle with slavery of our feeling nature is hardly possible in isolation from others; but it is no easy thing to be able to take advantage of group conditions. At the Prieuré, Gurdjieff told the people with him, "You have come here having understood the necessity of struggling with yourself and only with yourself. Therefore thank everyone who gives you the opportunity to do so."

The Thinking Center

The head brain is the one with which we think ourselves most familiar, but even specialists who have devoted a great deal of study to it fail to understand its real power. The reason for this is that it works in vastly different ways, according to the level of energy with which it is working. It is not enough to study it in its ordinary level of function.

Even at the ordinary level, the head brain of man distinguishes him from other animals. Man has a different relationship to time and space: he can look toward the past and the future and put his attention on things of different scales. He has a power of representation that can be quite independent of bodily stimuli, and this enables him to acquire a kind of knowledge that animals cannot. We can store and compare experiences and recognize regularities and repetitions; and from this we can do something to predict the future. We can form a picture of how the world works through the power of abstraction. With this knowledge we can enhance the power we have of action upon the world. We can see what can be done with different materials and what kind of instruments can be made. All of this belongs to the world of ordinary things. It does not give us freedom because it is nothing more than a reflection of the world of bodies.

As we are, our thinking works entirely in accordance with the state of our nervous system and the chemistry of our blood. When there is no external demand made of us, we spend most of our time in a dream state where mental images automatically form themselves. This is influenced and even dominated by our bodily sensations - what we see, hear, and touch - and by the condition of our organism, so that when we are in a healthy active state we have one kind of thought and when we are sick we have another. Sometimes the dreams in us take the form of pictures, but more commonly they take the form of words, inner talking, and conversations. Gurdjieff referred to this state as 'formatting', and said that as we are we do not have minds, we have only a 'formatory apparatus'. This apparatus is a mechanism in us that only turns over words with no contact with their meaning, and it is very dominant in us men of the contemporary world.

Yet it is through the inefficient and disorganized state of our thinking that we can first receive an impetus to work on ourselves. The mind, unlike the feelings or the body, can be told about the possibility of transformation. If we can learn how to use this madcap apparatus of ours that we call 'thinking', something productive can come out of it. The same associative mechanism that keeps us in the realms of dreams can also help us to work. It can be trained to keep an idea before us, a picture of how we can be. By this we become able to notice our slavery and blindness. But it is the next step that is crucial. Whenever we find ourselves in our thought aware of the idea of work, we should make a corresponding effort to practice what might otherwise remain only a possibility in our thinking. If, for example, we have the thought of being aware of ourselves, we should bring this into our bodies and become aware of our physical presence. Then from the two sides of thought and sensation we can try to become aware of our feeling state as well. In this way, our thoughts can become a reminder to work, and when this has become second nature to us, something can begin to change in our thinking so that it is not always so weak and passive as it ordinarily is.

We can think of what we call the mind as a 'sensitive screen' on which images, verbal as well as visual, arising from various sources are thrown. The usefulness of these images for our understanding and our ability to exercise some control over them depends on the energies at work. Ordinarily, it is the automatic energy which dominates, and this produces the dream state. With the higher energies, the instrument is the same and forms images in the same way, but their source is different. There begins to be expressed in us the fundamental urge of the thinking center: the urge-to-see. This urge gives us the need for things to make sense; but we should not identify it with the dissatisfaction that arises in us when things are disconnected and we fail to see how they fit together. The urge-to-see arises from within and it is inherently creative. We find ourselves no longer content to pursue a particular course of knowledge simply because we have been in the habit of doing so. We try to fit what we know into a larger and larger context. From the moment of birth we are reaching out to understand why the world is as it is, and the gradual organization of this is our intellectual power. Automatic thinking is a cul-de-sac from which nothing comes.

Under the influence of this urge we can study the world and ourselves with the realization that we are studying the same thing. This 'sameness' that we find is really to do with the world of will. One of the ways in which tradition expresses this is to say that 'man and the universe have the same laws in them', and this is also the meaning of Gurdjieff's statement that 'man is made in the image of God, that is, of the Great Megalocosmos'. The urge-to-see is really the clearest expression of will in us. When we are able to form mental images quite independently of our surroundings and of our own state, then we come into an extraordinary creative power. The thinking center then comes into its own. It becomes what it should be, a direct instrument of our own will. Then we can think what we choose to think and have the power 'to do', in Gurdjieff's sense of the word. But it is not until we have become balanced in the working of all three brains that it is possible for our thinking to 'have will'.

All this may seem very far away from the simple curiosity which is one of the lowest expressions of the urge-to-see, and so it is, but the same instrument is involved. When the creative energy enters to make it an instrument of our will, the head brain becomes the seat of what Gurdjieff called 'objective reason', the workings of which are quite beyond those of the ordinary mind. There are many gradations of objective reason, but all of them involve the ability to see directly what the world is about and what is really going on and how it is happening. This is a seeing or vision that is related to time differently from ordinary thinking. We see as it were 'in a flash', without need of any process. How high this condition is can be judged from the fact that even Man Number 4 does not have access to this sort of functioning.

The arising of objective reason depends on the formation of what are called 'higher bodies'. These 'bodies' are the fruits of transformation and they are of two different kinds. Besides the physical body, which is the carrier of man's functions, there can be a consolidation in the world of being which Gurdjieff calls the 'kesdjan' body and also a vehicle of will that he simply calls the 'higher-being body'. It is on the formation of the kesdjan body that a man depends for bringing organization into his thinking. It is on the formation of the higher-being body that he depends for the arising of objective reason. Through the higher-being body, a man can become subject to a will higher than his own and in this way become a universal instrument. The effect of such a trans-formation sometimes overflows into the thinking, in the form of visions or revelations, but the deepest illuminations occur entirely without the participation of the lower functions.

The ultimate act of choice that can open up for a man, in which man chooses his final destiny, is whether to be himself or to be God. He can choose to be separate or he can choose to be united; to live and act for himself or to become one with the Will which governs the whole world. Ultimately, the moment comes when he is able to see that either God must disappear for him or he must disappear for God. That is how it is, even though we have no means of understanding what it means.

The Structure of Man

Gurdjieff introduced a diagram of the centers in his talks in Russia during the First World War nearly sixty years ago. I myself saw him using it at the Prieuré in 1923, and although, when he came to write, he dropped it - and it does not appear in *Beelzebub's Tales* or his other writings - he certainly did not abandon it because at the end of his life he did speak about it and use it. Like much of the material that Ouspensky preserved in his *In Search of the Miraculous,* Gurdjieff may not have included it in his own books because he had discovered that people were taking it all too literally; they were not penetrating deeply enough into what it means, it all seemed too easy and straightforward. But I myself, in all the many long years since I first heard about it, have found it enormously valuable both for understanding my own nature and for talking with other people about psychological questions, though I have approached it from the direction of man's three brains in order to escape from the artificial description of the centers as if they were all roughly the same kind of mechanism.

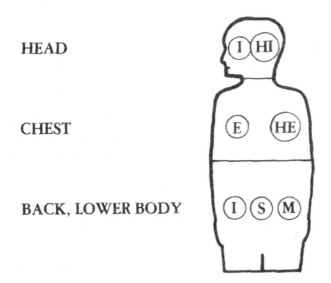

HEAD

CHEST

BACK, LOWER BODY

THE STRUCTURE OF MAN
FIG. 3.1

The diagram is a representation of the human body as a 'three-storied factory'. The top story is the head, the second is the breast, and the third the lumbar and pelvic region of a human body that is facing to the left. These three stories correspond to the three brains of thinking, feeling, and moving. But we can also view man in terms of his centers and then we find that he is no longer three but seven. On the bottom story there are three different centers: the moving center, which is concerned with our outer bodily actions;

the instinctive center, which is concerned with the maintenance of life; and the sex center, which works with a much higher energy than the other bodily centers[7]. In the middle story there is both an emotional center and what Gurdjieff called a 'higher emotional center'. All our ordinary emotional states and reactions belong to the emotional center, which is very much concerned with our own existence. But under the influence of the urge-to-be there can awaken the potential of the feelings to enter into higher worlds, higher levels of being and consciousness, and penetrate beyond time and space into the eternal reality. This is the working of the higher emotional center, through which we can arrive at peace and detachment. In the top story there is the intellectual center which deals with the world around us; but the urge-to-see is an urge to see beyond this world. We can picture a pure state in which there is an awareness of the whole meaning and significance of the world. Through this union is achieved the will by which the world is created and maintained. That which is able to unite with the Supreme Will is the part of us that Gurdjieff calls the 'higher intellectual center'.

In the whole man, then, there are three brains and seven centers. The higher centers correspond to higher levels of functioning. This picture of the perfected man is very useful in showing us how he does not always live in the highest state of consciousness. The cosmic energies are to enable man to communicate with God and to bring him into contact with the cosmic purpose. It is wasteful to use them to deal with material objects. The lower functions exist to deal with everyday life obligations. In this kind of existence that we have, there can be no final completion. The aim of the work that we set before ourselves is not to be rid of our human nature, but to transform it so that it is a whole in which each part does what it should do.

Three Make One

At first acquaintance, the various descriptions of man seem contradictory and even confusing: he is three, he is four, he is seven, he is one, he is many, and so on. The difficulty arises only if we take these various descriptions in terms of things that we can know; when we begin to see into the nature of our experience, they all begin to make sense because then we go beyond the out-

---

7 Gurdjieff said that the sex center reconciles the moving and instinctive centers.

side of things. Each of the various ways has a different starting point, a different question behind it, such as 'Who am I? How do I work? What is my principle of organization?' Nearly all these questions take us beyond the world of bodies or things, but not necessarily beyond our experience.

A great deal of the material that we have briefly sketched in this chapter is by way of explanation of Gurdjieff's 'four personalities', in particular, what he means when he says, '... in order to make possible the rounded perfecting of a man, a special corresponding correct education is indispensably necessary for each of these three parts, and not such a treatment as is given nowadays and also called "education". Only then can the 'I' which should be in a man, be his own 'I' ".[8] To illustrate what he means, he gives a picture of a man as a hackney carriage, in a state of ill-repair, pulled by a dispirited nag that hardly understands the difference between left and right and driven by a bored coachman whose interest lies in vodka and kitchen maids. The apparatus itself is going nowhere. It is a wasteful dream. All that can happen is that it is picked up by some chance passerby who wants to go somewhere. Gurdjieff elaborates this picture, which we have mentioned once before, in the most extraordinary way, and it does enable us concretely to visualize and understand the state of affairs in man without his 'own 'I' ". But what is this 'own 'I' "? Gurdjieff calls it the Master of the carriage, the horse and the driver. The Master cannot appear until many things have been put right. The driver has to learn how to communicate with the horse and how to consider its needs; the reins between them are really of a special substance that is produced when thought and feeling blend and is affected by all sorts of influences from the world of energies, or what Gurdjieff calls the 'weather', or 'atmosphere'. The 'grease' on the axles needs to be spread to give lubrication, and this has to be done by work with the body. The driver has to be able to 'hear' the instructions of the Master, and this requires what Gurdjieff calls 'ether'. All these various things have to do with the harmonization of functions and the concentration of finer energies. But still, who or what is the Master?

We have already made 'I' equivalent to will. In this sense, it is quite proper to say that each one of us has a real 'I' or Master, though in a latent condition. Our 'own 'I' " is not will alone but realization of will in what we are and in what we do. In this real-

---

8 *Beelzebub's Tales*, p. 1191

ization is our own reality. Without it, we are only an aggregate of components that must inevitably disperse, sooner or later.

It is in the nature of will to act as three. This is Gurdjieff's picture of the 'omnipresent active element okidanokh', which is also a representation of continuous creation. In the chapter called 'The Arch Absurd', he describes how the okidanokh split into three forces as it entered every new cosmic formation and how these three separated forces 'strive to reblend'. It is this that gives every new formation its own chance to be real, that makes it really a part of the great whole and not simply a cog in the world mechanical process. And in man, this splitting and striving to reblend of the three forces give rise in him to the three characteristic urges that we have tried to describe. The general names that Gurdjieff gave to the three forces were, for example, active, passive, and neutralizing, or affirming, denying, and reconciling. We can say that will is the universal affirmation, function is the universal denial, and being is the universal reconciliation.

The three forces can then 'crystallize', or take root in, the three centers: the affirming force in the head brain, the denying force in the body brain, and the reconciling force in the feeling brain. According to Gurdjieff, these crystallizations have to come through intentional education; that is, through work that is understood and properly guided, and then a man arrives at the point of having 'all three of the separately spiritualized parts' awake in him. In the ordinary, unawakened state of man, the three-foldness of his nature is constantly inherent in the food and air and impressions that he takes in, but remains below the threshold of his awareness, or provides only a fleeting 'shock' in which *djartklom,* or the separation of the three forces, results but has nothing to hold on to.

Thus, although thinking, feeling, and moving are all equally functions, nevertheless we can call the thinking center the very representative of will, the feeling center the very representative of being, and the body center the very representative of function. They are able to bring the universal reality of the three worlds of function, being, and will into an individual reality. This individual reality is the fourth personality of a man, his 'own 'I'', his wholeness.

The wholeness of man is equally the singleness of his will, the coherence of his being, and the harmony of his functions. The unity of function, being and will is the inherent 'divine spark' which is within us. We can as well say that this unity, the fourth personality, is to be 'discovered', as we can say that it is to be 'made'. In either case, there has to be a removal of the veils that hide from us our own reality, but this is a concrete action that is more than a mental change.

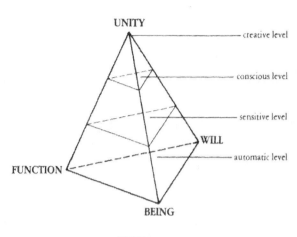

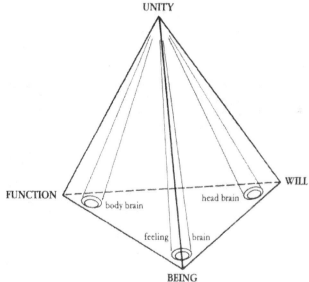

LEVELS OF FUNCTION
FIG. 3.2

His three centers reach toward his wholeness in their different ways, and the more they are in synergic relationship, the closer is their functioning to unity. This depends on the level of energy on which functioning takes place. On the automatic level, there is the dream state, in which we are the slave of every passing impulse, and the centers are out of contact with each other. Next, on the sensitive level, we can begin to notice the things that are going on in us and one brain can observe another. Then, on the conscious level, true self-observation becomes possible, when all three brains operate together and we can experience ourselves as a whole being. At the creative level of functioning, we can act under the initiative of our own 'I' and we can then become a being capable of self-creation, called by Gurdjieff Man Number 5. The balancing of centers is therefore a very great thing that can lead us beyond this material world into higher worlds, where our physical bodies can neither do anything nor support experience.

As we come closer to unity, the nature and meaning of our lives changes. Not only our perception and understanding change but how we can live. We do not exist in a vacuum. Our own development serves to bring us closer into contact with other beings, and also to bring us under the influence of what lies beyond existence altogether. As we become more real, we are more able to communicate with reality.

CHAPTER 4

Selves

When we talk about things we use one word, and this sufficiently indicates what we are talking about. We say 'chair' or 'cushion' and these single words are enough to connect us with all that we associate with the experience of a chair or cushion. With plants and animals and people, it is often much the same; we refer to them by their names and this is enough to connect us with the various associations we have formed about them. This way of going about things serves some purposes, but it is all on the surface and only captures the 'thingness' of things: how they are in the world of bodies where everything is outside everything else. We do not come into contact with the deeper characteristics of living beings and people through this approach.

We talk about ourselves as 'I' or 'me', also 'myself', but when we try to look at what these words signify, we find that they do not mean the same as each other, and what they refer to is not constant either.

'I' is the wholly subjective in us which we believe to be free. It is not the thoughts that are in me, or the feelings that are in me, or the bodily sensations. But to see that, for example, 'I' am not 'my body' is an enormous step.

'My body', 'my mind', and 'my feelings' are a part of 'me' and I can be aware of me, that is, aware of what I am. We cannot be aware of 'I' because it is always hidden, always behind, no matter how far we reach or dig into ourselves. We have linked 'I' to the will, and the will is never an object which can be known or sensed or felt; it is not even before us when we are conscious. Who would there be to see 'I'? The common idea that we can find an infinite regress in which one 'I' observes another and is observed in its turn and so on is really an incorrect way of describing the relativity of our consciousness. We have seen how one center can observe another and also how we can become aware of our automatic functions and even our sensitivity. None of this is to do with 'I'. What it has to do with is that 'me' is of different kinds, and exists on many levels. It is legitimate to speak of different selves that comprise 'me'.

When we use the word 'myself' in the same way that we use the name of an object, we make a big mistake. How is it that we can be acting in one way one minute and a minute later be acting in a totally contradictory way? If we begin to examine our behavior impartially, we can come to see that we are constantly shifting from one plane of existence to another and that for each of these planes there is a 'myself' that corresponds to it. The sort of *self* that is active depends upon the state of the functions that are operating. We must also remember that 'myself' is partially subjective and in every self we have to take account of a condition of the will. 'I am myself' is always true, but in as many different ways as there are selves.

We must make it clear that each of the selves we are going to talk about is strictly related to the physical body and its instruments. A self is an embodied state of existence and should be considered separately from man's possibilities of acquiring other kinds of body. The different selves make possible different kinds of experience. They are locations through which we can learn about what we are. They are organizations of function through which we can operate in this bodily world and come into contact with the world of life and the world of minds or people. None of them, not even the highest self, the 'true self', is able to exist without the physical body.

Man has by nature access to the cosmic energy of creativity, and this energy makes it possible for him to act, to come to real understandings, and to begin the work of transformation. This does not mean that he has a creative existence, that his own substance is creative. It simply means that the creative power can enter into the instruments associated with his body, as in sex. This is a most wonderful thing and is the source of man's potential not only to create outwardly but inwardly - that is, to become free. It is the same with consciousness, which can enter the instruments we have and bring them to a state of harmony and cooperation. This does not make man a conscious being.

With each of the energies, there is the possibility of a different kind of functioning, a different kind of experiencing, and a different kind of 'willing'. It is this which produces the different selves. With the accumulation of experience through life, the selves develop, more or less rightly and to a greater or lesser degree. If our 'center of gravity' moves toward the higher selves, this is a real advance in our being, and different opportunities are opened for us. We can then also talk about the making of a different kind of body, an inner body, which enables us to live in a quite different way. It is only when such a body is formed that we are no longer subject to the laws attached to our physical existence. This is quite different from the temporary experience we may have of higher levels that come through the higher selves.

In the ordinary state, the higher selves are dormant. Even then there may be moments of higher functioning, but we lack the organization of experience by which these moments can be more than dreams. This explains why people can have even very deep experiences but also in another sense *not* have them. The higher selves give us an organization of experience - a means of transforming energies - by which we can make a step into the higher worlds. They are not themselves the freedom that we seek.

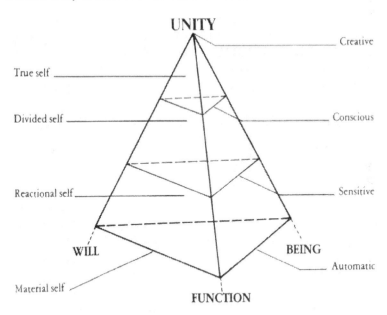

DIAGRAM OF SELVES AND ENERGIES
FIG. 4.1

Every self is a combination of function, being and will, which is organized in such a way as to make certain kinds of experiences possible. This means that a self has got its own set of functions. These are really the same instruments, but working more or less efficiently, more or less sensitively, with more or less consciousness. What the instruments of man can do is quite different on the different levels of organization. This leads us to the being aspect of the selves, which can be seen in terms of energies. Each self is characterized by a certain quality of energy, and when the corresponding quality of energy is not available, that self is latent, as if it were 'not there'. Using the terminology of our scheme of energies, we can say that there is a material self that works automatically; a reactional self that works sensitively; a divided self that works consciously; and a true self that works creatively. We can picture the four selves as four 'planes of experience' in the diagram of function, being, will, and unity. Each of the selves 'has a will of its own', and this introduces a hazard into our existence that is a very important feature of our human situation. Each of the four selves has some power to affirm itself as an independent entity or to open itself to the action of a higher will. In this way, each of the four selves can make a contribution to the embodiment of the real 'I', which is, so to say, 'hidden' in the upper point of the pyramid, at the point of unity. But they can also form a barrier to this embodiment. This leads to the question that is often asked in Gurdjieff's second series of writings, *Meetings with Remarkable Men*, 'How is it possible to come under the influence of higher laws?' This means, 'How can we be liberated from the prisons of our selves?' To understand what is required, we shall need an understanding of the laws under which man exists, which we shall try to develop in Part Two.

All our selves are needed if we are to come to completion and, far from destroying our lower selves, we must understand and regularize their workings to come into the higher ones. The lower selves are accessible to us in our own experience and in observation of other people. When they are in control, we are in the state of slavery and have no initiative apart from the interplay of our conditioning and external stimuli. Nevertheless, they do have a characteristic type of experiencing which we must learn how to recognize. We will begin with a study of the material self, that is, the man-machine.

The Material Self

It is through this self that man has power over all the other objects of the earth. It is supreme in the world of bodies, but it remains within that world and is subject to the laws of that world. The energy it works with is the automatic, very highly organized. The material self has all the functions of thinking, feeling, moving, instinct, and so on, but they operate without awareness. Gurdjieff called it the 'man-machine', but it is still a self and also has subjective properties. The material self can be a very useful instrument in dealing with the material world, but there is a danger that it will usurp our true human nature and act as if it were the whole man. Our conceptions of the world are largely formed through this self, and the experience it has is based on our bodily nature. Our conceptions of space and time are conditioned almost entirely by the fact that our bodies are solid material objects. This explains why our thinking is, for the most part, only useful in the world of bodies, the *ālam-i ajsām,* and cannot make sense of experience in other worlds. The apparatus of language belongs to the material self, and it develops almost entirely through contact with material bodies. A child begins to speak by naming material objects, coming later on to words for actions and even later to expressions of life and consciousness. It is because of this that we can very easily make the mistake of assuming that the laws which govern material objects are the laws which govern everything. Material laws include the impossibility of two things occupying the same place, and because of this we tend to believe that we cannot be both happy and sad at the same time, believing that happiness and sadness have the same discrete material natures as a table or a chair.

Our language, which is a very fine tool for dealing with material things, is actually an obstacle when it comes to trying to understand inner states and realities. The material self has no discrimination. It is able to think and speak, but it is insensitive to quality. It is able to talk about everything, but it reduces it all to the same thing. It is able to know about other worlds, but it always believes that the material world is the only reality. There are people who are dominated by the material self and, while they can be very powerful or successful in a worldly way, they have no feelings, no sensitivity. They will treat other people as if they were things and are therefore capable of great ruthlessness. This does not mean the man of the material self does not have urges, desires, pleasures, and pains. He has all of these, but they are all either derived mechanically from social conventions or they arise from the working of his animal instinct. He can desire power and domination over others, but it is all artificial; he is nothing but a machine. He can have very strong sexual impulses, indulge himself in food and drink, but it is all a sham; he is never able to enjoy life and his experience does not go beyond simple states of pleasure and pam.

It is inherent in the nature of the automatic energy, which is the quality of energy of the material self, that the man of that self does not notice what he is doing and never realizes what he is missing. He does not see that he is never really alive. His life is a charade but he does not have the energy with which to see through the pretense. But although he cannot be aware of what is wrong, he can be driven to seek for some feeling of existence. He has to adorn himself with success and with possessions to feel that he exists at all. The only kind of existence that he is aware of is material existence, and he depends on things. The man of the material self is not only interested in material possessions and money, though these are often important, but he has a material outlook on everything. We can speak of physical materialism, emotional materialism, sexual materialism, and intellectual materialism; in all of the functions, the only reality is material.

A 'body person', or a Man Number 1, of the material self lives entirely for the satisfaction of his bodily impulses. His only means of experiencing life is to have his bodily impulses stimulated. If he is a Man Number 2, centered in the emotional brain, then he is either a very negative and critical person who sees something wrong in every situation he comes into contact with, or he is a person with a great desire for power. Such a person is only satisfied in his relationships by the sense of possessiveness. He is unable to make compromises, because he is unable to see more than one point of view in a situation. Nothing really enters into him, certainly not the reality of other people, their feelings, and their experience.

A Man Number 3 on the material level can be very intellectual, very logical, but his idea of knowledge will be analytical and atomistic. He sees things in compartments and is unable to see things as a whole. It is not within the power of the automatic energy to bring about a unity of knowledge, so that while such a person may have a great fund of knowledge he has no desire or impulse to seek a deeper view of things, and is even suspicious of those who are drawn toward a view of wholeness. One of Gurdjieff's most important psychological conceptions was that of the 'formatory apparatus', which corresponds to the thinking center of the man of the material self. The formatory apparatus, powered by the automatic energy, is constantly associating, and this has become, in almost everyone nowadays, the primary tool of thought and action. It uses words as if they were material objects and is unable to discriminate between ideas; it has a fantastic ability to remember and associate words and ideas, and it is this 'formating' that we usually refer to as 'thinking'. It is so successful in dealing with the material world that it is sometimes assumed that it is a sign of true human intelligence. But intelligence is something that actually belongs to a deeper part of us.

A person dominated by the material self is in a truly pathetic condition. He can be outwardly successful but his life is, objectively speaking, wretched. He has no real experience of his own, and when the higher energies work in him they work apart from the self he habitually lives in, and he can only regard their action as a dream. He is constantly reaching outside himself for anything which can give him a feeling of existing at all. He is nothing but an empty shell and, because the material self is unable to exist independently of the body, when he dies he is completely destroyed forever.

Whenever I speak about this, I remember something which happened many years ago and made a deep impression on me. I had a very good friend who was a distinguished lawyer and a good man. One of his brothers was a very successful man - Chancellor of the Exchequer. All of his family were proud of his intelligence and helped him toward success, his brothers even going to work for a time to make money in order to help him with his career. But although everyone looked up to him, he had no feelings, no sensitivity and, somehow or other, all the feelings, all the sensitivity in his family had gone to his other brothers. When he died I went to his funeral because I was a friend of his brother. It was an unforgettable experience. When the coffin was brought into the chapel, where it was to be cremated, I had such a strong feeling of there just being an empty shell, a nut with no kernel. Everything had dwindled and dried up inside him, and I saw once and for all how terrible a thing it is when one allows oneself to be a prisoner of the material world. One may have everything externally but have nothing inside.

Yet we all have this material self, this automatic functioning of our centers, and it is necessary that it should be so. We could not become what we are to be without it. Our task is not to destroy it but to see that it plays its proper role. The material self should be the instrument for interacting with the material world. Everything that we do, such as breathing, eating, moving, thinking, and so on, is partially in the world of bodies. We have a role to play in that world. But if we are nothing but these mechanisms, and the corresponding energy transformations that keep them going, we miss the point of our existence. We have to learn how to separate ourselves from the mechanism. 'I' am not these associations, these reactions, these sensations that are going on in me; in much the same way as 'I' am not the brake, the accelerator, or the clutch pedal of the car which 'I' am involved in driving. We have to find ways in which this separation can be established in us, but when we use the word 'separation' we do not mean that these things have to be cut away from us as some sort of cancerous growth. The constant stimulation which arises through our sensations and our associations is necessary for us. It is the working of the automatic energy which maintains the 'tone' of our nervous system and the vitality of our entire organism.

By itself, the material self is nothing more than a machine 'running wild', out of control and serving no useful purpose. It is one of our tasks to discover the purpose of this self and train it to fulfill this purpose. The material self was often depicted in medieval paintings as a dragon. There is nothing to fear from dragons as long as we keep an eye on them. If we are off-guard, they can catch us out.

Although the material self is the instrument through which we can master the world, this does not mean that the material self by itself can be aware of the material world. It is simply *part* of that world, and when we are dominated by it we lose all sense of being in relationship with the external world; that is, we lose all sense of having obligations toward the things that we use. In his rightful place, man is a god in relation to material objects; but a sign of the man dominated by the material self is that he has no regard for the tools that he uses, but is more likely to be concerned with owning them. To treat the belongings of other people just as carefully as our own can have the most extraordinary results, results that will be quite unexpected. We suddenly find ourselves coming into contact with the world around us, with what we are doing, and with the tools that we are using. All this is quite impossible for the material self, which cannot see tools but only own them. When such an experience comes, we can see the material self for what it is: a machine.

In its rightful place, the material self has the all-important role of taking care of all our automatic functioning, all the habitual behavior we need for the balanced ordering of our lives. Even the perfect man has a material self; but it is subordinate to what is higher in him. We do not expect a chisel to decide for us what it will cut, yet there is a danger that we will let our material selves direct the way in which we live our lives. When this self is in its rightful place, the higher parts of our selfhood are left free to perform their functions, which are concerned with the higher energies of sensitivity and consciousness. These higher energies should not be wasted on tasks which can be done automatically. When we are concerned with material objects, the center of gravity of our actions can be the material self. But, as Gurdjieff expressed it, 'You can make as much money as you like, as long as it is only with your left foot'. The rest of us must not be swallowed up in materiality.

The Reactional Self

We can look at a picture and see it as a machine might, or we can be aware of it as well. What this difference is is quite obvious in our experience. In the second case, we have an experience of what it means to be alive. The automatic energy is capable of producing a description of the picture and, if it is a painting, of classifying it according to style and period and reproducing what other people have said about it; but in all of that, there is no one who is actually looking at the picture. The added awareness, which can put us in touch with the world around us, with other people, and with what is going on in ourselves, comes from the sensitive energy. It gives us the feeling of being alive.

The sensitive energy is essentially polarized in its workings, and all life is sensitive, governed by the poles of attraction and aversion. Sensitivity does not produce a neutral kind of contact with the world but a kind of experience with force and direction. It is for this reason that the self associated with the working of this energy is called 'reactional', but it must be distinguished from the state of conditioned reflex that belongs to the material level. The reactional self exists in our experience, whereas the material self is all 'outside'. In ordinary language, people talk about 'feeling' to point to the difference but each of the centers has its own sensitive reactional nature. There are instinctive pleasure-pain reactions, emotional likes and dislikes, sexual attraction and repulsion, mental yeses and nos, moving center 'want-tos' and 'don't-want-tos'. People living from the reactional self differ from those centered in the material self in that they can make contact with things, but they always do it in this either/or kind of way.

As we grow up, all our experiences work in us to organize the flow of sensitive energy. Without the action of a higher self, this leads to the acquisition of various habitual reactions with which we are identified. We said that each of the levels of energy really merges into the others, and there is in the sensitive level of energy a range of greater or lesser freedom from automatism. The power of response that the sensitivity has can be conditioned. When children are encouraged to follow their likes and dislikes, they are being 'educated' for slavery. Gurdjieff said about people who encouraged children in this way, 'Right to kill. Stick knife in back.' The proper role of the sensitive energy is to put us in touch with life and provide us with substances for our transformation; it should not be the dictator of our behavior. It is a terrible thing to see to what extent what we do is determined by the conditioning of our sensitivity, all the time going toward what we like and avoiding what we do not like, so that we live in a very narrow way. This is the life of what Gurdjieff called the 'false personality', which copes with all the real problems of life by avoiding them. It can even lead us into doing things that damage our health and well-being because the true sensitive power of discrimination between the healthy and the harmful, such as all animals have, is overlaid with all sorts of artificial reactions.

For the man of the reactional self, his likes and his dislikes are the 'truth': what I like must be good and what I do not like must be bad, and everybody else must avoid it, too. This kind of absurdity is a very powerful force in the lives of many people. If the reactional man is centered on his body, he will not do anything that does not 'feel good' to his body. This can bear no relation to what his body really needs. Because of the enormous capacity of the sensitive energy for being organized and structured, the reactional self can have all kinds of sexual predilections outside of the basic attraction between man and woman. None of these manifestations of polarity need to be stable and consistent. Reactional people can like a thing one moment and dislike it the next, but they will not be aware that this is happening. In any given moment what they are liking is 'good' and what they are disliking is 'bad'. They are intolerant of other people who do not have the same likes and dislikes and will find it hard to believe that their own reactions have ever changed.

The force that is in the reactional self is very seductive. This self will feel that the reactions it has are its very hold on reality. What has to be understood is that the reactions that take place in us do have a very important role in our lives, but they are only 'raw material' for our own being and not ends in themselves. What has to be learned is how to 'bear the clash of opposites' in ourselves, for it is then that the reactional nature becomes as it should be.

The avoidance of this clash or tension is characteristic of the man who is dominated by his reactional self. It prevents him ever from coming into contact with how things really are. Strength of feeling in him is really a barrier to understanding himself or others. Instead of having an insight into anyone, all he will ever know is how he feels about them. If he is mentally active, he will see everything as either right or wrong, true or false. He cannot understand ideas; he can only accept them or reject them. What he believes in is absolute for him and he cannot enter into any other point of view, though he probably believes that he is completely impartial and objective.

Recently, I was reading a book written about the history of Bukhara by a great savant. Although he has done more to widen our understanding of the languages of Central Asia than anyone for hundreds of years, he was nevertheless a very striking example of this sort of violent intellectual prejudice, all the more so because of his obvious intelligence. As he saw it, certain dynasties and people could do no wrong while others could do no right, and if I had not read many books about this and come to know it from many sides, I could easily have been taken in. I was astonished to see how his prejudice colored everything that he wrote, and that despite the fact that he was very intelligent he could not be impartial.

To begin to master the working of the sensitive energy in us we must study how it works in our lives. This is made difficult by the fact that we tend to identify with any state that happens to be present in us, and what we have to learn is how to direct our attention outside of 'ourselves' - that is, our states - to what is around us. If, for example, we find ourselves rejecting some idea, we have to get ourselves to see that '*Here* is this rejection in me; *there* is that idea which is being rejected'. We can train ourselves in this way, but at the beginning it is not so easy as it sounds. We have to enlarge our awareness beyond its narrow confines. This in turn releases energy in us, and if we are not careful, this new energy will be taken up by our reactional nature. The energy that is produced by our efforts to see can be lost in enthusiasm, excitement, or misery and self-blame. It is in this way that nearly all the opportunities released in the course of life, when by chance some larger awareness is produced in us, are wasted. The reactional self 'steals' the energy: we like or dislike what we see of ourselves and we get into some state that is as blind as what we had before the moment of seeing. To see ourselves without reaction is one of the first tastes of freedom.

To come to see, it is not enough to 'try to become more aware'. This in itself does not lead to very much. We have to struggle actively against likes and dislikes in us: do what we dislike doing and not do what we like doing; set ourselves to appreciate a point of view contradictory to what we believe to be our own; be active when we feel inertial and inactive when we feel energetic. Injunctions such as these are liable to be terribly misunderstood. They are taken to be an advocation of a masochistic life. But the fruit of their practice is rarely suffering, it is an enhanced sense of life. We become a little more free from the mutual exclusion of opposites and, instead of being at one pole or other, either being attracted or repelled, we experience the force between them in ourselves. This is the force of life that lifts us out of the mechanical life, and it is for this that the reactional self exists.

Only when the opposites can be experienced together in us can we begin to be aware of our own human nature. This nature that we have is something with enormous depth, and if we are caught by our reactions we are condemned to live only a surface existence, but if we can use the force of our reactions, we have a way of penetrating to what lies within us. The rightful place of the reactional self is that of a *generator of energies*, and the combination of opposites is that condition of transformation in which higher grades of energy can be produced. Just as with electricity it is impossible to generate a current unless we have learned how to separate the positive and negative poles, so it is only when we have learned how to separate the positive and negative forces of our reactional self that we can gain from our activities a source of energy for our inner work. A vivid life is one in which there is 'yes' and 'no' at the same time; affirmation and denial. When it is like that, the reactional self is the seat of an organ of perception of vast power which can help us to live our lives fully and to share in the lives of others. Far from leading to additional suffering, this way of life releases us from a great amount of unnecessary suffering. This is what Gurdjieff meant when he said 'sacrifice your suffering'. We have to come to realize that what comes out of the sensitive interaction we have with the conditions of life is not what we *are* but the energy that we can use to *be*.

It is only when we have become awakened to the reality of the higher selves that it can make sense to us that the material self is a machine for dealing with the world of bodies, and the reactional self is a generator of energies that can enable us to experience the reality of life. They are not complete in themselves but only instruments. We must explain something further about the training of the reactional self. This can only be done properly from within. It is of no value - in fact, it is detrimental - for people to be forced into contradictory situations against their wish. Conditions can be created in which it is relatively easy for people to recognize op- portunities for struggle, and they can be encouraged and guided to do so, but force only serves to stimulate the lower part of the selfhood. When the struggle begins to be established in this right way - that is, not for the approval or disapproval of others or for external reward but from within - then this is the way to an open- ing up of the next higher self, the divided self. Educating people in this path is a very high responsibility.

The Divided Self

The difficulty of awakening the divided self is illustrated in an Eastern story as it was recounted by Gurdjieff. In the story, man- kind is compared to a flock of sheep, and it is said that there is a magician who owns them. When he wants their wool he shears them and when he wants their meat he kills them. Because he is too stingy to put fences around his pastures, he has to find some other means of being sure that the sheep do not run away. Being a magician, he hypnotizes the sheep and suggests to them that they are immortal and that, far from its harming them, they will find losing their skins to be beneficial. Secondly, he suggests to them that he is a kind magician who has only their best interests at heart. Further, he suggests that, even if anything were going to happen to them, it would not happen this very day so that there is no need on their part to worry just now. And, as if all this were not enough, he suggests to some that they are lions and that nobody would dare to trouble them; to others that they are eagles and that they can therefore fly away when they need to; to others that they are men who can control their own destiny; and to others that they are magicians who can control the destiny of others. They are so contented by all of this that he is able to kill them and shear them without any problems whenever he wishes to.

There comes a nice little piece at the end of the story: the way that the magician keeps the sheep hypnotized is to beat them a little every day. These 'beatings' refer to the continual state of stimulation of the reactional self we are in, which inhibits the awakening of consciousness; the separation of consciousness from sensitivity. So long as we sleep in this way, we are prevented from seeing our real situation. So long as we are hypnotized by our own reactions, our likes and dislikes, our prejudices, our beliefs and habits of thought and all the rest of it, we are protected from seeing what Gurdjieff called, in the telling of the *legominism* of Ashiata Shiemash in *Beelzebub's Tales,* 'The Terror of the Situation'.

What we mean by the 'separation of consciousness from sensitivity' is being set free from the hypnotism of the reactional self. Then we can begin to see what it means to be dominated by the lower selves. A real struggle can begin, a struggle between the conflicting pulls of our higher and lower natures. The real property of the divided self is that it is drawn to live in two different worlds. This is due to the conscious energy, which can make connections beyond the limits of the sensitivity. On the one side, we are drawn out into the world, and this reaching out is the foundation of what we ordinarily call 'desire'. On the other, we are drawn within ourselves toward our higher invisible nature, and we can call this, as Gurdjieff did, 'non-desire'. The very seat of desire and non-desire is the divided self. That is why it is said that in every man there is a devil and an angel.

It is important to realize that the energy of the divided self is not in itself wise or good. It is the power behind the deepest urges that we have - consciousness. Consciousness is the first level at which the genuine normal urges that belong to the centers can take effect, but they are mixed with what comes to us from outside. Here are the drives to understand, to share, to live, to action, and so on, but they are usually adulterated by desire.

If we begin to work on ourselves in earnest, as time goes on we are bound to find that there is 'something' in us that wants no part of it. This 'something' wants to have its own way and does not want to recognize any master either within or without. Or else it is apathetic and only wants to be left alone. This self-assertion, however, is not the whole story. It is from the very same place in us that there comes the wish to be free of slavery and to fit into the whole, to serve and to understand what needs to be done. All of this belongs to the divided self and is the reason for its name.

It is not easy to see what the divided self is about. It is far deeper than the level of reaction. For the greater part of our lives, the divided self may be no more than a pattern that accompanies us from birth, and limits the kinds of relationship that we can form. We can only get at it indirectly, by finding out, for example, what we 'cannot do' in situations, such as take the initiative or keep to a plan and so on, which gives us a clue as to our type. The observation of our typical behaviors can lead us to understand that there is 'something' in us which is imposing a pattern of what is possible and impossible for us to do, that is not due to external conditioning or the state of our mechanism. This does not mean that we cannot live and experience outside our pattern or type, but to do this, a creative action is needed. Even as we are, the pattern is a pattern in depth, not like a blueprint, and it has a 'permissive' side as well as a 'prohibitory' one. Type is rather like a style of life that has almost infinite possibilities of variation. But we must remember that we are rather like actors who have a very limited repertoire of roles. It is almost impossible to make ourselves act in a way that is not typical.

Type is sometimes also referred to as 'character', but here the meaning is more directed toward the desires, aims, appetites, and ideals which are the foundation of our behavior; the content rather than the form. It is the needs for connectedness, for relatedness, that move us from inside ourselves, so that we are looking for something, reaching out to something, striving for something. All this gives our life and experience a certain 'shape' which can be recognized, but its recognition requires consciousness. Nearly everyone can have some feeling of what it means to associate different people with different 'animals. There does seem to be a real affinity between man and the various species of animal. But whenever we try to pin it down, it goes out of sight. It cannot be reduced to the sensitive level.

Jung showed something important with his notion of 'archetypes'. We can say that the 'animals' or 'archetypes' which form our character are taken from a source in which we all share, so that here we go beyond the limits of our private self. If we can really come to the core of this, we discover our unity with other people, and we see that we are dealing with the patterning of human nature. For someone who has penetrated into the archetypal world -

or the world of what Jung called the 'collective unconscious' - life is made harder. He becomes aware of the destructive forces in his own nature. He sees how much rejection of the total human reality there is in him. We have to be able to accept what we find in this world because it is rejection that binds us to the limited pattern of our own nature.

The limitation of our pattern is also what is called 'fate', the way of life and experience that is fixed in us at birth. It is 'we ourselves' who bind ourselves to fate, but how this comes about in us is not easy to see. It is seldom so simple as laziness or violence or the desire for domination. Something gets 'twisted round' in us so that we remain closed. Traits are 'positive' or 'negative' according to their source, though they may appear the very same thing. True pride, for example, is based upon contact with the inner richness of what we can be as human beings, and in its working is no different from humility, whereas false pride is ascribing to ourselves, just as we are, the qualities that only in reality belong to whole men and women. One pride leads us to God while the other seeks to inflate us in the world.

Unless we are free from the domination of the two lower selves, work belonging to this third level is ill-advised. The lower selves confuse the issue to such an extent that any effort to deal with the divided self is bound to be worse than useless, even harmful. We need to clear away the rubbish of the lower selves before we can begin to be aware of the hidden pattern of our nature. When this emerges, it can be very hard to bear. We begin to see how it is that we destroy our possibilities, reject, refuse to make sacrifices, all in the belief that we are holding on to our true reality.

As the reactional self is the door through which we must pass if we are to come into the world of energies, so the divided self is the door through which we must pass in order to come to the world of will.

So what is on the 'other side' of our own nature, our divided self, looks to us like nothing, absence, lack, whereas in reality it is there we have to go to find true reality. One of the few things that can enable us to pass through the door of the divided self is to see that we are helpless, to see that we cannot 'do', cannot in reality create anything from ourselves. Through the key of the pattern we have in our consciousness we can unlock many doors and achieve many things, but none of this is 'doing'. In every real step, we have to be stimulated by the creative energy within that we do not see. Will and energy are still apart. Our centers can begin to work together, and we are able to make all sorts of connections. We can be quite free of our reactions, but none of this gives us effective freedom because we still cannot change what we are.

The admission of helplessness is very subtle. It does not mean that we cannot achieve external results. It means that we see that we cannot change ourselves and that everything will remain essentially the same. It also means that we accept that there is within us a power which can 'do', but this power is totally beyond our awareness and we cannot come to it by any means at our disposal. This must penetrate our understanding, because understanding is the power of the divided self. Remembering Gurdjieff's dictum, 'Understanding with one brain is hallucination; understanding with two brains is semi-hallucination; only understanding with all three brains is real understanding', we can see that real understanding is possible for the divided self. But there is the understanding that binds everything to itself and the understanding that binds itself to the reality of things. It is in this second sense that Gurdjieff, in *Meetings with Remarkable Men,* makes Father Giovanni say, 'Faith comes from real understanding.'[9]

We can say that a man is, in a real way, his understanding. It is useless for him to say, 'Of course, there are things that I do not understand; of course, there are limits to my understanding'. He can even say, 'Yes, I can appreciate that there are hidden realities', but it is all just words. The opening of the understanding to the truly unknowable worlds is a very great thing. It has to be thoroughly disillusioned about 'doing', able to bear the realization that we are not the source of our own acts. We can have all sorts of experience, such as through meditation, when we become aware of something working in us that is not the result of our own initiative, but still we believe that this is something happening 'to us' and 'in us', and we remain at the center. What is higher remains at the level of an image for us; it is not a reality.

This does not mean that what is beyond our understanding is so remote that it will never have anything to do with us unless we become liberated beings. It does work in us, but in a secret way. What is before us in the work of transformation is the possibility of coming into cooperation with this working, and coming to the point of realization of *who we are.*

---

9 *Meetings with Remarkable Men*, New York, Dutton, 1963, p.240;

The True Self

The true self is whole. It does what it sees. What is done is done from the whole man. It is very difficult for our language to carry anything of what wholeness means. We believe that we know what is meant by saying that the 'whole is larger than the sum of its parts', but the very form of expression betrays that we are looking at wholeness in materialistic terms. At the very root of our difficulty is that here we have something that is beyond the reach of our awareness, even the fullest reach of this awareness in the conscious energy.

With the true self, a whole new realm of experience is opened up that has more to do with the will than with new content of our awareness. We can talk of creative action, but in fact nearly all our experience of creativity is 'after the fact', in the realms of sensitivity and consciousness. There is nothing here that we can objectify and look at in terms of something of which we can be aware. Words that we have, such as 'balance' and 'harmony', do point to something of the wholeness we are groping after. We can form some conception of what it means to be Man Number 4 in terms of the harmony of centers, but what this means in terms of being and will is still literally incomprehensible. It is only in the line of function that we are able in our thought to follow the ascent to the true self.

We can say that the reactional self can be the means of entering into the world of life, and the divided self the means of entering into the world of mind, but the true self is the means of entering into the world quite beyond life, the universal world which cannot be contained in bodies and separate existences. The doorway into the universal world is the real 'I', which is now a possibility. 'I' is the most hazardous point in the world. Because the true self is a whole, it can come under the authority of 'I', but here there is great uncertainty. The true self can identify with 'I' as a *separate reality*. This is *egoism*; it is not the same as the selfishness and self-indulgence of our ordinary state. The man of 'I' has real power. If he takes himself to be an end in itself, the center of everything, he has the power to create terrible disorder in the world. Gurdjieff described such a man as *hasnamuss,* which in Persian means 'soul of shit'. What is opened to the true self is the opportunity to exercise creative power. This can lead beyond existence in the path of service, or to an even deeper attachment to existence in the path of egoism.

All the ingredients of a man are derived from the greater whole, but at the point of 'I' there is a real risk of disaster. The greater whole is not only a machine in which every part has an automatically arranged position and function. The possibility of real freedom has been arranged for man, but on the way in which he realizes this freedom very much depends. He has not been given freedom. It is not possible to give freedom. Freedom must be realized, and it is always hazardous, and even depends upon hazard for its exercise and realization. The man who is able to go beyond existence and be detached from the powers of his body Gurdjieff called Man Number 5. Man Number 5 is beyond selfhood and he has passed through the barrier of egoism, but even he is not free from what he has carried up with him from the lower worlds. Only when the unitive energy of love enters into him can he finally be released from separation. For this, he has to enter purgatory and undergo the final purification in the agony of clear awareness of his separation from the Source.

All of this must seem very far away until we realize that in our own lives here and now the significance of the cosmic drama of 'I' is being enacted. To understand this we have to realize the literal truth of Gurdjieff's definition of *conscience* as 'the very representative of the Creator' and that it is produced in us by 'the localization of the particles of the "emanations of the sorrow" of our Omni-Loving and Long-Suffering-Endless-Creator'[10]. In many places, Gurdjieff describes how it is that, because conscience is completely outside the reach of our awareness, it has remained uncontaminated by all the influences that have reduced the other 'sacred impulses' of hope, love, and faith to factors of enslavement. Conscience is one of the most creative powers that we have. It has nothing to do with our training in morality. It is able to penetrate into the very reality of every moment, and one of the aims of work on oneself is awakening to the workings of conscience.

In Gurdjieff's picture of *Purgatory*, he has written over its gates the words 'Only-he-may-enter-here-who-is-able-to-put-himself-in-the-place-of-the-other-results-of-my-labors'. To do this is a very great thing. Gurdjieff himself said that it was 'the last thing for a man'. But even here and now it is before us. There is nothing so obvious to anyone who studies the workings of human nature as that all of us put ourselves at the very center of the universe, and have hardly any sense of the reality of other people. How can we begin to work at this, which is the antithesis of the

10 *Beelzebub's Tales* p.372

workings of conscience? Gurdjieff's advice was to 'bear the unpleasant manifestations of other people'. We have to realize that,
as we are, we forgive ourselves everything and others nothing.
Gurdjieff's advice directs us toward the experience of reality here
and now, in this very life. If we can even begin to practice what he
advises, we make a contribution toward the overcoming of egoism
in ourselves, so that 'I' may become a doorway toward God and
not toward objective hell, which is a separate reality.

The choice between union and egoism is a reality only for the
true self. Because we are not conscious of this self, it does not
mean that it is altogether irrelevant to our lives. The work that we
do is aimed largely at awakening the powers which bring us to the
point of decision between ourselves and God.

The true self is the vehicle of 'I', and there are influences that
enter our lives from within that originate at the level of this self. In
some sense, even if only to a very small degree, our own 'I' does
communicate with us. The authentic search for our own reality
begins with the true self, even if we are totally unaware of the action taking place. But to go from this stage, when our own reality
comes to us 'like a thief in the night', to something that can enter
our waking life, is a big step.

The true self is the proper domain of spiritual work, that is,
of work that goes beyond the transformation of energies into the
world of will. It is to do with this that Gurdjieff had some of his
greatest contributions to make to human understanding. Throughout *Beelzebub's Tales*, he reiterates that we are 'all children of
our common Father Creator Endlessness'. We men do not really
understand that this is so, and this lack of understanding is one of
the greatest curses on human life. As children of a common Father,
we can enter into the working of the great Whole, which Gurdjieff
expressed in terms of the three primal forces of the will: holy affirming, holy denying, and holy reconciling. These three are the
three cosmic aspects of will, function, and being.

We can extend our diagram of the pyramid beyond the central
point and arrive at other levels of reality beyond that of man with
real 'I'. These correspond to men Numbers Five, Six and Seven
in the terminology of Gurdjieff. They are in worlds beyond existence. They are 'men of will' who do not need physical bodies
to keep themselves together. They have 'bodies' that we cannot
imagine. We may 'discover ourselves' within this planetary existence, supported by the apparatuses which have been evolved

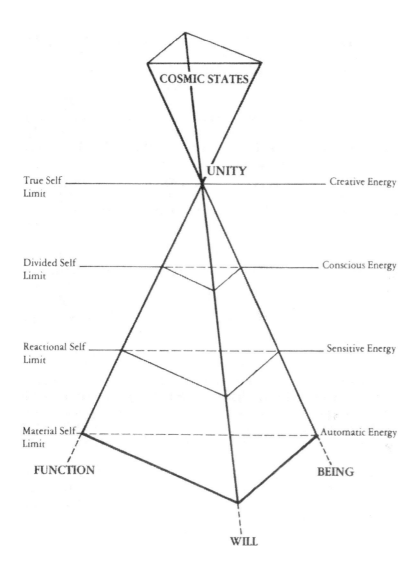

**DIAGRAM OF FOUR SELVES IN RELATION TO EN-
ERGIES AND UNITY**

FIG. 4.2

through living beings, and given the help of forces that work for the maintenance of the whole solar system; but to evolve to the condition in which we can be creative workers on such a scale in our own right would seem to be impossible. What we shall have to try and understand is that the whole idea of separate existence has to be abandoned on the other side of 'I' For us, this will appear as pure annihilation..

We have used the picture of land and sea to talk about the difference between the worlds of bodies and energies, or being. Beyond the sea is the air, formless, omnipresent, and invisible. The air can be our symbol of the spiritual reality that touches us everywhere, and without which nothing is possible.

PART TWO

LAWS

PREFACE

I vividly remember one of the students on the Fourth Sherborne Course asking, 'What worlds can we hope to reach during this course?' My immediate thought was, 'What an idiot!' Mr. Bennett simply said, 'You can go as far as you can.' But I am not quite sure. He might have said, 'You can go as far as you wish.' Then he spoke the last poem that Francis Thompson ever wrote, and I wish that it were possible to reproduce the way he said it. The best that can be done is to reproduce the poem entire and say that very obviously Bennett agreed with every word, and saw the meaning of every line.

A.G.E. Blake

THE KINGDOM OF GOD
' *In no strange land'*

O World Invisible, we view thee
O World Intangible, we touch thee
O World unknowable, we know thee
In-apprehensible, we clutch thee!

Does the fish soar to find the ocean,
The eagle plunge to find the air –
That we ask of the stars in motion
If they have rumour of thee there?

Not where the wheeling systems darken,
And our benumbed conceiving soars! –
The drift of pinions, would we hearken,
Beats at our own clay-shuttered doors.

The angels keep their ancient places;-
Turn but a stone, and start a wing!
'   Tis ye, 'tis your estranged faces,

That miss the many-splendored thing.

But (when so sad thou canst not sadder)
Cry;- and upon thy so sore loss
Shall shine the traffic of Jacob's ladder
Pitched betwixt Heaven and Charing Cross.

Yea, in the night, my Soul, my daughter,
Cry,- clinging Heaven by the hems;
And lo, Christ walking on the water,
Not of Genesareth, but Thames!

CHAPTER 5

The Seven Worlds

Nearly seventy years ago, when I was a boy, I read two books, both written in the 1890s, that had a considerable influence on me. One was called *Flatland* and the other was, I think, called *The Fourth Dimension*[11]. *Flatland* is a story of people who live on a flat surface and are therefore two-dimensional instead of three-dimensional. The people are all triangles and squares and circles and so on, and they have various adventures and romances and whatnot; but the main point of the story, which the author takes great pains to bring out, is the limitations of a two-dimensional life, the things that can and cannot be done. There are many things that we can do very easily in our three-dimensional space that cannot be done in a two-dimensional space, a flatland, because in flatland all movement is limited to the plane surface. For example, you cannot tie a knot in flatland because in order to tie a knot you would have to get out of the flat surface to pass the threads over and through one another. You can picture this fairly easily for yourself: just picture a flatland where it is not possible for one flatlander to slide over another and you will see that, although your threads can curve and bend quite easily, you cannot pass them over and under each other because that would mean going out of the flatland.

At a certain point in the story, of course, there comes an intervention from the third dimension, that is, from three-dimensional space such as we have. This is a very peculiar occurrence for the flatlanders, because they do not have any conception of a solid body, and when a sphere passes through their plane surface, they simply experience this as a point which grows very rapidly into a circle and somehow diminishes and turns back into a point and then disappears altogether. It was very strange and inexplicable that something could just materialize out of nothing and grow and shrink and disappear, but they thought of it like this because they could not conceive of any other world other than their own. After reading this book I began to think for the first time about

11 *Flatland*, E. Abbott, and *The Fourth Dimension*, E. Hinton.

the possibility of there being different worlds. The second book, *The Fourth Dimension,* was a much more mathematical book about four-dimensional space. The author gave a number of exercises to help the reader try to visualize four-dimensional bodies, such as a four-dimensional cube called a 'tesseract'. You could try to visualize what it was like by seeing what would happen to it when it passed through our space, in the same way as you can visualize what would happen to a cube that was cut down to two dimensions when passing through a plane surface. When I was a boy, I was interested in all this and used to practice a great deal trying to visualize different sorts of arrangements, different kinds of possible worlds, and I think that this practice did help me a great deal later on. I started this when I was about fourteen or fifteen years old and continued it for many years afterwards. When I said that these books had a considerable influence on me, it was because they made me realize that it was possible that there were worlds quite different from the one we know.

Our life in a three-dimensional world is much more free than life in flatland, but life in a four-dimensional world is even freer, and has possibilities that we can hardly imagine. At the same time, there are various properties of three-dimensional existence which cannot be found in a four-dimensional one. For example, we said that it is not possible to tie a knot in a two-dimensional world, and this is fairly easy to see, but it is also not possible to tie a knot in a four-dimensional world. The four-dimensional world is so free that all knots slip away through the additional freedom of movement that is possible. It is exactly the same as giving a circle trapped inside a ring in the world of flatland the degree of freedom of our space so that it can slide over the enclosure. In four-dimensional space, knots do not hold and the links of chains separate without any resistance; vessels that are closed for our world are open, and a 'container' in this higher-dimensional world is something totally different from what it is in the world that we know. We have got to try to see that the different worlds are different not because they have different things in them but because they have *different degrees of freedom.*

Both Abbott and Hinton had a vision of what the real differences were between different worlds and tried to express their vision in the form of images. We have the difficulty that our thought is based on this world of sense experience, the world of three-dimensional bodies. It requires a special mental effort to imagine any other kind of existence. Ordinarily, when people talk about 'higher worlds', they reduce it all to some sort of silliness. We are conditioned by the world of bodies and fail to realize that we have possibilities of a totally different order to those that belong to this world. When higher worlds penetrate into our own we make the same kind of mistake as the flat-landers did when the sphere passed through their world: they could not imagine that anything with the nature of a sphere could possibly exist and they changed it all into something they could think and talk about in the way they were accustomed. Our way of thinking and talking even makes us experience what is going on in a conditioned way. We can even use the material of the two books we have been talking about to reinforce our habits of thought.

What we want to get at is the real substance of these images of the higher worlds, the possibility of being transformed and becoming different *kinds* of people. We have tried to describe different degrees of 'being human', but the important thing to realize is that the differences involved are not differences in the world of bodies but differences in the world of being, in the depth and coherence of consciousness. The world in which we live corresponds to our being. The being of the ordinary undeveloped man such as we know and as we are is only capable of maintaining itself in a world very like the one in which we physically exist. If our level of being changes, we can live in a higher world. We acquire a 'container' for what we are that is different from a physical body. But this does not mean that our existence in the ordinary world ceases. Transformation means being able to live in more than one world.

A great mistake, one that is very common, is to think that the higher worlds are more 'fairy-like' or insubstantial than our familiar one. This largely comes about because we use such words as 'finer', 'subtler', 'more refined', and so on to describe the quality of experience in them. We ourselves have also talked about a 'spirit world', and our ordinary associations will easily make us think of it in terms of ghosts and similar insubstantial entities, when it is quite unlike that. In reality, a transition from a lower to a higher world is one from a less substantial state of being to a more substantial one. Going back to the example of *Flatland,* flat-landers have no thickness. In our world they would crumple into nothing at all, whereas in their own world they are even cognitive beings with indestructible bodies. In the same way, all that we take to be solid, enduring, with properties of inside and outside, would not at all appear like that in a higher world. Our bodies, on which we rely for our existence in this world, would appear to be flimsy and insubstantial. In fact, solid bodies as we know them could not exist in a higher world.

All this is illustrated very well in another book which made a strong impression on me, and which some of you may have read, C.S. Lewis's *The Great Divorce*. This man had very great insights, real intuitions, about the nature of the higher realities, and he managed to convey some of his insights in his writings. He describes here three worlds. One is a lower world, a world of separation, of divorce, where the whole tendency is toward isolation and getting more and more shut up in one's own subjectivity. This lower world, which is entirely dreamlike, with no substance to it all, is his representation of those who have rejected the purpose of life, and have lived just for their own egoistic ends and have become shut up in them. The higher world, the world of reality, the spiritual reality, is incomparably more solid. It is inhabited by those who have gone beyond, have become free. The third world is the ordinary world we know, the world everyone starts out in, which is in between the other two. The story tells about the fate of people after death. Those who have formed something in this life, who have acquired what we would call a soul, are able to enter into a higher world, whereas those who have not acquired anything for themselves in this world, who have rejected that possibility, have gone to the lower world. But it is possible to move from the lower world to the higher one, and those who become free wish to help those in the lower world to escape.

There are half a dozen different episodes involving different people who are brought out of the lower world and given a chance of entering the higher world, and only one is able to respond and become free, because the spiritual world in comparison to the lower world is intolerably substantial. The free beings, the ones that have a soul, have more substantial bodies than the others. The ones who have not become free are insubstantial, ghosts in comparison, and when they are placed in front of this possibility of being helped out of their state, they cannot take advantage of it. Lewis gives a beautiful description of this, telling how they find themselves in a meadow of a higher world and they cannot bear to stand on the grass because it is too strong, too substantial for them. They cannot bear the contact because it is as if they were standing on needles, whereas those who have gained something during life are substantial enough to bend the grass down.

Once you have experienced something of the nature of the higher worlds for yourself, you can see how valuable these images are, and that a person who is able to write something like this has had direct experience of the difference between one world and another. The truth is that the material world is the thin world, the insubstantial one. This has often been said by people who have had visions - mystics and so on. They experience some state and reporting on it afterward say, 'I saw that this world is nothing but a shadow, and it is the other world that is real.' Unless you have had some experience of it yourself, and are able to hold it in front of you, it is hard to understand what they are saying.

Our way of approaching this will, first of all, be through the *energies*, since these determine the kind of experience we can have. The different energies correspond to different levels of being, each having its own degree of freedom, its possibilities and impossibilities. Different energies also have different gradations of substantiality, which make different kinds of existence possible. We can go further and say that each of the worlds we shall speak about has its own kinds of energies. There are the more restricted, limited energies of the physical world; there are the freer energies of life, and there are the energies beyond life which act with even fewer restrictions.

Depending on the energy which is present, two people who are externally in the same situation may be in very different worlds. If a higher energy is present in one of them, he will be able to think, feel, and act with greater freedom than the other; he will have more possibilities. He may only experience this without understanding it, and fail to see that he has entered an 'inner world' which is not a dream. For him, for example, 'choice' has become a reality; whereas choice is not a reality in the world of bodies. If we 'work on ourselves', it is possible to concentrate an energy which brings us into the world where choice is possible. There is no movement in a physical sense - it is a displacement from one plane of existence to another, which cannot be observed in physical terms. This can bring with it a feeling of great joy and release, but what is important about it is that we have acquired something of the substance belonging to a higher world, and therefore have a place in it. If it were not for such temporary displacements into other worlds, we would have no possibility of transformation, no possibility of gaining material for understanding our true human potential. But it is a totally different matter to secure a permanent place in a higher world.

The world that is natural, though not ordinary, for man is centered in the sensitive energy, ranging from the automatic energy below to the conscious energy above. The man living in this world is sensitive to the workings of his mind, his feelings, and his body. He is capable of working successfully with the automatic energy without being caught up in the flow of it, and he can also separate consciousness from sensitivity. It is through this separation, which is probably what Gurdjieff meant by 'remembering oneself', that the natural man can become open to still higher worlds. By all this we can easily see that we are not living in the natural world but in a lower one.

Unnatural Man and Supernatural Man

Man can live a life centered on energies other than sensitivity. If the energies are lower, we can speak of 'unnatural man'. The energies of consciousness and beyond lead us up to 'supernatural man'. In speaking about both of them we have difficulties. When we are in the unnatural state, we do not see it for what it is; for that, we have to 'wake up' and assume the perspective of the normal human world. The difficulty with the higher worlds is rather different: we are not absolutely cut off from them, but when something of a significantly higher order comes, we fail to recognize it for what it is. It is important to get rid of all the inappropriate pictures we have about higher worlds that are embedded in our thinking.

One step down from the sensitive world is the world of automatism. This we call the world of 'sleeping man'. In this world we are only occasionally able to be aware of the world around us or even of what we are doing. This always comes as a surprise to people who have not discovered the enormous power of the automatic energy to organize the most complex, but routine and habitual activities. Our eyes look but we do not see; our ears hear but we do not listen; our minds associate but we do not think. We may think that we are choosing, but in fact everything happens as in a machine being fed with a mixture of programs: first one, then another, all according to external stimulation and internal interaction. Compared with the world of sensitivity, it is really 'flatland'. It is the world that is proper to animals, not to men. In this world, we cannot observe ourselves. We may think about ourselves a great deal; we may have all kinds of emotional ups and downs, but in none of it do we see anything. Sometimes this is called the world of 'blind' people, the *monde des aveugles.* While we are in it, all our judgments and opinions are totally false. It is typical that we will find fault with other people for something that we ourselves may, at that very moment, be doing.

In *Beelzebub's Tales,* Gurdjieff distinguishes between what he calls the *Itoklanoz* and the *Foolasnitamnian* principles of living. The first is proper to all two and one-brained beings: vertebrates and invertebrates. Only the second is proper to a three-brained being such as man. It operates when the sensitivity is not conditioned, and it is open to the organizing power of the higher conscious energy. Then it is possible to begin to live according to the true 'sense and aim of man's existence'. The world dominated by automatism has the sensitivity of only slavish reaction, bursts of emotion and sensation that swallow us up. In this world, we have no possibility of seeing what the point of our life is. There are built up around us all sorts of absurd artifices which provide us with an alternative to real life: a landscape of opinions, fashions, habits, entertainments, means of manipulation, words, and so on that are utterly futile. This is the sort of thing Gurdjieff means by the 'unbecoming conditions of ordinary being existence established by them themselves'. We are deluded by the power of thought in us which gives us power over the animals and the rest of the material world. This is a real power, but it belongs to the physical world when it is automatic. We no more control it than we control anything else. In the same way, we can see that certain sleeping people are adroit at manipulating other sleeping people; but the one is no more free than the other.

The bits of sensitivity that come to us in the automatic world are our 'peak experiences'. In reality, this world is terribly dull. Nothing can really happen; nothing can change. All the time we are dependent on some kind of external stimulation to keep us going, to provide us with a certain momentum, but the sensitivity that is in us can be aware of the tedium of it all. People doing dull and repetitive work will throw a spanner in the works or go on strike just to introduce something new, some kind of feeling. It is often the case that we find some negative emotion gives us some feeling of existing because we have nothing else in us that is at all close to life. Negativity is even sought after to alleviate the flatness of the world.

Below the automatic energy is the vital energy. Man can even descend into this world, where no kind of experience is even remotely possible. This is the world of things. We can become en-meshed in it. We can think of it as the 'last dregs of automatism', the shadow of the shadow of living experience. Our attempts to escape the mechanical world through negativity draw us into a world of complete delusion, where the force of emotion makes us feel that we are really human and fully alive even though we are in a sub-human state. This is why identification with our negative emotions is such a terrible thing: we become *less than automatic*; we live entirely inside a false image of the world and ourselves that can only subsist at all according to the vital level of energy. This state is lower than that of the animals. In the New Testament it is called the 'outer darkness', the place of weeping and wailing and gnashing of teeth.

So long as our lives are lived in these lower worlds, there is no possibility of changing. Change is only possible in the world of sensitivity, which reaches to the conscious level. The world above the natural world is centered on consciousness, reaches down to the sensitive level and up to the creative level. It is 'four-dimen-sional' in comparison with the world of our ordinary experience. Here, certain kinds of restraints disappear and we find that we are no longer tied in knots. In this world, there is a different vision. Seeing is no longer a great effort, but we live in seeing. If we say that there is a world of blind people and a world of one-eyed peo-ple - and that 'in the country of the blind the one-eyed one is king' -then the world of consciousness is a world of two-eyed people. This is the world of the men or women who have found their own 'I', their own master. The central aim of our work is to enter into this world, for then transformation becomes a reality and a deeper kind of work, real spiritual work, is possible.

It is very difficult for us to live in this world, because it lacks many of the supports to which we are accustomed. We will re-member how it is that the containers which are fully enclosed in the three-dimensional world are no longer enclosed in a world of four dimensions. What is closed in the three-dimensional world is open in a higher dimensional one. All of this is important for our understanding, because we have to grasp what it means when we say that we do not, as we are, have anything that can contain the conscious energy. We can have a moment of seeing, one in which we see and understand everything in a quite different way, yet almost before it has come to pass in our experience, it has slipped away again. We are not organized enough to hold the experience. Thus it is, that we cannot enter the world of consciousness until we have a 'something' that can contain conscious experience. This something is called a 'body', but we have to understand this word in the general sense of being a container for experience rather than something with arms and legs.

A great deal of what is said about 'inner bodies', 'higher bodies', 'subtler bodies', and so on is so much nonsense because it has no practical foundation. It is so often assumed that we have them as a matter of course and even that they give us experiences similar to the ones that we know, but only nicer. The reality is that these 'bodies' are to be attained through inner work, and are not possible at all for people living on sub-human levels.

The false idea that the body of the conscious world is like a ghostly spirit of little substance comes from the fact that this body can move in a region that is inaccessible to the physical body. Gurdjieff calls this body the 'body *kesdjan*'. It can exert an influence beyond and even independently of the physical body, not because it is tenuous and able to slip out through our pores or anything nonsensical like that but because it has added degrees of freedom. It is not possible to recognize the operations of this body, even if it were developed in a person standing before us, because they cannot be observed in the physical world. The transformation by which it is made is an inner, secret one that is outside ordinary perception. Because we do not actually see what this body is, we run the risk of either getting lost in fantasy about it or of dismissing it altogether as an imaginary, entirely subjective experience. We are just like the Flatlanders who speculated about the appearance of the sphere, trying to reduce it all to what they could think about in terms of their ordinary 'flatland' experience.

There is a still higher world that is centered in the creative energy. Here, only in the lower limit is there any consciousness. This is a supra-conscious world that reaches up to the unitive energy of love. It is the world of 'great doing' where events take place totally invisible to the mind and awareness. It is beyond space and time, beyond number, and beyond separation. It is totally free from the limitations of existence and can be entered only through the sacrifice of our separate nature. In this world what seems to us to be impossible is a reality.

We can call this the 'five-dimensional world', and the corresponding five-dimensional container is a body of a still higher order to the body that can bear conscious experience. Gurdjieff called it the 'higher-being body' and sometimes the 'soul'. It is possible to talk about this world in this abstract sort of way, but it is hardly possible for us to form a mental image of what it is about, let alone actually experience what it means. There is an almost insurmountable gulf between us and this world that makes it almost impossible for us to understand it. We are aware because we have been told through Revelations that various manifestations of Higher Beings have worked on the earth, but we never see them as they are. Instead we look at them according to the limitations of the world we are in and see separate saints and prophets, and occupy ourselves with comparing and contrasting the things that they have said. In reality, they are neither many nor one; neither a set of separate individuals nor just the same as each other. The distinction of one and many does not apply at all in the world to which they belong.

Perhaps we can form some idea of this higher world by saying that it is possible for beings that live in it to choose whether to exist or not to exist. There is no longer any need for dependence on an existential support of any kind. The 'higher-being body' is capable of forming the instruments that it needs whenever it needs them. To go back to the language we were using in the earlier chapters, we can say that this world is the very medium of will, or we can even call it the 'world of will'.[12] Even the duration of life can become a matter of conscious choice. There is the power to do. What happens can be entirely independent of anything that has taken place in the past. Nothing is fixed because there is nothing that has to exist in order to be.

Incomprehensible as all this is for us, there are higher worlds still. The penultimate world is centered in the energy of unity, or cosmic love, which underlies everything. It is this energy which redeems the whole of creation and makes possible the return to the Source from which everything comes. We associate the world of redemption with the highest figures of mankind, with Abraham, Moses, Buddha, Christ, and Muhammad, but that is where it ends for us. What we see are the images of these beings 'sent from Above', not what they are. Beyond the 'Above', a word that

---

12 This seems to contradict what was said about the universality of will, being and function. Here the 'world of will' means the realm of will that is not enmeshed in existence. In Sufism, this is the realm of the universal, but 'created' Spirit, *ruh-i kulli* and the individual spirit. The same word spirit, ruh, is used to refer to both will in the cosmic sense and also the energies which are its instruments. Hence the *ālam-i arvāh* the world of spirits, or the world of energies. The 'world of will' is the world of acts which do not depend on an existing apparatus. It is unconditioned, or spiritual.

Gurdjieff uses for the penultimate world, is the beginning and end of all, the Unfathomable Source.

To make anything useful out of these descriptions of higher worlds we need to be able to bring ourselves to see the limitations of our thought and understanding. This is not the same as saying, 'Well, of course I can't possibly understand these things. If you say it is like that, who am I to dispute it?' We need the practical approach of struggling with ourselves until we can actually see how narrow and flimsy our thinking is, and how it is that the kind of thinking we have is derived. We need to be able to confront the experience that we have, without the screen of associations and pictures that is produced by the formatory apparatus. Then we can find a different attitude to everything we enter into.

It is necessary to learn how to stop reacting to ideas and be able to bring them into confrontation with experience. This is especially important for what we are about to embark upon, which is in some ways far more abstract than anything that has gone before. But although it is difficult to grasp at first exposure, once people have learned how to relate it to their own experience, it becomes possible for them to understand and talk about things which otherwise would be too elusive.

Being Under Laws

We have just looked at what the idea of different worlds could mean from the standpoint of energies. Now we have to go back to our starting point and ask what can be made out of the proposition that higher worlds are 'under fewer restrictions' than lower ones. What this means, first of all, is that what is *impossible* in a lower world can be *possible* in a higher world. What can happen and what cannot happen depends on which world we are in. For example, all the worlds that we can be aware of are subject to separation in space and succession in time. Things depend for their identity on not being something else. The higher worlds do not suffer under such constraints: 'here' and 'there', 'past' and 'future',' 'me' and 'not me' do not exclude each other. However, even these higher worlds are subject to some conditions, though we can scarcely imagine what these mean. Gurdjieff in *Beelzebub's Tales* often talks about 'higher events' as proceeding 'according to law'.

Laws are an expression of will: this kind of thing can happen, but that kind of thing cannot happen. The more laws there are, the greater the constraints, and the greater the constraints, the more 'fragmentary' the corresponding mode of existence. Events become more and more dependent on other events, until nothing can happen at all unless a collection of circumstances brings it about.

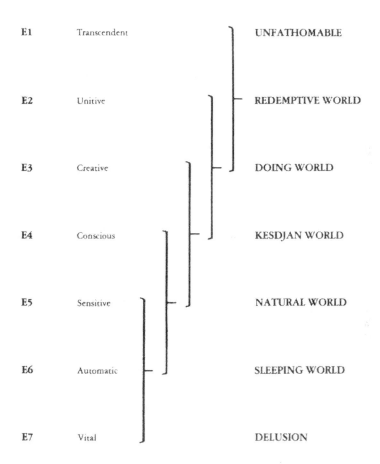

SEVEN WORLDS IN TERMS OF ENERGIES
FIG. 5.1

We see that what we are arriving at by thinking in this way is something that looks very much like the physical world that is studied by science, or like the world of bodies in which everything is outside everything else and anything that happens tends to be canceled out by other things that happen. This is the world of thermodynamics and probabilities. But we can also see what it means in terms of obvious facts like 'you can't get a quart out of a pint pot'. Things are so fixed that they can be counted and measured; so interdependent that nothing can really change because of the inertia of the total complex.

What we are after with the work of transformation is to come into a condition where we are under fewer laws. None of our real problems can be solved in this world. In this world, we are too dependent, too enmeshed with other things. We cannot see what is going on. In the world of sleeping people, the 'inner world' is divorced from the 'outer world' and we only dream about doing things. Nothing can change because there is not a degree of freedom in which change is possible.

It is not difficult to get some idea of what it means to come under more and more laws. If we join the army, we come under military laws, and these are in addition to those of civilian life. We cannot go where we like when we like; we have to perform duties that are given to us arbitrarily, and so on. If we break some of the military laws, we go into prison, where the restrictions are even greater. The doors are locked against us and every part of the day is scheduled for us. Everyone who has ever been in prison knows what this feels like, and also how it feels when released: the first explosion of freedom has a tremendous impact. The transition between worlds is just like that, only a far deeper experience. The Fathers of the Church used to pray to be released 'from the prison-house of my sins'. Our ordinary state is like that of a prison, and this image appears in many of the Sermons of the Buddha. We ourselves have often used the image of 'slavery' to describe the automatic state of man, though such a man is in slavery to his own conditioned nature, rather than to an external master.

The relief at being able to have our own thoughts, our own feelings, and our own actions should be unmistakable. It is on this that we have to base a great deal of our understanding of what it means to make a transition from a lower to a higher world; that is, to come under fewer laws.

The way in which Gurdjieff talked about the worlds was built on the idea of the Law of Three. This is the law of 'how things happen', and it could be expressed by saying that 'nothing can happen unless there is brought about a combination of three independently arising forces having the nature of affirming, denying and reconciling'. Ouspensky reported Gurdjieff's presentation of the scheme of worlds in his *In Search of the Miraculous*. There it all looks very abstract. Gurdjieff says that the highest world is where the three forces are indistinguishable, and he calls this World 1. The next world is where the forces are distinguished, and this is therefore called World 3, in the sense of the 'world of three'. Then comes the world in which the three forces enter into combinations, and this is World 6. And so it goes on with Worlds 12, 24, 48, and 96. All the numbers refer to how many laws there are, so that in the highest world there is only one law, whereas in the lowest world there are ninety-six laws. What these various laws could possibly mean is hardly discussed and it all looks like an exercise in simple mathematics. But Gurdjieff's way was to put material into the hands of people for them to work with, and come to see for themselves. What people had to bring was their own struggle to understand. What he provided was material from very extraordinary traditions, which would be almost impossible to discover from the experience of a single human life. This is particularly true of his formulation of the law of three.

Teaching about the law of three exists in very many traditions, East and West. We can read about it in the *Tao Teh King,* but perhaps the oldest expression of it is to be found in the Sankhya philosophy of India, which is more than two thousand five hundred years old. The Sankhya teaching about the three *gunas,* or qualities of nature, had a profound effect on all of Indian thinking. It describes the nature of the three gunas - *rajas, tamas,* and *sattva* – in various ways, and says that there is a primal state of purity in which they are all One. From this One comes the three qualities, but not mixed, and from the three come the mixing that produces all the diversity of the world. All this is very close to Gurdjieff's explanations of the worlds. What was more original in the material that Gurdjieff brought was his great insight into what it means for people to be able to see for themselves the working of the law of three. His special precept was that man as he is 'third force blind'. Because of this, he never sees how things really work, how they come about, how they can change. He is always in a world of pushing or resisting and does not see the reconciling force. It is only when we can perceive through our head, our heart, and our body together that the law of three becomes a reality for us.

Gurdjieff gave quite another expression to the idea of different worlds in *Beelzebub's Tales* than the one which appears in *In Search of the Miraculous,* often going to the other extreme of the abstractions reported in Ouspensky's book, but we shall save most of this material until later. What we have to bring in at this point is that the Creation only begins with World 6. Worlds 1 and 3 are 'uncreated'. It is only when the three forces come into combination that there can be said to 'be' anything at all. World I we shall call 'The Unfathomable'. It is totally beyond any being. The three forces are indistinguishable; they are one. This will appear to us to mean absolute nothingness, because nothing can be distinguished from anything else. Here being, freedom, action, purpose have no meaning at all. Then comes the world in which the three forces are distinguished: World 3. This world is the link between the Unfathomable Source and the Creation, and we can talk of it in terms of three forces or three laws. It is impossible to conceive. Who can represent to themselves a state of affirmation that is not an affirmation toward something, toward some denial or resistance or field of action? None of the three forces can be pictured apart from the others. At best, we can extrapolate from our experience of function, being, and will, as we did in Chapter 1. Yet Gurdjieff says that it is possible for a created being to come into this world. In *Beelzebub's Tales,* this corresponds to the degree of 'objective reason' that Gurdjieff calls the 'sacred *anklad'*, which is only 'three degrees' removed from the Reason of Our Endlessness: clearly a reference to World 3. Between World 1 and World 3 there is a barrier which cannot be penetrated from the lower side.

All the great religious traditions speak of these higher worlds. There must therefore be something important about them that we need to know. World 3 is the seat of the Buddha, the Supremely Enlightened One. In Sufism, this world is the *Beit-ul Ma'mour,* the abode of God. In Christianity, it is the Holy Trinity. Beyond this world is the Void, the Godhead, the Unfathomable: World 1. World 1 is the ultimate Source of all the other worlds, but World 3 does not arise by a creative act. That is why in Christianity there was introduced the phrase 'begotten, not made', to speak about how it is in the second world. World 3 is divine because it exists only through love.

The interaction between the three forces gives the six fundamental laws of the Creation, which is World 6. If we call the affirming force 1, the denying force 2, and the reconciling force 3, we have a very short and convenient way of referring to the six laws. Each of these laws, as we said, is a combination of the three forces; and what distinguishes them from each other is the order in which they combine. Thus, there is the law 1-2-3, called the law of expansion, or the law of involution. It is by this that diversity is created. Then there is the complementary law of evolution or concentration, which is expressed as 2-1-3. By this law, diversity is able to return to unity, or things are able to return to their source. The law 3-2-1 signifies a third law, called the law of freedom. Through this law, it is possible for free initiative to act in the Creation. Then there are the laws to do with the order and maintenance of the world. First, the law of order itself, 3-1-2, which says that everything has an inherent pattern. Then the law of interaction, 1-3-2, which is the law of universal connectedness through which everything can interact with everything else. Finally, there is the law of identity, 2-3-1, by which everything can preserve and affirm its own nature. Taken all together, the six are the fundamental laws of 'world creation and world maintenance' which Gurdjieff said are proper to the understanding of a true man.

World 6 is the world of unity in diversity, but it lacks the distinction of one and many. The part of us that belongs to this world is the same for all of us. It is from this world that there comes the unity of life. Only he may enter this world who has shed his own individuality, his own 'I', and has nothing of his own. In the very careful exposition of Mahayana Buddhism, he is called the *Bodhisattva*, the 'pure spirit'. His characteristic is compassion. He renounces his own liberation into the final state so that he can retain a hold on physical existence, and be able to work with creatures. He can participate in all creatures; he accepts the being of all creatures; and he is the source of the help that comes to us. World 6 is the world of the highest mystical experience, of being without the separateness of existence.

Below this world, we come to World 12, the world of individuality. The number of laws is doubled. There are parts, distinctions between inside and outside, this and that, which make individuals possible. World 12 is the first world in which we can count and therefore we can form some idea of it. It corresponds to the world of the man who has his own 'I' and it is the world of all individual wills. There are not many wills, as there might be many objects; all wills are one. There are all the laws of World 6 but, in addition, there is another set of laws to do with the manifold, the multitude of separate existences. In this world there is both the One and the Many, and because of this the number of laws is doubled.

The will is like the air. The air is all one, but enters into the breathing of separate creatures. In the lower worlds, the will, just like the air, serves to keep things going, but in World 12 the will is the agent of creative power. Time and space do not apply as they do with us. In this world they are mastered. Here, decision is a reality: what is decided *is*. All our expectations about this world are an obstruction. Getting into this world is not like becoming better or superior versions of what we are, it is attaining the freedom 'to do'. We live under the absurdity of taking all the limitations and restrictions of our mode of existence, where we are separated from ourselves and from others by the 'materiality' of the world we live in, to be what we really are.

When we use the word 'materiality' here we mean it in the sense that the more conditioned a mode of existence is, the more it is 'material': fixed, inert, uncreative, and predictable. The more 'spiritual' a mode of existence is, the more it can change and transform. In the higher worlds, there is less and less of a mode of existence in which everything is just a combination of already existing materials. The substance of the higher worlds is 'ever new', able to create its own forms and not have to derive them from external sources. We have to understand that our ideas about what 'substance' is are almost entirely derived from our experience of the very lowest worlds. But 'substance' is entirely relative to the worlds. The substance of ourselves as they are is too conditioned or too 'thin' to be engaged by 'I'. The substance of World 12 is totally different because it cannot be contained in the ordinary worlds of man. Therefore, it is true to say that for us true individuality 'does not exist'. Taking all this into account, we can begin to see that the approach to the worlds we are taking through laws must lead us to the same conclusions as the approach through energies.

In the next lower world, World 24, events are subject to actualization in time and space. This is something that we can set ourselves to understand. We call this the 'world of essence', meaning the world in which a man's inner life can begin to be real. This is the world in which we should be living in a normal life, just as the proper world for animals is the lower one of World 48. It is probably the world that corresponds to the feeling people have about being 'really human', and 'being oneself' has a meaning here that it entirely lacks in the lower worlds. In our own special language we can express all this by saying that it is the world of *selfhood*, in which will is committed to existence. As well as the separation between individuals of World 12, there is now also an internal separation. If we say that this is the world of the divided and the true selves - the lower selves, we must remember, are externally dependent in a way the higher selves are not - we can see that internal division is the rule. In the divided self, it is obvious, for it is in its very nature to be pulled in contrary ways by our 'higher' and our 'lower' natures. As for the true self, it is poised at the threshold of the 'I', under the hazard of whether or not it will allow itself to be an instrument of the will.

WORLD 1	UNFATHOMABLE
WORLD 3	DIVINE WILL
WORLD 6	COMPASSION
WORLD 12	INDIVIDUALITY
WORLD 24	ESSENCE
WORLD 48	PERSONALITY
WORLD 96	DELUSION

SEVEN WORLDS IN TERMS OF LAWS
FIG. 5.2

The world of the selfhood is dependent on internal states, and this introduces a whole additional set of laws and further conditioning. Hence, twenty-four laws. Within this World 24, there are various 'places', and experience is not all of a kind. Experience in the divided self is not the same as experience in the true self. We can say that the true self corresponds to the higher world of

World 12 as it manifests in World 24. However, this self is still attached to existence. It cannot maintain itself in World 12, the world of individuality. The maintenance of our existence in World 24 depends on our being sensitive in all three centers. To maintain ourselves in World 12 we would have to be able to concentrate conscious energy.

Again, we can begin to realize that all the various ways of talking about man we have followed - in terms of centers, Gurdjieff's 'personalities', selves, energies, laws, and so on - are concerned with the very same thing; but it is a big mistake to try and reduce any of these ways to any of the others. If we hold them before us, each as an independent vision, they will illuminate each other. As we change from one way of talking to another, we can help ourselves to avoid the almost inevitable automatisms of thinking that ruin any hope of understanding things beyond the physical world.

When we introduced and discussed the idea of different selves, we frequently made use of the idea of being 'dominated by' one or another of them. We can now begin to understand this idea in terms of being under the laws of a given self and see that, though it is possible for the conscious energy to work in the divided self, the divided self is not a conscious state of being. Similarly, though the true self is subject to the working of creative energy, it is not itself of a creative substance. All the selves can be instruments or masters: that is the hazard. When they are instruments, the laws of a higher world can operate. When they are the 'law unto themselves', they bind us to a lower world. We can also say that they are the very means by which it is possible to pass from one world to another. The true self, for example, is the self through which we can be prepared to enter into the world of individuality. We have to learn to see in a different way, concentrate different kinds of energies, and 'be able' to relinquish something of our conditioned state of existence; to 'sacrifice'. The building up of a substance of an 'inner life' gives us a 'body' or 'vehicle' with which we can move in the world of twenty-four laws. Then we can 'learn' what is needed to become free of twelve of the laws and enter another world.

World 24 is founded upon free sensitivity, which simply means that we are aware of what is going on around us and inside us, without being caught up in any of the machinery. People believe that in fact this is how they are, 'I am aware of myself; I am aware of my surroundings'. The beginning of real work comes with a thorough disillusionment on this score. It is a very extraordinary thing that people can picture this natural state of man and not take any steps to verify whether it is true for them or not. It may seem an unkind thing to say, but by far the greater majority of men and women living today exist in the lower world of World 48. This is the *world of personality*, where there is a distinction between objective and subjective states, so we cannot be connected to things as they are. This distinction means that things can happen to us as if we were not there. Hence there are twenty-four laws which have to do with our existence as objects. The twenty-four laws coming from World 24 belong to our subjective state, which means that all 'higher things' are really just dreams. We have no means of discrimination. We can even make efforts, but they only serve to strengthen our conditioning. All sorts of artificial constraints arise between us in this world, so that we are entirely separated from one another, and can only communicate with each other from the outside. Our experience of time is now subjectivized, dependent on our mental, emotional, and physical states. The sense of time in the world of essence is quite different, because there we can be in touch with the pattern of things.

World 48 is the world of our material and reactional selves. It is through training of our reactional self that we can be awakened in World 24. But if we are dominated by it, all our experience is distorted by how we 'feel', that is, our lack of objectivity. The material self is the machine. If this self takes control, then any sensitivity that is produced in our organism becomes 'negativized', its relative freedom turned into a greater slavery. So it is that we come into the final and lowest world, World 96, which we call the *world of delusion*.

It is very important to understand this world because it is at the root of all our psychological problems. We are connected to it by what Gurdjieff called 'the crystallized consequences of the properties of the organ kundabuffer'. He supposed that a certain organ was implanted in man a long time back in prehistorical times that forced him to see reality 'upside down'. This was deemed necessary because man's evolution was to be arrested, and if man saw this, he would be in revolt. Later, the organ was removed from the presence of man, but by that time, there had been established certain conditions of life which perpetuated the consequences of kundabuffer. The 'crystallized consequences' are all those impulses which arise in us that are unworthy of man, such as 'self-love, vanity, swaggering, cunning', and so forth. Living in this state of delusion, life is lived for pleasure alone, and when our pleasures are interrupted we fall prey to various negative emotions which cause us to lose ourselves altogether.

Everything to do with this world is abnormal. At least, the personality can do things in the world: can perform duties, calculate, wrap up when cold, and so on. The state of delusion is far beneath that. It is totally occupied with things that have no reality at all. What it takes to be freedom is abject slavery; what it takes to be real life is just empty wastefulness. It even engenders all sorts of diseases. Gurdjieff also said that it shortens the length of our existence. This is one of Gurdjieff's most important insights into the reality of different worlds. We only truly exist in World 24. In the next world, World 48, we are, so to say, 'marking time' and time spent in this world is not a real duration of life. But in World 96 there is even 'negative time', where possibilities of experience are destroyed and squandered. To see how often we are in this world can be a very hard experience, and no one can possibly accept how often we are in it unless they come to see for themselves. But unless we see how it is, everything that we do aimed at liberation will be contaminated by the delusions of this world. We need to build in ourselves some sense of objectivity. The negative states are so powerful that they swallow us up, and they are then impossible to see. To see, we have to struggle with our negative emotions. This is the reason of the injunction, 'do not express negative emotions'.

There are ninety-six laws because every one of the laws of World 48 has a negative counterpart. We can say that what is worse than being a machine is being a machine that believes itself to be God.

Real Understanding

I have been developing this picture for you because it is really necessary if you are to have any kind of image of what it really means to be transformed. We see and touch the world around us, but we do not realize that it is not this world but the higher worlds that are substantially real, and we cannot understand this until we have begun to experience it for ourselves. To do this we have to learn how to exist differently, how to exist in more than one world at a time. Altogether we have spoken of seven worlds, all of which can influence our lives. So far, we have spoken as if these worlds were quite separate; and while this is largely true in terms of the interactions that can take place between them, they are all nevertheless coexistent. All the worlds penetrate everything existing. We do not have to change our place physically to enter a different world, but we have to learn how to place ourselves under the influence of higher laws which are present here and now. Practically speaking, to study this system of worlds in detail we have to study all the various laws which apply in each world, as well as the ways in which one set of laws can be superseded by another. All these various orders of laws are workings of the law of three in one or another aspect or combination, acting with correspondingly different, as Gurdjieff termed it, 'degrees of vivifyingness' in the different worlds. We cannot study them and their operations theoretically, but only by coming to see them operate in ourselves. The practice of observing ourselves itself places us under different laws, and gives us the possibility of experiencing our existence in more than one world at a time: the one who observes is not the one who is observed, and they reside in two different worlds under two different sets of laws. If one tackles the scheme of worlds in this manner, with this investigative attitude, it becomes a very valuable framework for thought, and a useful instrument for putting our understanding in order.

For the most part, as we are, we live in Worlds 48 and 96. We may do various mental exercises of the sort which enable us to form some sort of mental image of different dimensions, higher worlds. We may read various descriptions of the different worlds which describe them more or less convincingly, but there is the very great danger in all of this that we will not interpret these exercises or descriptions correctly. The idea of the system of the worlds is very valuable, but we can mislead ourselves with it because it enables us to speak about things that are not within the reach of our senses, and that we cannot point to. The scheme itself is the result of influences from the higher worlds, a symbolic language that we cannot use and correctly understand until we have had some corresponding experiences of our own. We ordinarily confuse understanding with the ability to talk about things, to use words convincingly: in reality, understanding is non-verbal. Understanding a certain law, for example, involves seeing and participating in its action in and upon us. Like the being of which it can be said to be a measure, understanding is hidden, inward, a result less of changing what we 'know' than of changing ourselves and the way in which we exist. To understand more, we have to *be* more, have to become transformed.

The true test of our understanding is not that it gives our ordinary selves more to talk about, but that it enables us to create these higher worlds within ourselves, to enter into the higher worlds which, until then, must remain for us only words. And to make this entry, we may find that we have to learn how to empty ourselves of all that we ordinarily acclaim as our 'riches', all our 'understanding', 'attitudes', 'opinions' and all the rest of the material that has become fixed in us over the course of our lives. If we can empty ourselves, can be empty inwardly, then everything can enter into us. We can have everything if we can learn to separate from our ordinary selves, learn how to get out of the way. It is the hardest thing to empty oneself, but if we can once learn how this is to be done, then everything can come.

CHAPTER 6

The Law of Three

In order to be able to change, we have to understand, in a real sense, the law of threefoldness and how it is altered and limited in the passage through the various worlds. People who grasp this law intellectually are very rarely nearer to it than those who feel completely lost. It is one thing to be able to deal with these matters in words and quite another to live them. At the very start we all suffer from a tremendous drawback: the working of our centers is dominated by polarity, so that everything we look at, everything we feel and think and sense is experienced in terms of two forces and not three. For us, three forces are higher-dimensional, and Gurdjieff expressed this by saying that 'Man is third force blind'.

We see everything in terms of affirmation and denial, yes and no, like and dislike, and so on, which is sometimes called the 'pairs of opposites'. For the moving center there is action and repose, activity and passivity. We are either restless, looking for things to do with our hands and bodies, or we are the opposite, slothful and indolent, when even the thought of any kind of physical work tires us. In the instinctive center, the sort of dualism we find is one of pleasure and pain, sickness and health, instinctive attraction and instinctive aversion. This center is working all the time to keep inner processes in balance through its polar sensitivity, adjusting to too much or too little acid in the blood and so on. The emotional center works according to like and dislike; it makes us seek out the pleasurable and shun the unpleasant. If an experience is emotionally neutral, the emotional center does not work at all because neutrality is not an independent force. The intellectual center has yes and no, agreement and disagreement, acceptance and rejection, knowing and not knowing. If we look at one object and say that it is a chair and then look at something else, we say this is not a chair. This way of dividing things belongs to our ordinary mechanical logic.

In all the ordinary working of our centers, it is very rarely that we experience the opposites at the same time. Usually, our experience is dominated by only one of the two forces. This leads, as we shall see, to a fundamental misunderstanding of what affirmation and denial mean. But in the natural state of man it is the simultaneous experience of the two forces that gives him the power of choice. Because he is able to experience pleasure and pain, like and dislike, yes and no, at the same time, he is able to see that it is the law that all opposites cancel out each other. It is in the very nature of things that pleasure and pain balance out in life, but this is quite outside the experience of personality in World 48. If the personality is active, inactivity is not real for it; if it is full of inertia, it cannot conceive what it is to be energetic. If it is in a pleasurable state, pain does not exist, and vice versa. Once we really begin to see that this is so, we can understand how it is that we do so many things that are contrary to our true welfare. For the personality, all that is real is the force that it is experiencing at the given moment. If there is pleasure, there is nothing unpleasant, and life is 'all roses, roses', but if we get into a bad state, life is just horrid. The utter absurdity of experience in World 48 has to be seen to be believed. For all we might read about it, the facts we see for ourselves will catch us completely by surprise.

In World 48, we are like mechanisms, seeking for pleasure, wanting to be with people that we like, attracted to ideas we agree with, and all these things we believe to be 'good'. What is painful for us - the people we do not like, the ideas we disagree with, and the rest - are all the things we believe to be 'bad'. However incoherent or blind it all is, we live in a world where there are 'yes' things for us and 'no' things for us. We believe them to be quite separate, and that it is possible to have the one without the other. Because of this lack of realism - which is a lack of *seeing* - we are bound to regard the 'no' things as harmful or even evil. We do not have too much trouble forming some idea of the cosmic role of the affirming force. We can picture God the Creator, or some creative power, but we can have no understanding of the cosmic role of the denying force, because we always see it as negative. In reality, the denying force is equal in stature and importance to the affirming force.

In *Beelzebub's Tales*, it is said that His Endlessness, the Source, was obliged to create the existing world in order to have a source from which the place of His Abode could be maintained. It is within the power of His Endlessness to create something that is really independent. Gurdjieff builds up a picture of how emanations from the Abode of His Endlessness, the Holy Sun Absolute, went out into the space of the universe and, beginning to act at certain points, brought about the concentrations called Second Order Suns, which we call stars. These became a denying source in relation to the Sun Absolute; that is, they became a field of action. It then became possible for the emanations from the Sun Absolute to take on the reconciling role in the creative action originating in the stars, out of which came the 'return to the Source'. Creation has a necessary role to play, and it cannot be thought of as negative in any sense.

The parity of the Creator and the Creation is made clear in another description Gurdjieff gives of the three forces, calling them 'God-the-Father', 'God-the-Son' and 'God-the-Holy-Ghost'. We cannot think of the Son as negative. Somehow or other the Father, the creative power, has to be able to express itself, affirm itself, and therefore the Son is begotten, and enters the world to become the medium through which the Father can be expressed. Christian theologians have been convinced by some kind of intuitive experience that the Son is in no way inferior to the Father. The Son has a different, but in no way inferior, role to play in the cosmos.

An example of affirmation and denial that is very often used is that of man and woman, and it is said that the man stands for affirmation, the first force, and the woman for denial or receptivity, the second force. However, this has had the result of making people think that a woman is in an inferior position, or that she must always be passive according to some social criterion. This quite misses the point. We must see that woman is equal to man; that the sexes are truly equal. The difference is that they play different cosmic roles, both of which are equally necessary for our human completion, and these roles do not come out in the medium of social conventions but have an inward, hidden nature. It is only when there can be a meeting of equals, a meeting of mutual acceptance, that these cosmic roles can be a reality.

Perhaps our blindness to the importance of the denying force is most forcibly seen in the difficulty we have of equating the cosmic roles of God-the-Son and Satan. They are essentially the same, but because Satan is the adversary, the very personification of the denying force, we find it terribly hard not to think of him as negative. Yet without temptation, and without the force of resistance, the transformation of individuals would not be possible, the workings of the world would not be possible, and the purpose of the creation could not be fulfilled. All this is not simply theology. It is the very reality we find when we begin seriously, in practice, to work on ourselves. The very foundation of this work is the establishment in ourselves of the struggle between 'yes' and 'no'. Our liberation becomes possible when we begin to struggle with our own 'denying principle'. It is through our own denial that we are able to transform.

One-force living corresponds to World 48. It is only in World 24 that we are able, through what we call the 'freeing of the sensitivity', to experience two forces at the same time. While we are experiencing one state, we can also experience its opposite; while we are agreeing with an idea, we can also experience disagreement with it. Unless we can do this, it is not possible to understand the second force, the denying force. Even in World 48 we can come into a state where, for a time, the sensitivity is freed. We must learn how to use these opportunities. The understanding of all three forces properly belongs to World 12, in which it is possible to see things as they really are. There we are able to see that there is something apart from both affirmation and denial which is a source of freedom and that it is through this third force that wholeness comes.

There is a great deal that can be learned about the working of the three forces by actualizing them in the experience of our centers. The head brain corresponds to the affirming force, the body brain to the denying force, and the feeling brain to the reconciling force. Whenever we set ourselves to understand something, or to work in a different way, all the brains can be involved. Ultimately, what we are after is expressed in a prayer that is quoted by Gurdjieff in *Beelzebub's Tales* 'Sources of Divine Rejoicings, Revolts and Sufferings, direct your action upon us'. This prayer is addressed to the formation of the higher bodies in ourselves. The seed of our spiritual body is in us, or is in our 'I'. This is the source of rejoicing. In the course of our transformation, our physical body is the source of revolt. What has to come is so much 'otherwise' to our ordinary selves, with their thoughts and feelings, that this 'body', this entrenched mode of existence that we have, must be denial. When we pray like this, we can become aware that all of us, all of what we are, is nothing but denial. We can begin to understand that our ideas of the meaning of affirmation have been based on the experiences of self-will and self-assertion. Freedom comes when we can deny ourselves before some hidden obligation. This is the way of what Gurdjieff called 'intentional suffering'. Only through such suffering can an unlimited affirmation be reconciled with a conditioned existence. But what this suffering means can never be explained. All the suffering that we know is linked to emotions of misery, fear, attachment, and desire. A suffering that is linked with rejoicing will seem to us either absurd or a perversion.

It is no easier to understand the cosmic working of the three forces than it is to understand the prayer. It is possible to form a mental image of a cosmic situation in which the three forces are exemplified, but all this does is to give us material for the intellectual brain. To get understanding, we have to be able to feel the content of this image and enter inside it. That requires of us something that is very hard: that we should be able to bring real experience before us, and see it for what it is. This means that we have to arrest our habit of 'thinking about' experience, which wastes experience and prevents us being realistic about our lives. We have to put away all this 'thinking about', all this associating and 'formating', and *see*.

The cosmic situation that we will talk about is one that touches every human being. We have to begin by seeing it in that way. All of us participate in it. We would not exist at all unless it were for this. It is the very key to our humanity. No one is lacking in experience of it, awake or asleep, saint or sinner. What we are going to look at is the coming together of man and woman in the conception of a child.

Father-Mother-Child

A cosmic situation is one which expresses the laws of creation itself, that is, all the six fundamental laws of World 6. The dominant experience we have of man and woman is one in which there are only two forces, the polar world of sex. We rarely understand that nothing can come out of the polarity of sex without the entry of some independent factor. Man and woman have to have something in which they can share. They can sense the need of something that has to happen between them if they are to be able to help each other to be what they are. They may be drawn toward each other in the sexual act, or complete one another in some mutual interest or undertaking, or they can come together in some situation of conflict or competition; however it is, there is nothing that is stable unless something quite independent, of equal force, enters the situation.

In ordinary situations between man and woman there is attraction and repulsion, agreement and disagreement; one takes the initiative and then the other. If now we say that it is when they have a child that things become different, it is liable to be misunderstood. This is not how it is in the world that we know, World 48. In that world, the child is seen as a material factor, as an intrusion or a mutual dependent. In the higher worlds, the coming of the child is an independent factor that changes the whole situation. Even in our ordinary language, we make the change of talking about 'father' and 'mother' instead of just 'man' and 'woman'. The child is not a part split off from the father or a part split off from the mother, but it has something of them both in such a way that it is able to be the means of relating them. This corresponds to the simplest way that we have of looking at the third force: that it is the result of the contact between the affirming and the denying impulses.

We will find all the six laws operating in this situation, but the primary manifestation is that which begins with the maternal force. In the world of personality it is not obvious, but in the natural world we can see how it is that the woman is the initiating factor in parenthood. It is the woman who attracts the man to her. Because of her need to be a mother, she has the power to arouse in the man his paternal power. The maternal awakens the paternal. Through this comes the union by which the child is conceived.

If we put this in terms of our symbolism, we have the mother carrying the second force, force number 2, which arouses in the father the generative or active force, number 1, and from their union comes the child who carries the third force, number 3. We write this down as:

2-1-3 the triad of evolution

This is how the renewal of life takes place, not only in man but in all forms of sexualized life. If this power of attraction were not present in the female, then the relationship which allows a new being to come into the world would never be initiated. Through this conjunction, a new being carrying with it a new potential has entered the world with new possibilities for development. When the mother looks at the child, she sees it in terms of its potential, what she or he will become; it is in this way that the mother recognizes the third force being manifest in the child. We can also say that the woman-mother acts upon the man-father to release in him the third force, the potential of a new life which is set free, and we can also say that the woman converts the affirmative force that she has called to herself into the result, which is the child. All these different ways of speaking about it are right.

When we look at the event from the standpoint of the sexual act itself, it is the man who plays the initiating role. It is the father who inseminates, plants the seed, in the woman. Seen in this way, conception is an act of the transmission of life from generation to generation. The man sees in the receptivity of the mother the means of fulfilling, transmitting, renewing, and opening out the future; all of which is realized in the child, the carrier of the third force. Where the woman is the initiator, we look to the creation of a new possibility in the new life come into the world, but where the man initiates, the emphasis is on the transmission of the existing possibilities of the race. It is these possibilities that the father transmits with his seed, and the child, carrying the third force, can become in his turn the transmitter. In the visible world the child, and in particular in Western society the son, becomes the representative of the father, transmitting in turn the seed, the line, and even the calling of the father, completing his work. Where the father initiates, we have the triad of involution:

1-2-3 the triad of involution

We can understand it in terms of the chain of generation and transmission. We can say that the third force here is the means of keeping up the continuity of the world. Without the third force, the chain of transmission comes to an end. The relationship is sterile if it does not result in a child.

So far, we have looked upon the child in its role as third force as the *result* of the act of procreation. This is the easiest way of looking at it because it corresponds to how things happen in time. The first two triads everyone can see and recognize. What is difficult to see is that the child also has a power, and has been the initiator of his own conception. What is it that really moves the woman and really moves the man? The child, unborn and unconceived, an essence looking for a body, is the force that awakens the maternal initiative of the mother. It comes from another dimension. In the ordinary world, we can have one force acting along one line and another acting along another line. Both these are in the flatland of ordinary experience. Mechanical calculation can tell us what the resultant should be of these two forces. But even in terms of what we are able to see, we know that what comes out of the two forces is often quite unexpected. There is at work some independent influence from dimensions not contained in flatland.

There is a beautiful fable of Robert Louis Stevenson called *The Poor Thing*[13] in which all this is described. He evokes an extraordinary image of the unborn child that acts irresistibly upon the woman, in spite of her aversion and reluctance, so that she is bound to move toward its conception, draw the man to her, and enable it to be born. The child before conception has no body and does not even exist in the world of spirits, the *ālam-i arvāh*. It is just the will-to-be, pure will, pure third force. In saying that it acts upon the woman, so that she draws the man to her, the triad has the form:

3-2-1 the triad of freedom

There is no way in which people who have not been awakened in their higher centers can really see the child outside of space and time, in its unconditioned state. It is in this realm that we were given the possibility of being born *before we existed*. In the Muslim tradition it is said that before we are conceived, we choose this life.[14] What all this means can hardly be understood because we can form no conception of acts of will outside of existence. The kind of 'decisions' that we know are really responses to already existing situations. The child before conception is not at an earlier time but in a higher world, where free decision is a reality.

There is not only the decision to be born but the choice of where to be born, through which parents, and with what heredity. This is an act with greater limitations because it is an act of commitment to the existing world and its condition. The new life that comes carries a certain pattern; it has a shape and a form, and these are inevitable limitations. The most obvious is the genetic pattern through which the child has its hereditary endowments, half of which come from the father and half from the mother. At the moment that the father's seed enters the mother's ovum, the pattern of the physical life is fixed. Then there is the pattern of fate, which does not originate from the father and mother but is said to be fixed by the environment of planetary influences at the moment of conception. The physical heredity and the 'astral' heredity, or fate, are both fixed at the moment of conception and are the laws that govern the new life. The mother is the receptacle of

13 *Fables*, Coombe Springs Press, 1976
14 Bennett also referred to the legend of Er, the son of Armenius. Er is severely wounded in battle and goes into the spirit world, where he sees individuals choosing their lives. Plato *Republic*, Book X. The problem with Plato's descriptions – at least as they are translated – is that individuals are identified with minds. But it is the will that chooses, decides and commits.

the pattern that is transmitted through the father. Fixing the pattern is what we call:

3-1-2 the triad of order

This triad is the power to be conceived at such and such a time under such and such influences through such and such parents. When we look at certain familial relationships we sometimes wonder and ask ourselves how it comes about in families that there are certain patterns of birthdays which are grouped about a very small number of days. It very often happens that there is a connection between the birth dates of members of the same family that comes from the power of children to have themselves born in conditions that correspond to what they require.

Besides the physical pattern transmitted genetically and the 'spirit pattern', or fate, there is a higher level of order that can be called *destiny*. If heredity comes from World 48 and fate from World 24, destiny comes from World 12. The child's destiny is unique, given to the child independently of who his parents are. It does not come from them and it does not come from anything at all 'outside' of the child. We can say that it comes from God. It is to do with what he has to fulfill by being born, and it is through this that there is a power to choose the corresponding conditions of life. But it does not have unlimited power. Sometimes, a match cannot be made between the pattern of destiny and the conditions of life. The conception will go wrong: there is a failure to conceive or physical difficulties or a miscarriage, something which prevents the destiny from being embodied. Or it may be born and it will turn out that the fate or conditions of life do not permit the destiny to be realized. Children with very high destinies are very rare in the world, and special conditions are arranged in order to ensure the conditions of their conception and birth.

All of us have a unique destiny which we are called upon to fulfill in this life. This is a task not only of making the most of our physical heredity, nor even of coming to terms with our fate, but of becoming such men or women who are able to fulfill the reason why we came into existence. For that, we need to come under higher laws. It is not a matter of something that we have to 'do' which we can be told about and know. It is our *dharma*, the 'rightness' in our lives.

When the third force acts as the link between affirmation and denial, we have the two remaining forms of the triad. Firstly, we will take the case where the mother is the initiating force. It is through the child that she is able to require the father to provide a home. She becomes the homemaker, the unifying and stabilizing factor that holds the home together. The child entitles the mother to demand of the father that he should play his role as head of the family, but it is better to say that it is through the child that the family has an identity, and it is through the child that the couple becomes a family and the three are one whole. Thus:

2-3-1 triad of identity

When the father is in the initiating role, we see something different. The two roles, that of the man and that of the woman, are reconciled by the child. The father's work in the world becomes the task of providing for the family. He has to sacrifice some of his freedom. At the same time, the family cannot be geared entirely to his work. All that he can do has to change because of the presence of the child; then his powers and his potential find a different purpose and he becomes connected with the future in a different way. The mother has to provide the environment for the family. Her own independence is curtailed. The child gives both the father and the mother a bond of mutual acceptance which is expressed in all the interactions between the affirmative force of the man and the receptive force of the woman. This gives:

1-3-2 triad of interaction

We see how the third force appears quite differently according to the position it occupies in the triad. It can be the result, it can be the initiator, and it can be the bond of union. The pictures we have made of the six triads are fairly easy to grasp. Ordinarily, it is not possible to have any direct intuition of these things. The only way in which a direct perception is possible is from a higher part of ourselves. The descriptions we have given are more in the way of pointers than of abstractions which we can talk about and think we understand. In the worlds that we live in, experience does not correspond to these descriptions because all sorts of extraneous things come in making it difficult for us to see any of the forces clearly.

We can say that there are six different manifestations of the third force, yet in all of them it is the same, it is still the child. But this brings us no nearer to seeing that this is so. We ordinarily assume that we know what it means to be a father or a mother or a child, but all we know are the externals. In the world of bodies, all that we know is that there are male bodies, female bodies, and child bodies. The cosmic situation is quite invisible.

The power of the child is mysterious. Before he is conceived, he awakens the mother, but after conception his power does not cease. It continues as she bears him and for long afterward. It is something deeper than our ordinary emotional states, a bond far beyond that of flesh and blood. Sometimes we look at children whose parents are totally different in appearance and we ask in astonishment, 'How is it possible that he is like both of you?' Yet we have not really come close to seeing what it means that the child is able to be both the child of his father and the child of his mother. In many ancient myths the idea is expressed that we come into this world by some act that we cannot understand and which we have lost contact with.[15] Yet everything that is in the lower worlds is the result of an act of that kind. The law of three works in everything everywhere, but we are in the country of the blind.

The Descent of the Worlds

The laws 'begin' in a world beyond space and time, and even beyond existence, where everything is possible. It is only when we have become so transformed that we have gone through the emptiness in our center that we can come to see the reality of such a world. We are talking about World 3, where each of the three forces is able to sustain itself independently from the others. There are no triads, no combinations, because the forces are completely free. This condition lies beyond what we can see, even when everything has become still in us. Affirmation here requires no denial, no field of action. It is only when the three forces issue forth from this world, and enter into combination, that different forms arise that we can recognize.

In World 6, there is a commitment to existence and we have the six laws, which we have called involution, evolution, freedom, order, identity, and interaction. But there are no separate existences. This is the universal world, the world of universal will.[16] All the laws of this world originate in World 3, but in its turn, World 6 is a source of laws for the existing world. Where World 6 is the source, we have the lower worlds of separate existences. The impulses which enter into combination in the lower worlds can

15 This idea is wonderfully portrayed in Doris Lessing's *Briefing for a Descent Into Hell.*
16 In Sufi terminology, the Universal Spirit, *Ruh-i kulli.*

either come directly from World 3 or through the commitment to existence of World 6. To distinguish between these 'committed' and 'uncommitted' impulses, we call the first 'essential' and the second 'existential', giving these words a different sense from that philosophers use. Also, when we use the symbolism of the numbers 1, 2, and 3, we differentiate between essential and existential impulses by marking the latter with an asterisk (*). So, for the completely essential law of involution we would write 1-2-3 and for the completely existential we would write 1*-2*-3*.

The completely essential laws which originate in World 3 are to be found in all the lower worlds.[17] What distinguishes the lower worlds is their addition of conditioning or their extra laws. The lower worlds are so thick with laws that we are reduced in the end to causality and thinghood: all that happens is dominated by separate existence. Impure or existential impulses originate at various levels as we go down the worlds, each new level adding more conditioning.

All the pure triads of World 6 are transmitted down to World 12, but, in addition, there are originated another six laws which carry the results of commitment to existence. (see Figure 6.1) In World 6, the laws are those of the pure plan or idea of the creation. In World 12, the plan is still present, but also there are the laws which derive from the plan in manifestation. The unconditioned essential impulses that originate in World 3 enable the creation to be more than a limiting mechanism. Each level transmits something of its own. Even in World 96, the pure plan is to be found, but it has been 'buried' under a succession of limitations, and 'canceled out' by the negative laws of delusion.

Gurdjieff talks a great deal about this combination between the essential and the existential in the chapter 'Holy Planet Purgatory' of *Beelzebub's Tales*. One of the things that he says is that there is a primary creation which begins in this solar system. Because of this he calls the sun *deuterocosmos* - second creative source. If we look upon the sun as a secondary creator we can represent the creative action of the sun as 1-2-3* in contrast to the creativity of the prime source, 1-2-3.

---

17 In one lecture, Bennett described World 3 in terms of the three laws: involution (1-2-3), evolution (2-1-3) and freedom (3-2-1). This seems to contradict the idea that World 3 consists of the pure forces uncombined. However it helps to open up a new perspective on the six laws: interaction, identity and order appearing as the counterparts of involution, evolution and freedom.

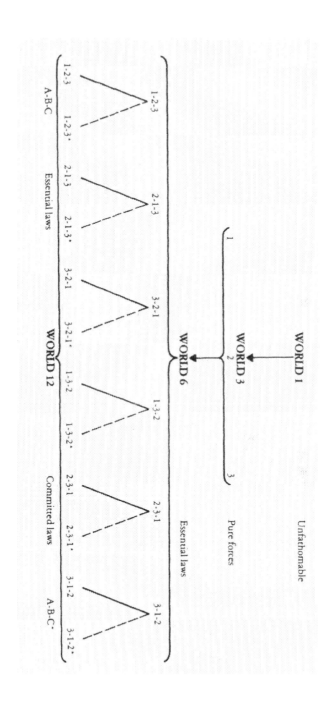

ARISING OF LAWS OF WORLD 12

FIG. 6.1

What this signifies is that everything that starts in the sun is already limited because it is committed to the line of creation of only one out of thousands of millions of other suns. Although its creative potential is vastly greater than anything we can possibly imagine, in comparison to the ultimate source it is very limited. However, the conditioning comes in only with the resultant force 3* and not in the initiating force 1. This is because the creativity of the sun is *essentially the same* as that of the prime source, or Sun Absolute, and it is limited only in its manifestations.

The solar world is the same as World 12. Half its laws terminate in an existential impulse, which is another way of saying that half the laws have to do with individualized existence. Even in these, however, it is useful to remember the dictum, 'will is unlimited in its essence, but limited in its operations'. In World 12, all initiative is unconditioned but half of the results carry the consequences of separate existence. These consequences are a privation from only one point of view; from another, the restrictions upon entities and events imposed by existence make possible the realization of the demands of essence in ways that essence itself, despite its greater freedom, cannot achieve. This is the purpose for which the creation has come into existence: that there might be an independent return to the source. But whether this independent contribution will be made in any particular instance or individual is not assured, owing to the same limitations of the existing world.

To get a general picture of the descent of the worlds, and how they pass one into the other, we can use the situation of military command. At the top is the commander-in-chief. He has a *vision* of what the army can achieve. The *decisions* that he makes, with the authority that is behind them, go down through all the ranks, and even the least private is affected by them. But they also go through subordinate commanders who have to introduce something of their own, because all the details cannot be provided from the top. Each of them *interprets* the top decision in terms of the limitation of his command. This inevitably results in the loss of simplicity. *Commands* at the lowest level become the merest fragments, and the possibilities of confusion grow at every level of descent in the hierarchy. Using our symbolism, we say that the creative vision of the commander in its pure form, before any commitment to action, has the form 1-2-3. It is wholly unconditioned. When the decision is taken which issues forth in an order, the triad takes on the form 1-2-3*: the army is then committed to a course of action. In this triad, the second role is played by his advisers, who help him to translate the vision into operational terms. The actual command is the third force, 3*. What is transmitted reaches the next echelon, which is in the receptive role. At this level, there is a limitation of vision. The presence of the pure triad of the commander gives rise to a new form in those second in command: 1-2*-3. This is the triad of 'limited vision'. Those at this level are the first in the position of both receiving orders and giving orders. The orders that they give will be based on the partial understanding that they have; nevertheless, through the orders that they receive, they have an authority and power of command of their own. What originates with them takes the form 1-2*-3*. The commands that they issue are dependent on the specific conditions that they are familiar with. Further, there is now a multiplicity of commands. Communication between the different subordinate commanders is never perfect enough to ensure that all harmonize fully. Mistakes are made, and there are gaps which no one notices. Two subordinates may try to do the same thing and get in each other's way. Their ideas about timing may be different. The minimization of confusion is staff work, how the second force fulfills its role in response to the commander-in-chief's affirmation.

When we reach the lower levels, we find the dependent forms of initiative. The original vision is still 'there', but now it is in the state of mind of the soldiers. The unit commander partakes of the commander-in-chief's vision in his own affirmation with the form 1 *-2-3. What these forms mean is that the higher vision has taken on the limitations of the experience of men who are 'in the fray'. The orders of the unit commanders then have the form 1*-2-3 and 1*-2*-3*. They are entirely concerned with specific actions, but the first calls on the unlimited side, the 'heart' of men. As we go down through the various levels, we can now see how command becomes increasingly multiple (see Figure 6.2).

Nothing happens until the commander-in-chief issues an order; then everything else at all the other levels is set in motion. The original vision 'involves' down the chain of command until it reaches the fighting men who then act under a whole series of orders: the general order of the commander-in-chief, together with specific commands from the subordinate commanders at various levels, down to the battalion or company commanders with whom the soldier is in direct contact. But the original vision is with the ranks also. There, it is the quality of command, the authority it carries, and the confidence that it generates. If the commander-in-chief is a Napoleon or a Genghis Khan, his name alone is enough to inspire everyone with a belief in victory. It is because of this overall affirmation, this hidden vision of the ultimate commander, that the ordinary soldier feels that he can carry out what he has been asked to do. This is the mystique of command that is able to inspire everyone, even if the leader is rarely seen by the soldiers. Overlaying the action of the pure triad 1-2-3 there come all the other triads originating at different levels: with the second-in-command, through the need for interpretation of the overall plan, and with the unit leaders, through the contingencies of battle. The further down the line that orders originate, the more the response of the soldiers is going to be based on actual experience of the merits of those who issue them and the less it is going to be based on mystique. The vision of the ultimate commander is often very remote, and the only means of participating in it is through the 'magic' of his name. As we go down the scale, what the soldier has seen with his own eyes counts for more and more. He does not expect his company commander to be a Napoleon, but is satisfied if he knows him to be resourceful.

There is, of course, a very great difference between the hierarchy of the army and the hierarchy of worlds. In the creation, while there is always an involutionary process continuously taking place, there is also a corresponding evolutionary movement 'from below' and the working of all the other fundamental laws. If we had taken the law of evolution to study, we would have taken an example like the food chain to illustrate it. But we have enough material to enlarge our picture of what is meant by 'essential' and 'existential' impulses. We can say that the existential, limited forces are concerned with the facts, with what is actually going on, whereas the essential, unlimited forces are concerned with the pattern behind what is going on. Here our ordinary usage of words is very awkward. It would be convenient to use some such word as 'idea' or 'ideal' for the essential triads, but these words have been corrupted by their association with minds and thinking. As things are, we have no language at hand for talking about matters of the will which does not end up by reducing it to a human function. We use the word 'pattern' to signify the combination of unlimited impulses which is given form in the conditioned worlds we know. In the military example, the pure pattern is symbolized by the creative vision of the commander-in-chief. We assign this to World 6. In World 12, there is a commitment to action, and a command is given that expresses the pattern in a particular form. What is now working is both the pattern and the manifestation of the pattern.

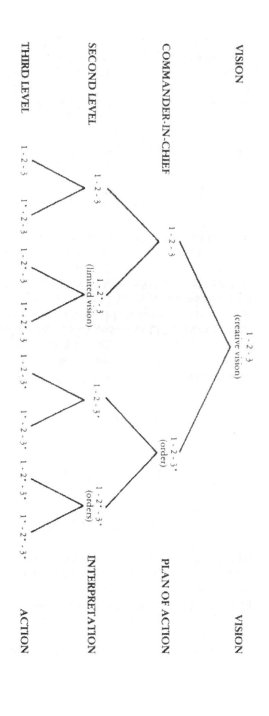

MULTIPLICATION OF COMAND THROUGH DESCENDING
LEVELS
FIG. 6.2

At the next level, the commanders have got to see what is issued to them 'in their own lights': they interpret. In the symbolism this is shown by the *middle* term becoming conditioned. The interpretations become mixed with the original commands, and there are now four sorts of command. All this belongs to World 24. At the next level, there are the commanders who have got to go out and tell the men face-to-face. They have got to 'order' in an existential sense; tell the men what to do. This is a great change from the beginning, where the creative vision is a perception of possibilities and the original command is to realize them. To see something and to commit oneself, or one's army, to its realization is totally different from taking this or that actual action. All of this is signified in having the first term conditioned in the lowest world, World 48, in which there are now eight sorts of instructions.

The Pattern of a Child

The cosmic situation of father-mother-child really belongs to World 6. In the world we know, women attract men at any time, and the idea that the woman attracts the man at the moment when there can be a conception is quite beyond any of our experience of sex. What we experience is a world of haphazard interactions between men and women. It is almost impossible for us to see what could be meant by the child, as yet unconceived, initiating the attractive power of the woman toward the man by whom it can be conceived. World 48 is an abnormal world for man, and in it everything is seen 'upside down'. Our sexual lives are disordered, but the more disordered they are the more we believe we are being 'free'. In *Beelzebub's Tales*, Gurdjieff talks about the 'conscious reproduction outside of themselves of new beings similar to themselves'. In World 12, the world of real man, 'man without quotation marks', there is no movement toward a child until the child itself calls it forth. This is an act of freedom. Freedom cannot begin in either the father or the mother, or the man or the woman. Man and woman cannot unite themselves. The only point of freedom is in the third force.

In our symbolism, we write the law of freedom as 3-2-1. Here the child awakens the woman to being a mother, and the future mother awakens the man to being a father. In this way, the triad of evolution is formed: 2-1-3. It all seems very simple. Why is it that we do not see these things and, instead, see only confusion? The answer is that it is very unlikely that we can ever experience anything in this pure form because our experience has all the other forms in it at the same time. Our experience is a 'mix-up' because we are a 'mix-up' and what can happen in our world is a 'mix-up'. When we say that we are 'in World 48', this means that we are the very stuff of World 48: distracted from seeing anything as it is, including ourselves, because we are not merely in a 'state' of confusion, we are in a world of confusion, and confusion is in us. Through the practice of 'stilling the mind', some of this confusion may lift itself from us; but even in this quieter state we are still very far away from the pure and 'simple' world.

As it enters existence, is born, and matures, the child enters into worlds of greater and greater conditioning. We must understand that the whole movement is a being sent away from the source in order to return, for in the return the creation serves its purpose. The conditioning of existence is a reality and part of the scheme of things. Yet it introduces a very great hazard. It is through this hazard that we can be transformed, for what is open to us is far more than the kind of development in which a seed grows into a flowering plant. The seed and the plant are in the same world. What we have to do is to change the world that we are in.

The nature of a child comes from three different kinds of pattern. There is, as we said before, the pattern of destiny, the pattern of fate, and the pattern of heredity. When these patterns enter into the workings of World 48, where the child is a separate existence interacting with other separate existences and he communicates with them and with himself from the outside, he comes into the full hazard of conception in a body. The three patterns interact with the contingencies of external events, such as environment and education.

What we mean by the pattern of the child is the form that the triad of order takes in him. We write this triad as 3-1-2. This is the pure form. The force 3 represents the child, the force 1 the father, and the force 2 the mother. The child enters into a certain heredity, that is, into the genetic combination of the particular father and mother. This we write as 3-1*-2*. Here we are representing the child in his unconditioned nature, and saying that he exerts some kind of selective influence on the embodiment that he will enter. What comes in this way belongs to the world of essence, World 24, and it illustrates what we mean by using the word 'essence' in describing this world. In World 24, the genetic potential that comes from the parents 'belongs' to the child, is intrinsic to his 'real being'.

It is different in World 48, where we have the completely existential triad: 3*-1*-2*. By putting the first term as conditioned,
we mean that the child takes his body *to be himself.* The pattern
is that of an animal and the third force is simply part of the existing world. The child is an organism that is born, grows, and dies.
The triad of 3*-1*-2* is the law of selective breeding, where the
concern is entirely with external characteristics, such as strength,
appearance, and measurable intelligence. When the same kind of
attitude is in the child, he runs the risk of losing contact with his
own essence.

Planetary heredity, or fate, is represented as 3-1*-2. In this
form, again, we suppose that the child has some power of choosing an appropriate fate, that is, influencing the time and place of
his conception. The reality of such a thing as the 'right time' is
non-causal. Many people feel that something or other influences whether or not a particular act of sexual union will produce a
conception. The 1* in the middle represents how it is that the act
of fertilization is irrevocable, not merely in the physical sense but
also in the sense of fixing the 'psychic' characteristics. Tradition
associates the transmission of character more with the father than
with the mother, but what matters is that a pattern of experience is
fixed from what is dominant at that time in that world, World 24,
the 'planetary world'.

A human being who possessed all the possible characteristics
of men would be unrecognizable; he would have no sense of selfhood, and relationships would have no meaning for him. The feeling we have with every human being that they are 'somebody',
when it is not just a reaction to their bodily existence, is a response
to the pattern of their nature. This pattern, which we call character, is one of the most important tools for our lives. It enables us
to deal with the problems of life, but not with why we are alive
at all. When it rules us, we cannot get near to the place of transformation.[18] The character is material to work with, not an end in
itself. It gives us a place to start from in the natural world of man,
World 24. In World 48, it becomes 3*-1*-2. This is the pattern of
life that is bound by fate. We talk of being 'the prisoner of fate',
but the only thing that existence can imprison is something that
itself exists.

The triad of destiny is written: 3-1-2*. This is only a limitation
insofar as the child has to come into existence to fulfil a task. His

---

18 Character and fate belong to the divided self. The place of transformation is the true self.

existence, which separates him from his own essential reality, is not intended as an end in itself. There is some high form of action that requires that we accept translation into a living body, but in our world, World 48, it gets narrowed down to a sort of affirmation that we ourselves are unique, and our physical existences are somehow uniquely important. We lose track of what is the purpose of it all and, particularly, what our own purpose is. We mistake what is existential and material for what is essential and spiritual. The triad of 3 *-1-2* can be thought of as 'destiny blindness' and, through it, our lives are occupied in chasing shadows.

In the scheme of worlds, we can say that the pattern of destiny is in World 12, the pattern of fate in World 24, and the genetic pattern in World 48. However, there is also an essential form of the genetic pattern that belongs to World 24. We can now make sense of Gurdjieff's definition that essence is 'what a man is born with'. After birth, the child enters a world of separate existence, in which his own selfhood can develop. This is when the actual can overwhelm the essential in him. The results of his interaction with others and with the world crystallizes out into a shell, or *personality*, which is a device for dealing with the world of outside things, things known indirectly, the world of bodies. The personality is not a being and has nothing of its own, but it can usurp the true inner world. Then essence 'does not develop' and the adult forms who lives in his personality and has the 'consciousness' of personality, not his true consciousness.

The personality exists in World 48. Being under the laws of World 48 means that we are separated from our own inherent pattern. Everything is a matter of force, momentum, and inertia; and the events of this world do nothing for our inner life.

The highest thing in us comes from World 6. This is altogether beyond the limitations of the world we know; it has nothing to do with the father and mother at all, or with the conditions surrounding the conception, or even with the power or influence which the unconceived child exerts over its embodiment. It comes from God. Here the unconditioned third force is divine. God endows the child with will, its 'I'. It is this which makes man in the image of God. The ultimate triad is 3-1-2. Our will, our own 'I', is that which enables us to take our place in the enlarging harmony and become 'a help in the administration of the enlarging world' - because we can be *free*.

It is a very great thing to become awakened to the reality of will, and thereby become a 'conscious instrument' of the purpose of the creation. This is so unlike any way of working that we can imagine, that even the word 'conscious' will mislead us. We are in the condition Gurdjieff called that of 'slaves to all universal purposes'. Everything serves the great purpose, without exception. Either we serve just as a thing, a body through which certain energies can be transformed, or we come to serve as 'I', freely. When we serve as a thing, when we take the material world to be the only reality, when 'I' is not even a possibility for us, the gift of will becomes 3 *-1-2. Under this law, we believe that freedom belongs to the visible world and also that we 'have' freedom. But not even God can give men freedom. Freedom has to be realized.

The absurdities of World 48 are so difficult to convey because they are the very medium in which we live, and through which we have been formed. They make us believe that higher worlds are 'dreams', 'far away', 'imagination', 'like this but only better', 'absurd'. They make us live in an order that comes from this world, and blind to an order that calls us from the higher worlds. The higher order is given to us, but we are not compelled to fulfill it. The choice is ours: to live in a way in which Great Nature exacts her payments automatically or to pay our own way through what Gurdjieff called 'conscious labors and intentional sufferings' so that we can become free and even 'help God'.

The practical beginning of work is making the transition from World 48 to World 24. This is simply in order to get into the world where it is possible for us to be ourselves, and free of the laws which make us dependent on things outside ourselves. What is 'in our essence' is represented by the four laws:

3-1-2	Free will
3-1-2*	Destiny
3-1*-2	Fate
3-1*-2*	Heredity

In World 48, these laws are added to by laws which take effect through the apparatus of personality, the laws of the 'man-machine'. These additional laws are imposed on us by the conditions we find in the world around us, and they are in that sense artificial, something grafted on to us. It is these laws which keep us in the country of the blind.

CHAPTER 7

The World of Delusion

If we begin to examine our lives impartially, we see that we live much of the time in an unreal world, an unreal state. So much of our time and energy is spent on things that are really unimportant, things that in a year's time, or a month's, or possibly much less, we shall have totally forgotten these things because they have no significance for our lives as a whole. We find in ourselves sensitivities to all kinds of things that do not really matter and have no significance for our essence at all, while things that do matter do not touch us. Every one of us is endowed with all these immensely rich possibilities, made, as it is said, 'in the image of God', yet all of this we throw away. We hold on to a picture of ourselves which justifies all our actions and refuse to look at the nullity behind the facade, at the waste there is in our lives. Every so often we are forcibly reminded how little we make of our lives, but it is very rare that anyone sees objectively the extent of the absurdity of human life. We are so accustomed to living these meaningless, absurd lives, and seeing others do so too, that we do not see how far from natural this is. Something has entered human life which is not natural, and we have this strange condition of an inverted world which Gurdjieff referred to as 'the abnormal conditions of ordinary being existence established by them themselves'.

In World 48, half the laws are initiated by conditioned impulses. These laws cannot be related to the whole of us, or to the whole of the situation we are in. What we experience through them is an action in which we are not aiming at anything but furthering our own point of view, even when we are trying to do something which is objectively right. They make us what is called 'self-centered', but what we are centered on is not even what we really are. It is the apparatus of the personality that gets stimulated by some impulse from the working of external laws. Our dependence on external supports engenders egoism in our selfhood. Every impulse that arises in us says 'I', but we cannot see that these fragmentary 'I's have almost nothing to do with each other, that they are just happening in the personality. Because of all this, we are not related to the whole in an independent manner, and we cannot even begin to know what it is to 'work on ourselves'.

But something far worse is wrong with our lives. We destroy what we want to preserve, and throw away what we need, and even know we need. Even our dependence in World 48 has some reality to it. In the world of unreality, World 96, there are negative laws, laws of destruction, waste, and unreality. The power of delusion is expressed by Mulla Nassr Eddin in *Beelzebub's Tales*, 'What might not happen in this world? A flea might swallow an elephant!' Using the words of a well-known proverb, we make mountains out of molehills and molehills out of mountains. It is not a matter of morality; that we are wicked, bad, or evil. It is a matter of reality and unreality. It is this fictitious life that destroys us, not the failure to live according to some code of morality. All the great moral codes and traditions have been introduced into the life of man to protect people from the consequences of living this unreal life, but because we are unable to carry out all of their injunctions inwardly, in our hearts and minds and bodily impulses, these codes cannot serve us as a means of liberation from the nullity of our lives.

Gurdjieff gives an explanation of the origin of this world of delusion in terms of 'the organ kundabuffer'. He takes great pains to show that the delusion in which man lives is not something for which man is to be blamed, not a consequence of his actions, as it is presented in some religious ideas of 'original sin'. He puts it down to the conflict between the laws of existence and the laws of essence. Because of the commitment to existence, 'mistakes' are inevitable. According to Gurdjieff, some kind of cosmic mistake was made at a point in man's evolution. Very much higher powers than man decided that, for the sake of preserving the overall order of the solar system, which they believed at that time to be threatened by an external intervention, man should transform energies only automatically and not consciously. They implanted in him the organ kundabuffer, which prevented him from seeing his essential nature. Later, when the apparent threat had passed, the organ was removed from the presence of man and he once more had the possibility of becoming an independent responsible being. Unfortunately, by that time, he had somehow or other been caught by the consequences of his buffered state. Since that time, the properties of kundabuffer had passed from generation to generation, and today we find in ourselves the inability to face reality.

We 'see reality reflected in our attention upside down'. Instead of wanting to be free, we want to be slaves. Throughout *Beelzebub's Tales*, Gurdjieff gives strings of different sorts of behaviors unworthy of man which he says are 'consequences of the properties of the organ kundabuffer', but they all amount to the desire for what is not real.

In World 48, each of the fundamental six laws has eight forms. In World 96, in addition to these, there are forty-eight negative counterparts. The effects of the positive and the negative laws cancel each other out and nothing really happens at all. Needless to say, when we are in World 96, we are totally unaware that this is so. We cannot experience more than one force at a time. We are subject to pleasure and pain as actual facts, being unable to realize the compensation that reduces them to null events. We react to them blindly. Pain appears to us as a state of unredeemed negativity because we are blind to the compensatory pleasures which exist elsewhere in the whole. Pain is pain, but we add on a negativity that is delusion. The most ephemeral pleasures delude us into fantasies of well-being. There is not only the blind mechanicality of World 48, there is a 'perversion of the will' that even destroys the fruits of our automatism. As soon as any sensitivity appears in us, we pour it down the nearest 'sink'.

It is in practice very hard to see the negative triads at work, but once we have caught a glimpse we can never understand human life in the same way again. People say, 'Well, we can accept all that is said about being mechanical and asleep. We understand the idea that there is more or less awareness, and sometimes this can get pretty low so that there is just a set of instruments ticking over with no one there. But how can there be this almost *deliberate* negativity? We can be blind - all right. But we cannot conceive how it is that we are supposed to be turning our backs on reality.' It is difficult to see, but that is how it is. It is even evidence of our state of delusion that in the face of all that goes on in the world about us in the conduct of human affairs, where nearly everything that happens betrays an overwhelming passion for unreality, we continue to believe in ourselves as reasonable beings. What we have got to look for is this additional layer of futility that holds us in sleep, but is worse than sleep.

The law of involution 1-2-3 is the law of the creative process. The affirmation engages with a field of action and something is made out of it. In its negative counterpart there is all the appearance of doing something, but in reality there is just the opposite.

If there is a job or task confronting us, instead of doing something about it we only sit around and talk about doing something, or we even daydream about doing something. Having spent all our time in dreaming and talking, we find there is no time actually to do anything. We have spent the time in believing that we are about our business, but in doing this we have wasted the possibilities that were open to us. The real creative power enriches existence by opening it to the possibilities of higher worlds. The negative counterpart impoverishes existence by wasting even the possibilities that it has. What should be done is ignored, and what does happen is out of place. It is not even self-centered; it is totally unreal. We are pretending and we are also completely caught by the pretense. All 'creative activities' which have no essential aim behind them sooner or later degenerate into play-acting. It has horrendous effects not only on the lives of individuals but also on a much larger scale.

Whenever undertakings are initiated in ignorance of the limitations of our human powers, they invariably finish by perpetuating just the sort of evils they were designed to avoid. Work that ought to be done is not done, and what is done is given a false name. Through the power of the law of three, it all fits together in consistent unreality. The real task is avoided, resources are used up pointlessly, and what comes out of it cancels out what is useful. Part of what it is, is called 'building castles in Spain': talking, planning, dreaming that never results in anything concrete. We can give this the name of imagination, but what is meant by this is more than ineffective mental activity. Possibilities are being used up to no purpose in the belief that, on the contrary, something useful is happening. When something or other tangible comes out of it, we imagine this quite useless and inappropriate result to be just what is right, believe it to be what it ought to be, and fail to see it for what it is. All this is 'useless imagination', to be distinguished from the creative imagination that results when we are able to place ourselves under higher laws that open the way to new possibilities. Useless imagination is not simply a kind of harmless inefficiency of the mind; it is *unreal* and *destroys* possibilities instead of creating them.

The triad of evolution, 2-1-3, is the law of our return to the source, but in its negative form, it is the law of our disappearance into ourselves: self-love. The law of evolution requires the lesser to be sacrificed for the greater. To evolve, we have to learn how to separate ourselves from our ordinary selves, to leave ourselves behind; to become an independent being and not a dependent personality. Negative evolution is where we feed ourselves, feed our illusions about ourselves, strengthen our own egoism. In a talk he gave on freedom, Gurdjieff said that before we can learn how to become free from outside influences - which he called the 'greater freedom' - we must first learn how to be free of ourselves, our vanity, and self-love. As long as we have self-love, nothing from the outside, good or bad, can come in. We can make efforts, but in the negative world they only feed our illusions: something wrong is crystallized in us. Then all the work we do turns sour. We are deluded into believing that we can evolve to satisfy self-love. To an outside observer we present the absurd picture of someone trying to become what he or she is not and never can be. Having the form, but not the substance, of work on oneself, this 'essence-egoism' is perhaps the most insidious of the negative triads, for very often results are obtained which appear to be favorable, and can only be seen to be worthless from the standpoint of a higher world.

Self-love is the very denial of the reality of higher worlds. Gurdjieff called freedom from this delusion of oneself the 'lesser freedom', which must come before the 'greater freedom'. Self-love is not simply a matter of liking oneself a great deal; it is a turning away from the reality to be found in higher worlds toward an imaginary reality believed to be inside one's existing self. The reality is not there and never can be.

Identity is existence according to one's essential pattern: 2-3-1. Negative identity is existence divorced from that pattern, to be what one is not, to be a nonentity. Work on ourselves begins from the realization of our own nullity, that as we are we are not real and that we are not yet what we ought to be. But if we do not recognize the possibility of transformation, whenever we are brought face-to-face with our own nullity, we are in *fear*. The full realization of our nothingness brings us to transformation; its avoidance in fear drives us to deny our own mortality, our own inevitable death. Fear is the root of our self-destructive activities: to hide from ourselves our 'essential nonexistence', we build ourselves a mask that is a projection of our fears; we call friends enemies; we seek momentary pleasures at the expense of enduring satisfactions; we cling to sleep as a protection. This has nothing to do with the workings of instinctive fear, which has an important role to play in physical preservation. Indeed, it is not like the working of any of our functions: a thought, a feeling, or a sensation. It is not even a state of consciousness. It is in the will. Trying to escape the fact that we cannot say 'I Am', we *fear*.

In the real worlds, all the forms of interaction, 1-3-2, serve in the universal exchange of energies through which the universe is maintained and fulfills its purpose. Everything is connected to everything else so that all of it is useful in some way. But in the negative world, there is *waste* and wasteful interaction. Unnecessary activity is undertaken which only leaves existence the poorer. It has no essential aim. What is done is worse than useless; all it does is to diminish our possibilities. In the real world, every situation has an essential pattern which can be more or less realized through corresponding kinds of action; but the useless activity of World 96 can prevent realization altogether. This is not only an individual catastrophe, it has consequences for all of the earth. Not only do we as individuals find ourselves 'masturbating away' our wealth, as Gurdjieff put it, but waste has become an inherent law in the common life of whole peoples, giving rise to needless pollution, destruction of resources, and the extinction of other species.

We have to see that much of what we do is absurd and unnecessary. It serves no purpose and gives us no benefit; nothing can come out of it, and we probably do not even want to be doing these things. We are not even compelled to do them by the workings of our automatic machinery or by external forces. They have no place in the scheme of things at all. It is a startling thing to see how much of our time is taken up by waste.

The inversion of the law of order, 3-1-2, is not disorder but order in the wrong place, which we can call *subjectivism*. Objective order is the pattern of what is possible and impossible, which, in the lower worlds, issues as the conditions for existence, such as 'space', 'time', and so on. But when we are dominated by the negative triads of order of World 96, we take our own accidentally formed views and opinions to be the criteria of truth and of possibility itself. We blandly assume that our subjective attitudes, which have been formed in us solely due to the action of our environment, are to be taken as the reality by which all experience can be tested. The general absurdity of this is not hard to see: what is objectively insignificant becomes most important; and we ourselves occupy the center of the universe. Unable to participate in any will other than our own, we are undisturbed by those opinions contrary to ours because they are obviously wrong.

We live in a false world. The good thing of the moment is an eternal good. The bad thing will be bad for all time. It is all so unreal that we are not only cut off from essence, we are out of touch with existence. We can see this in our attitudes to time. We take it that there is no other line of actualization in time than the one that we are in; we believe this line of time to be that of universal time. We live in an imaginary past and an imaginary future because we cannot live in the real present: we do not exist. We are not able to see the limitations of our lives and so we cannot see anything about what can be done in the future. We fail to see that in order to be here and now, we have to *be.*

Perhaps the nature of our subjective blindness is most clearly shown in our inability to experience, even in thought, our own inevitable death. Although there is nothing more certain than that each one of us is mortal and may die at any moment, because this fact is not in us it means nothing to us. We may fear death, but we are quite unable to confront it. Death is one of the most significant facts of human life, obvious to everyone, yet we can go on living as if there were no such thing. To see this in ourselves, we can try, when we are with other people, to become aware that we and they are mortal and must inevitably die.

We now come to the most extraordinary aberration that we have. It is the inversion of the law of freedom, 3-2-1: identification. Identification plays an important role in Gurdjieff's psychology. It appears many times in Ouspensky's books, *In Search of the Miraculous* and *The Psychology of Man's Possible Evolution.*

"It is one of the earliest ideas that I was introduced to when I first came in contact with this teaching. Identification is a false freedom, the illusion of freedom, where we feel free because we are doing what we want to do. Instead of finding ourselves, we lose ourselves in what we are doing, and then what we are doing may be free but we ourselves are enslaved. People can also become lost in what they are doing even if it is not what they want, even when it is something they have no choice about. When we are in this state we feel any interference with what we are doing is an encroachment on our freedom. If we are, let us say, cooking in the kitchen, we become so excited, so identified with what we are doing that if anyone comes and tells us that we are not doing it the right way, we become offended and feel that we are being interfered with. We feel that our freedom consists in doing it in our own way, but what freedom we might have had we have given away, and, having had a possibility to be free to do anything, we have chosen to become slaves.

"When we are identified it is true to say that we are no longer ourselves at all, because we have transferred our sense of our reality to something outside of ourselves. We even make it somehow seem valuable to be identified, praising a man who is really wrapped up in his work or spending vast sums of money for the latest sensational, that is, identifying, book or film. We become the slaves of everything that we are doing, enslaved by all the people we meet and the situations we enter into, and yet there is this terrible absurdity that in all of this we think that we are free.

"We can, for example, be struggling with ourselves, trying to hold back the expression of some negative state, while we are boiling away inside. Then suddenly we let it all go and, while objectively we are throwing away all that we had gained by making that effort, we feel better for it, feel free, and justify it all by saying that we wanted to be sincere. We have let ourselves be controlled by this negative triad, yet we feel good, feel all the better for it, because we do not even suspect that such negative states have no place at all in anyone who aspires to the name of *man*.

"Or, again, we find this state in ourselves quite clearly in regard to our possessions. All of us have some possessions we are attached to, as we say, or identified with, and if there is any danger of their being lost it is worse for us than if we were to lose ourselves. I can remember a very striking example of this which took place long, long ago when I was in one of Ouspensky's groups. We were talking about the difficulty we were having in remembering ourselves and he said that in order to remember we had to have a reminding factor. He continued that to have a reminding factor we would have to sacrifice something that was precious to us, put away from ourselves something which we valued. One woman said to him that she was becoming desperate, that she had been trying to do something for several months and had been unable to do anything. He told her that she should look around her home and find something that she really cared about and sacrifice it. She looked very embarrassed for a moment and then said, 'Well, to tell the truth, I have a very beautiful old tea service at home which I inherited complete from my mother, which I'm attached to.' His reply was, 'Break one of your Dresden cups and you will remember yourself.' The next week she came in a genuine hysterical condition, saying, 'I have been so agonized by what you said about my Dresden cups. I could not break a Dresden cup even if it were to save my soul.' His answer to her was simply, 'Do you see what is meant by identification?' "

Our personal relationships are constantly being spoiled because we are identified with people and what they may be thinking or feeling about us. Someone has only to make the slightest little gesture and our inner world is filled with all sorts of emotional reactions. Anything at all can be exaggerated to the most absurd lengths. A word of criticism and we believe that we are hated outcasts. A nod and we believe ourselves to be acknowledged as wise or supremely important. In all of this, nobody else has made us identified. We ourselves have done it. When something shakes us out of the state of identification, there is something very disagreeable in realizing how lost we have been; we can hardly bear to acknowledge the truth.

When we are identified, our vision of the world is terribly small. The present moment shrinks to a point. But when we are totally identified, utterly lost, we believe ourselves to be most free, that we see everything that is real. At first, when we come across this idea, it is almost impossible for us really to accept that we can ever be identified: other people, yes, but not us. But once we have really seen this in ourselves, when we have tasted the bitter reality of it, it is no longer possible for us to look at ourselves as we did before. We can no longer 'sleep in peace', as Gurdjieff put it. That is why self-observation must be undertaken with the resolution not to stop at any barrier, not to flinch from anything that is discovered, and not to fail to follow up the inferences that inevitably follow from what is seen.

When I was working in one of Ouspensky's groups, we would meet only once a week but would spend months and even years trying to come to an understanding of just how these negative laws worked in us and how, once we had understood their working, we might supersede it, how we might place ourselves under the influence of higher laws. In reality, there are not two different approaches to this work, one which deals with the negative laws and one which deals with the higher laws, the essential laws. Every time that, through struggling with our negative states, we come to a point where we are able to separate ourselves from ourselves and observe ourselves impartially, we are not only coming to understand how the lower laws work in us but are also, at the same time, creating a place in ourselves that is free from their influence, that is working under different laws. And every time we approach any theoretical study of higher laws, of the laws of essence, which is not founded on work on ourselves, then whatever our subjective sensations may be, we are not experiencing the action of higher laws, but only the action of our imagination. Gurdjieff said more than once that this teaching originates from a conscious source. To understand it we have to be able to approach it consciously, to be able to approach it *through* and not *from* the machinery of our ordinary selves. We can say that the whole theme of negative laws is of immense importance for an understanding of human psychology in general, and of special importance for an understanding of the psychology of our possible development provided, of course, that it is all approached in the right way, that is, practically, in terms of our own negativities and our own mechanicalities. And, though we ourselves are the only proper subject of this study, it is not something which we can do alone.

CHAPTER 8

Above and Below

Most accounts of the possible destiny of man are of no use to us. We fail to realize that they talk about different modes of being, different worlds, different kinds of functioning. It is almost impossible for us to see that words such as 'awareness', 'body', action', 'self' mean quite different things in different worlds, and even have quite contradictory meanings. Our thinking tends to invent a picture of at most two worlds: this world and the next, heaven and earth, spiritual and material, and so on. Then we assume that this life is in one world, the next life in another, or our bodies are in earth but our souls can be in heaven. We have the absurdity that the things we know nothing about like 'soul' are assigned to some other world and yet we continue to talk about them as if they were something that we could know.

The division of reality into two worlds confuses and puts together things which really belong to different levels. So, for example, the mind of man is treated as something spiritual when it is, in its ordinary working, just a function of the planetary body. We abuse many important words like 'immortality' and 'heaven' by using them without even stopping to ask ourselves whether we have the least idea of what they refer to. Worst of all, we use such words without having any means whatsoever of finding out what they mean. We have got into the habit of believing that when we have some mental picture or other which we associate with a word then we 'understand' what it means, in spite of the fact that this picture, in all probability, has just been 'picked up' by chance and we have no idea how we came by it. Without a practical means of verification, all our thinking and talking and picturing about 'higher matters' is worse than useless. Gurdjieff called this activity, which is objectively harmful, 'wiseacring'. The tragedy is that wiseacring is considered by a vast number of people as a sign of high intelligence.

Whether we are 'believers' in higher worlds or 'disbelievers', our situation is the same as long as we lack real understanding. Such understanding can only be founded on 'self-experiment' and observation, so that at least we know what is meant by 'delusion', 'mechanicality', and the 'natural state'. Unless we have some grasp of how it is that as we are we live in different worlds, all talk of genuinely higher worlds is only a matter of subjective opinion. We hardly realize how widespread is the disease of using words with no attention to what they mean. It is one of the major barriers to our development. In his sermons, again and again, the Buddha says that it is useless to talk about whether the soul exists or does not exist, or whether the perfected man, after his death, continues to exist, or whether he both exists and does not exist, and so on. It was not until long after the time of Buddha that the language of the 'worlds' was developed, and it became possible to talk about these things in a more precise and reliable way. Even then, all of it is useless until we have learned how to verify the idea of worlds for ourselves, through our own experiences. Using the scheme of seven worlds just to clarify concepts is a dead end: we will still get into contradictions and confusions unless we have learned how to make distinctions based on our own experience.

The truth is that this life is lived in different worlds by everyone. Even when we spend most of our time in the world of sleep, World 48, there are times when we are in contact with World 24, and able to be in direct contact with things. As we learn more about the practical significance of these worlds we can come to understand that there are a number of indications by which we can tell whether we have moved from the laws of World 48 to those of World 24. We can also come to understand the typical ways in which we descend below personality into the world of delusion, World 96, and what this world is like. Understanding of the higher worlds does not come to us through self-observation alone, but by struggling with the 'impossibilities' of our lives, under the guidance of those who have gone before us.

There are three different ways of approaching the idea of different worlds. The first is through the study of the levels, the powers, the different bodies of man himself; that is, through a psychological system. The second is the cosmological approach, which has a somewhat different treatment in the writings of Ouspensky than it has in *Beelzebub's Tales*. In this approach, the different worlds are shown in their correspondence with different levels of the cosmic structure: the sun, for example, corresponds to World

12; the planets to World 24; and the earth to World 48. The third approach is the one which is most readily accessible. It relates the different worlds to different states or qualities of experience, and it is through this that we can practically verify what we are taught.[19] In reality, the different approaches are concerned with the very same thing, though at first it is difficult to make much out of the cosmological ideas. We are constructed in the image of the great Megalocosmos. When we understand ourselves, we understand the universe. As we are, we neither understand the world nor ourselves.

Levels of Man

The first three kinds of men in Gurdjieff's system, Men numbers 1, 2, and 3, correspond to people like us and the people we know. Because we tend to live in a way that is dominated by the working of one center, all our actions and perceptions are liable to be lopsided and incomplete. We can have no real picture of either ourselves or the world. Most of our life is lived in World 48, under all forty-eight laws. Man Number 4, who is able to maintain a balance between all three centers, is able to live in World 24. He has something established in him which is free of the dependent laws of World 48, and he can be said to be the 'man of the way', the man who is seeking in a practical way. He is able to balance his outer life (lived under the laws of World 48) with his inner life (lived under the laws of World 24). He has accepted 'work' as a guiding principle of life and this has built a 'center of gravity' in him corresponding to World 24. But although he has entered the natural world of man, he has gained nothing that cannot be lost. Only when the second body, the body kesdjan, has been formed in him, and is able to function independently of his physical body, will he be firmly established.

Man Number 5 is firmly established in World 24 and is able to come under the laws of World 12. Gurdjieff described him as the man who is 'fully himself'. All that he knows, the whole of him knows. What he sees, is seen by the whole of him. He does not have to draw on anything outside of himself in order to be

---

19 See the quotation from Baha ad-din Naqshbandi in the Introduction. In Sufism, there is the term *dhawq*, or 'taste', which designates this approach. The taste of different worlds comes to us from the higher centers, or the 'angels' Bennett was a master of cultivating *dhwaq* in people, and enabling them to keep it pure.

himself. He has reached the unity of being, will, and function that escapes us in the lower worlds. Being able to exist in World 12, he is able to form the 'higher-being body', or higher part of the soul, which gives him a direct instrument of the will. In this further transformation, he becomes Man Number 6.

Man Number 6 goes beyond the particulate or individual will. He is really able to enter into others. This means that he is able, in his own experience and action, to enter into the higher process by which the will that is one becomes many. All will is will, but to realize this requires a strength of being that is far beyond us. With this strength, Man Number 6 is able to enter into the workings of World 6. The events of that world become a reality for him. He is involved in the creation of destiny. If we say that he is under the direction of a will that is higher than his own, and that he has become free of his own will, this will appear to our thinking as a state of privation where his individual freedom has been superseded by the workings of a juggernaut. It is not like that. World 6 is not impersonal in the sense of lacking individuality. It is the world out of which can come the creative working of individuals.

WORLD 3		COSMIC WILL
	Man no. 7	
WORLD 6		UNIVERSAL WILL
	Man no. 6	
WORLD 12		INDIVIDUAL WILL
	Man no. 5	
WORLD 24		SELFHOOD
	Man no. 4	
WORLD 48	Man nos. 1, 2, 3	ONE-CENTRE FUNCTIONING
	↓ (delusions)	
WORLD 96	Unreal existence	

GURDJIEFF'S SCHEME OF SEVEN MEN
FIG. 8.1

In Gurdjieff's notion of 'objective reason' there is hidden a very profound understanding of reality. Objective reason is in contact with the working of essential laws. These laws are not laws as we know laws, that is, limitations to do with the conditions of existence. Essential laws are the very spirit of creation; to do with the marriage of the limited with the unlimited. In them the reconciling force is the will of God. Objective reason is in fact the power of entering into the working of these higher laws. They are not laws 'outside' to be studied, but to be participated in through purity of being. When objective reason is taken to its fullest heights, man becomes Man Number 7 (see Figure 8.1). He is infused with the energy of love and can enter into the workings of World 3. This is the limit of what is possible for a created being, and Gurdjieff calls this gradation of reason the 'sacred anklad'. Here the creation has reached its highest point of return, and created beings have become divine. But we have to try and understand this in terms of the whole purpose of the creation, and not simply as the development of a particular kind of being in whom we have a subjective interest. There must be, in the scheme of things, an ultimate point of return. Here man, life, and the universe become united in a common act of service.[20]

The Facts of Experience

We must start from an understanding of ourselves as we are. Our lives are lived mechanically and are full of useless negativity. Most of the time we are carried along by momentum and do not even notice what is happening. Passing almost all our time in dreams, we end up with nothing but dreams, and we ourselves have nothing but the substance of a dream. We only remember our dreams to the extent that we notice them; what is not noticed is lost forever. But if we ask ourselves how often we have been in a state of noticing over the last week, or over the last day, then we will find that very little has remained with us. We will find thoughts about what we have been doing; we will find routines to do with our daily activities; but in none of this will we find any real experience, any real material of concrete memory. Nearly all of our life disappears because we do not enter into the experience at all: we are not aware of ourselves, we do not see what is going

---

20 The real meaning of *worship*, for example, is this return to the source. We do not praise God by giving him applause for his cleverness, but by entering into the 'uphill' stream of evolution.

on. All that is happening is only happening to the machine in us, the personality, which has no being of its own. We have become so accustomed to living in this state that we fail to see how abnormal it is. Experiences are so dependent on outside things, that when these outside things are not there, the experience cannot exist.

The narrowness and restrictions of our lives are not noticed. We are like people living in cities with their half-poisonous atmospheres and their extremes of noise and congestion and stress, which are harmful to the whole of us, who have become so accustomed to it all that we fail to notice the damage that is being done to us. It is only when we go out into the country and breathe fresh air, and are surrounded by peace, that we realize that we have been living a strained and artificial life. Even then we may find that we miss all the poisons and are so disoriented by good air and silence that we cannot bear the natural world.

Awakening into higher worlds is a relief, but we have to have something in us that wishes for relief, that is not totally addicted to slavery. When we awaken into World 24, we can see World 48 for what it is: a state of existence in shackles. We can realize that in the world of personality, we have been dreaming about doing things and about experiencing things, but not actually doing anything or experiencing anything. Then we can understand that nothing really beneficial can happen in that world: it is the pretense of a life, not living.

Unlike World 96, World 48 is not a negative world. There are higher laws which come into it from above. It is possible to experience something directly. Because of this, we can be aware, even through our personality life, that something is wrong, that something is missing, even when things appear to be 'going right' for us. In World 48, we are alienated from ourselves by our dependence on outside stimulation. Even when we do something that is exciting and positive, there is always something that we feel to be lacking. This feeling of incompleteness was marvelously expressed by the Buddha, 'Impermanent are all component things. Nothing comes into existence but bears the seeds of its own dissolution'.

When we are under the laws initiated by existential impulses, the situation is really much worse, for then we have no initiative of our own and we are depending on something being done to us. This is very far from the true state of a human being; but it has become accepted as a normal thing. We are dependent on our interest being aroused, our functions stimulated, so that some activity can get under way in us. Even when we notice this, we still cling to the absurd belief that we are something in our own right. The laws which work in us in this utterly mechanical state are those which are initiated by an existential impulse, such as 1*-2-3. Gurdjieff says that these laws have lost 'half the force of their vivifyingness' and they place us partway between the condition of free beings and inert things.

We should be clear that dependent states take up most of our time, whether we are dependent on things or on other people. It is only by chance that we come under the working of another kind of law and are able to feel differently about ourselves, see what we are looking at, or make contact with the actual situation in which we exist. Living as we do, we are incomplete and we need to be supported by outside factors, not only to maintain our existence but also for our inner workings and manifestations. Our so-called 'inner lives' are nothing but a mirage of our mechanical lives. We feel that we are only half alive, but so long as we try to introduce something through external channels, such as reading books or expanding our social life, our efforts will not only fail to give us more life, they will make us even more dependent on what is outside us.

We have to learn to be uncomfortable in this state of sleep, of not really being alive. This will draw us toward the laws of World 24, enable us to be attracted toward the higher worlds. Our minds may be full of all sorts of ideas of self-improvement, but none of this will do anything. What matters is the inner attraction toward what is more real. No matter what grasp we have of the theory, no matter what feelings are engendered by particular experiences of seeing the facts of our sleeping state, all of it will remain subjective data in one or another of our brains and will have no effect at all on the whole of us. Until we have become able to recognize our dreams as they are going on, no change is possible for us. It is not enough to know with our minds that we are asleep, or to feel with our hearts that we must work; we must be able to confront with the whole of ourselves what it means to be asleep.

In *Beelzebub's Tales*, Gurdjieff in the guise of Beelzebub says over and over again that the duration of life of three-brained beings on the earth is constantly diminishing. If we take this literally, it does not make sense since we men are, on average, living to a far greater age in the physical sense than at any other time. But what he is talking about is the real, substantial duration of our lives, which depends very much on how much experience in essence we have. This means how much of our lives is spent in World 24 as opposed to the dream-like state of World 48. There is far less content to life than there used to be because we are tending to live more and more in the world of personality, World 48. In this world, time is very strange. We appear to be experiencing things as they happen, so that we ourselves are present as tomorrow becomes today and today yesterday, but when we really look at it, we are hardly there at all. The world has not even 'passed us by'; we have not been there at all to experience a world process, or even be blind to it. The yesterday of World 48 is thin and insubstantial, but the past that has been lived in World 24 is alive in a way that our personality memories can never be. We can say that a minute of life in World 24 has as much life and content in it as a whole day of life in World 48.

Until we have come to see the world of personality for what it is, we will cling to the belief that something significant can be done while we remain in it. It is very hard to break with this belief, and it is one of the things that takes a very long time to be established in us, but until it is established, we will go on chasing after objectives which have no practical reality. For practical work, we have to come to the condition in which we are able to see our sleep as it goes on; so that here and now we realize the truth of our mechanicality. It does not matter how many experiences we may have gathered of seeing that we are in the state of sleep; it is still necessary to watch how much time we spend in World 48. It is no good saying, 'Well, now I have really learned that lesson and I really see that I spend a great deal of time asleep, I can go on to something else and leave that behind'. We see one time that we do not actually taste the food that we are eating, but every time that we eat we have to try and see whether we are tasting or not.

We speak of liberation 'in this very life', but this also means in this very moment, not a bit yesterday, a bit today, and a bit tomorrow. If we do not work now, we never work. We have to educate ourselves into this way. At first, we can learn to examine our day and what we have done, and ask how much of it had any meaning at all and, if it had a meaning, then what kind of meaning it had. It is not necessary that we should be in an active, initiating role for an action to have substance, but the point is that what happens in our lives where we are just objects might just as well not have happened at all. Later, we can learn how to be active toward this research and realize the importance of struggling with habits and, eventually, come to the point of understanding what can be generated in us by initiating the struggle between 'yes' and 'no,' that is, of separating ourselves from ourselves.

The part of us which sees what is going on, which sees how things are, can be called the 'as if I'. What observes is under fewer laws than that which is observed. The more this part can be kept from reacting to what it sees, the better for us. Reaction can spoil everything. In a flash, an observation becomes an occasion for self-damnation or self-praise. We become pleased with ourselves or plunged into misery. It is not easy to come to the ability just to see. At the same time, we have to realize that this observing part is not the real 'I'; it is simply playing the role of 'I'. This is harder than it seems because the mechanical laws of World 48 can tum everything round, and turn this observing part into what is known as 'work personality'. The only protection is in the purity of seeing. What sees is nothing in itself and should never be given a material identity as if it were a 'something' in its own right.

The real tragedy of World 48 is that so much of what happens to us in that world has really nothing to do with 'us', that is, with our own nature, our own essence. We wander off the line of our own life and we experience things in a way that is not even according to our character or fate. We have the uneasy feeling that what we are doing is meaningless. Gurdjieff spoke about all this as being under the 'law of accident'. In our symbolism, we can write this law as $1*-2*-3*$, the completely existential form of the law of involution.

I remember when I first heard about this many, many years ago. One of the things that Gurdjieff said about it was that it was the first of the laws of World 48 from which it was possible to free oneself. As soon as we are able to really commit ourselves to working on ourselves, to commit ourselves from an understanding of the need for work, that is, as a result of having created in ourselves something not on the level of World 48, then this law of accident is no longer able to take hold of us in the same way. Then we can come under the action of laws that give what happens to us a meaning. Then instead of our lives always being blurred and confused, mixed up in a way that is characteristic of World 48, things begin to happen to us, whether pleasant or unpleasant, which really belong to us.

When we begin to become free from the law of accident, our relation to the world of sleep changes. We are able to recognize when we have gone off the rails into some mechanical form of life. Then our sleep can act as a reminder for us. We know the taste of sleep, and we know the taste of real life. The taste of sleep tells us that we are not working, or that something is missing in the way that we are working. Then we have to make some effort to separate ourselves from ourselves and bring the higher laws to life in us. It is closely analogous to being sensitive to what is called the 'muscle tone' of the physical body, but in this case, what we are working with is the 'psychic tone' of our inner life. Work on oneself is needed, first of all, simply in order to bring ourselves into the natural state of World 24. This does not require that we are perpetually in a condition of strain, just as the preservation of muscle tone does not require that we are constantly lifting weights. Much of work on oneself belongs to the normal life of a man, and it is a great misfortune that education completely neglects the welfare of our inner life.

As we said, we cannot really assume that we have a permanent place in World 24 until we have a 'body' that corresponds with that world. This inner body, or second body, can be represented as something constructed out of the sensitive energy, so that we can understand how it is that a way of life in which sensitivity, as soon as it becomes available, is used up on reactions, and cannot possible lead to making a substantial presence. Our World 24 experience is really a shift in the balance between the dependent and the independent laws of World 48. Half of the laws of World 48 are the same as those of World 24, and it is this that enables us to have the taste of a real life without yet being established in the higher world. So we find, for example, that after struggling for a long time with a certain negativity toward someone, suddenly all the difficulty is lifted and we have the most wonderful satisfaction. But however much we may wish to prolong this state of freedom, it only lasts for a certain time, and then we return to the original condition.

Such an experience can cause us great distress, but we must understand that it is simply evidence that there is a great difference between a temporary state and a permanent change in our being. Sufi terminology is particularly useful in helping us to understand the distinction. In this terminology, *hāl* or 'state' is distinguished from *makām* or 'station', that is, from the level of being that is permanently established. We can understand this distinction in terms of the different 'men' of Gurdjieff's system. Man Number 5, for example, has all sorts of powers open to him because he has another kind of body, the kesdjan body, which enables him to 'move' in the inner world. Because of this body, his *makām* is quite different from ours. Yet someone may have a change of state, a *hāl*, which temporarily gives him the same sort of powers over himself that Man Number 5 has all the time. This does not mean that he has acquired the being of Man Number 5, but that he has come under the laws of World 12, which Man Number 5 always lives under. He has, so to say, 'shifted sideways' in a lower world so that for a time he is no longer subject to the more existential laws, whereas the transition to the being of Man Number 5 is a vertical shift from a lower world to a higher one. A change of *hāl* is then a change that results from coming under different laws while remaining in the same world, while a change of *makām* is going from one world to another. It is very important for anyone who seriously wishes to work on himself to understand this distinction. We must learn not to be identified with changes of state. If we allow ourselves to become identified with them, and look upon them as a test of progress, then they actually become a hindrance to us.

It can happen to us that, in meditation, for example, we come under the action of a higher law, possibly one that is too high for the level of our being. Then we may find ourselves in a *hāl* that is, let us say, very terrifying. If we fail to realize that this is only a state that has come over us which will soon pass, we can become identified with it and it will turn into something negative that will damage our whole attitude toward the work. Similarly, a state of ecstasy can produce all sorts of illusions about ourselves, such as that we no longer need to make the basic efforts to maintain a natural state because we believe that we are above it. States of bewilderment and hiatus, or absence of consciousness, can also catch us up. This is not as it should be. Nearly everyone requires the guidance of people who have learned, and really understood, that states are only part of the process of the work and we do not need to get lost in them. Lack of this guidance accounts for a great many of the blind alleys and aberrations that come out of the search for a higher kind of life.

It is only when we can separate from our states and see them as they are, that is, as the temporary manifestations of different laws, that we can begin to work without looking for reward, for the sake of the work itself. Then we can take states as they come and let them go as they will. If some state is terrifying, we no longer feel that everything has gone wrong; if another state is very beautiful, we do not then believe that we have changed our level of being. When it is like that, the states that come can be part of the normal process of transformation and we can get our lives more into balance. Then we can have real experiences in which our essence can grow because we have learned how to keep from spoiling them. What usually spoils them is that personality identifies with them, and robs them of their freedom by bringing them into World 48. When they are unspoiled, what we are experiencing belongs to World 24.

Essence experience of itself does not bring us into the full life of World 24. For that we need to have our own selves. This means, using the language of the various selves of man, that the true self must be awakened. The four selves of man are balanced between the existential and the essential laws. They form a bridge between our own 'I' and the outer world of bodies. The material and the reactional selves belong to World 48, while the divided and the true selves belong to World 24. For the moment, we will not consider how it is that when we are dominated by the lower selves we come under the laws of delusion of World 96.

The World of Selves

In its right nature, a self is a bridge between higher and lower worlds. For a full life, we need all the apparatus of the physical body. We have obligations in this physical world and we need instruments with which to fulfill them. But in the 'upside-down' situation of ordinary man, the instruments assume command and we lose ourselves. When the lower selves are in command, we are closed to the action of higher laws and we are out of contact with our own essence. This is not as it should be. The lower selves should be able to perform their functions in the lower world of World 48 without entrapping 'us' in them. World 48 is the 'outer world' of all our external actions, and the true 'inner world' should exist on a higher level.

The outer world contains our material and reactional selves. The material self is subject to all the laws of this world, all the forty-eight laws. It is automatic because inner and outer events are not distinguished and everything is on the same level. Everything is tied to events in the external world. However, because even in this self there are the effects of higher laws, it is possible for us to become confused, and believe that we are free, that we are something. This is an illusion, since in the material self there is nothing that can hold an inner experience together. Everything that happens to us is attached to something material.

The reactional self has more freedom. It is open to the action of the laws of World 24, but in itself it belongs exclusively to the outer world. The reason for this is that the reactional self in its right place is the instrument we have for perceiving the world of life. In every contact that we have with the outside world there is latent an inner experience. When we *notice* something, what we notice may be just some external object, but there is a taste of life that we are alive. Noticing is a *hāl* that brings us under the laws of World 24. If we look at the reactional self in purely functional terms, simply as an apparatus of reaction, it cannot make sense that the very same thing brings us under the laws of delusion and also brings us under the laws of our own essence. It can only make sense when we clearly see the difference between being the slave of our reactions, being able to perceive through our reactions, and being the master of our reactions. In the first we are in the world of delusion; in the second we are having essential experience, though we are still in all probability in World 48, while in the last we are awakened in World 24 through the realization of the higher laws of our higher selves. What the reactional self has to bring is not the mechanical abilities of the material self, but the possibility of inner experience. This is what it means when we say that the reactional self, while existing in World 48, is subject to only half the laws. It corresponds to the inner, life side of our experience in this physical body.

But the reactional self cannot lead to independent being. All it can do is enable us to be in contact with what we are thinking, feeling, and doing, which in its turn enables us to work in such a way that the reactional responses we have can provide us with energy from which a true inner being may be fashioned. The *hāl* of the reactional self is very important for our work on ourselves. It is momentary and can go one way or the other, toward essence or toward personality. Until it is mastered, the true inner life cannot begin.

The divided self belongs to World 24. It is the self of our astral inheritance and is subject to all the twenty-four laws. Here, life can form into a pattern and we can talk of being ourselves, but features of our character can be exaggerated - we can be full of pride and overvalue our own understanding. All that the reactional self has as state, *hāl,* the divided self has as *makām,* or being. So, although it is under the very same laws as the reactional self, the divided self is more free. It exists in a different environment. It is able to move into higher states and conscious, and even creative energy can enter it. These higher energies are able to organize the sensitive energy, and it is in this way that an inner being begins to be formed. All this, however, does not free the divided self from the limitations of its own pattern. We may remember that this self is poised between the essential and the existential laws and thus is not able to see itself objectively. It will mistake its own directives for those of the true 'I' and remain within the boundaries of fate. Essence will grow, but remain fixed with the characteristics it had at birth. *Purification* only becomes possible with the awakening of the true self, which exists under only twelve laws. As the awakening of the reactional self in World 48 gives us the feeling of life, so the awakening of the true self gives us the feeling of 'authority' in ourselves. Being under the laws of World 12 enables us to decide and exercise the powers of the will. We can struggle against ourselves in quite a different way because we can see ourselves as limited, see the blindness that is inherent in our understanding of the world. But struggle in World 24 is not the same as in World 48, which we tend to experience in terms of the pulls on our sensitivity.

It is through the action of the true self that the essence can become the place into which 'I' can come. This 'descent' of 'I' is also an ascent of being into World 12. The mastering of the lower worlds is the way toward attaining the higher ones. To have the powers of 'I' before the essence is purified would be a terrible thing. Gurdjieff said that when this happens, all that has been 'crystallized' in the essence has sooner or later to be 'decrystallized', and that this can only be done through the most terrible suffering.

We can now picture to ourselves that the divided self is a bridge between Men Numbers 1, 2, and 3, on the one hand, who exist in World 48, and Man Number 4, on the other, who exists in World 24. Man Number 4 can live according to his own essence, and can have the creative experience or states of the true self. But mastery over World 24 comes only with the purification of the true self and the transition to Man Number 5 (Figure 8.2).

The Taste of the Natural World

World 24, the natural world of man, is within World 48,[21] but it is hidden by our dependence on external things. What we depend on may take the form of anything around us: the clothes we wear, the opinions of others, the pictures in our minds, fixed reactions, words, and so on. All this dependence we refer to when we use the word 'personality'. The personality is really part of the external world and should deal with things that require no initiative and no inner experience. But when we live in the world of personality we believe that the impulses coming through the personality are 'from ourselves' and the various associations produced in our brains from these impulses are our 'inner life'. The laws which apply to the working of the personality are those which are initiated by an existential impulse. In other words, what starts them off is 'contingent', not essential to ourselves. The proper role of the personality is to deal with events that do not require 'our own' attention. But when we identify with the personality, the laws of our essence are bound to those of the personality and we lose the independence of an inner life. This should not be misunderstood. It does not mean that the inner life is right when it is cut off from the external world. That is a mistake that is often made by people when they begin to realize that the kind of involvement we have in the external world robs us of something. The true inner life is independent, but not separate. It is only when it is independent that we can actually be aware of the external world without distortion

In the personality, our interaction with the world is under the law 1 *-3 *- 2*. We do not make contact directly. Our interest has to be stimulated: sexually, emotionally, intellectually, physically, and so on. Almost invariably, it is through only one of our brains. We look at a chair and what we really see is just the concept; we do not see the wood, the finish, the fabric, the design, the solidity, or anything concrete. We are looking through the word 'chair'. If we want to sit down, we go and find a chair, but all we experience of it is 'a something to be sat upon', and very probably we will not even be aware of actually sitting down on it. Or it may be 'my grandfather's chair,' and all we are then experiencing are the emotional associations attached to it. All the time we are in the situation of having to be stimulated in some way in one of our brains,

---

21 The idea of World 24 as within World 48 – and, as is said later, of World 12 being within World 24 – corresponds to Gurdjieff's notion of inner octaves. Cf. *In Search of the Miraculous*, p. 136.

and then experiencing what we are brought to look at through the collection of conditioned responses and secondhand information that personality is made of. We never see things save through an image we have of them. We are always falling back on some previous experience and fail to see what is in front of us in the moment. This is true whether it is something in the external world or an idea that we are trying to understand. Always there is some picture in the way.

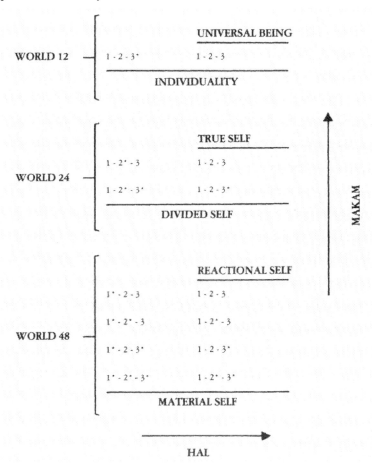

PLACE OF SELVES IN WORLDS ILLUSTRATED BY LAW OF INVOLUTION 1-2-3

FIG. 8.2

But in the *hāl* that temporarily suspends the dependent laws of personality, the experience is radically different.

For example, we can be studying some idea, and be quite convinced that we have become thoroughly familiar with it, when quite suddenly it is as if the scales have dropped away from our eyes and we begin to see its essential life. The experience is always fresh. We may be looking at something we have looked at a thousand times and then all at once realize that we have never seen it before. With young children there is much more of this kind of thing because they have no formed personality to set up the conditioned kind of interaction. Small children can very often look at a thing and see it without depending upon any words or previous images. For very many adults, this is impossibly rare. One of the greatest difficulties of our existence is that although we come into the world with this capacity for essential experience, it all becomes covered over and buried when we are filled with all sorts of information and ideas acquired from our environment. This layer of second-hand material governs all our interactions with the world, as well as shaping our ideas about ourselves, who we are, and what we are capable of. As the content of our personality, it should help us to carry out our daily activities in the world. Instead, it is virtually all there is to us.

Normal people, that is, people who are able to live in World 24, also have to have a certain amount of this 'information extraneous to their essential nature', but this personality in them is relegated to a subordinate role while their capacity for direct experience takes the position of initiative. Such a person is awake and alive to what he is doing, and this is what makes the life of World 24 so much more satisfying than when we are caught in World 48. It does not mean that in World 24 we have gone beyond the limitations of our existence. We see things according to our pattern or type, which is represented in the middle term of the law 1-3*-2*, but this is free of what we have been taught and what we have picked up through the surrounding circumstances of external life.

What is true for our contact with the world around us is also true for our contact with ourselves. In World 48, our identity comes under the dependent law 2*-3 *-1*. This means that we experience ourselves only through asserting ourselves against an external impact. Somebody offends us and we 'take up arms' and defend our position or stand up for ourselves and our rights. The initiative is in some reaction to external events and the outcome is in what we call 'self-assertion'. All of this is totally embedded in external events and really has no inner content. It is a fictitious sort of identity with the shell of the personality in the middle to keep it going. It works through either praise or blame. Somebody gives us praise and we go around 'swaggering' or exhibiting about it or indulging in internal exhibitions of this 'recognition of our true nature'. Beelzebub more than once advises his grandson Hassein that if by chance he should have to live on the earth, he should always with everyone use flattery so as to avoid being attacked by victims of 'wounded pride'.

In World 24 we are able to be present to ourselves quite spontaneously. Our identity does not depend on anything outside of ourselves, but arises from the quality of our inner state itself. The essential law is written as 2-3*-1*. All the laws of World 24 have this quality of immediate awareness about them. Freeing the initiating impulse from external conditioning is the way toward a genuine inner life. We can do a very great deal to cultivate the taste of essential laws, but it is difficult to prevent the personality from robbing us of their benefit because we are always looking for results and changes and confusing *hāl* with *makām*. They come about in quite different ways. A change in *makām* is not directly a process in time, and the meaning of time is different in the different worlds.

Essence experience seems to give us more time because we are able to sustain ourselves in the present moment. In the personality, the present moment is always leaking away into the past and into the future through associations. We are caught up in things and have no time. We are unable to make a real contact with a past event and we are unable to hold a vision of the future. But what happens to us when we are under the laws of World 24 has a depth that enables it to hold together. What we have experienced in an essential way remains alive. We are able to make a connection with the future and prepare for what is to come. We have a place in the course of events and are not just a bit of flotsam tossed on the surface of external happenings. Under the domination of the personality, we are under anxiety about things which are outside our control and blind to things which are inside our control. We do not see how our inner state can influence what is possible. We are living according to a mechanical line of time. With the essence, we can see what is potential as well as what is actual; and this gives us the possibility of real choice. Choice changes the meaning of time.

The central characteristic of World 24 is that of being our own selves. This is quite different from the state of striving to be oneself that belongs to World 48. Ordinarily, people try to be independent by getting away from the influence and domination of other people. They strive to have their own opinions, their own means of support, their own house, to be their own boss, to make up their own minds, and so on and so on. In other words, they look for identity in terms of external things. But in World 24, we are independent because we are ourselves, not because of external things that we have acquired. The freedom of the essence is not a freedom from external constraints but a freedom to be what we are. It is substantial freedom. Because of it we are able to do things that are very difficult while living in World 48. There will be kinds of task that nearly always cause us great difficulty and which we can never do unless there are circumstances which give us a support, but under the laws of World 24, we find that this all becomes wonderfully easy. It is as if something else takes over from us and sees it through. For example, we nearly always find it impossible to speak to someone about an embarrassing topic unless they themselves provide the opening. Then one day we find ourselves quite free from all that nonsense in us and there is no hesitation. Then we are surprised when all the old inhibitions return and we can feel very keenly the suffocating effect of the dependent laws on our lives.

The freedom to be and act from our own selves is still only a relative freedom. In World 24, we are still apart from other people, and therefore living in a world which is no bigger than ourselves. The sense of relief we have at living in our own essence may quite delude us. Going from the world of personality into the natural world may be compared to emerging from a dark cave into a valley. The valley looks as wide and long and bright as anything could ever be, and we can completely fail to grasp that there are other valleys and a whole world to discover.

The change in going into World 24 is remarkable. There is a sort of division between inside and outside in the personality, but it is really spurious. Just as in human groupings we say some people 'belong' and others do not, so we say that some things 'belong' to what we are but other things do not. There is no essential difference between those who belong to a given group and those who do not; and there is no essential difference between what we say is inside us and what we say is outside us. Almost all of what we call our 'insides' originated outside us, and there is no reason why any of our ideas, our beliefs, our habits, all that gives us this spurious sense of uniqueness, should be ours apart from the fact that things happened to fall out in that way. So long as we are dependent beings we are not any more distinct from others than we are from ourselves. Our being apart from other people is only a reflection of our alienation from ourselves. Ordinarily, our lives flow according to mechanical laws and things simply happen as a clock, when it is wound up, runs on until its spring is unwound. When we are able to enter World 24 we begin to live our own lives from our own initiative, independently of what is going on around us. We become truly separate, distinct beings, each with our own self-nature and with an independent inner life.

We can come into contact with other beings, but we are not able to enter them, and we can rest content with what appears to be the inexhaustible possibilities of our own nature. It is quite another step to realize that the freedom we have acquired is at the expense of rejecting others. We strive to become free of the dependency of World 48, and it is all too easy to believe that the sense of security, confidence, and independence we have in World 24 is really based on something permanent. It is not so; even in World 24 'nothing is permanent, everything has an end, everything wears out'. The 'body' that corresponds to this world, the inner or kesdjan body, is still corruptible. It can be thought of as an organization of sensitive energy that coheres through time; all intentional efforts to work on ourselves bring about a certain growth of this body. It does not grow as a plant or physical body grows and it is not strictly true to say that it comes about through a process in time at all but, as we have said, the condition of time is different in the different worlds. The sensitive energy is inevitably subject to disorganizing influences that win in the end. It is only when this body of sensitivity, capable of surviving the death of the physical body yet still itself mortal, becomes the foundation for the arising of the highest part of man, the soul, that a man is truly immortal. This highest part can be related to the organization within ourselves of the energy of consciousness, as well as to the attainment of our own will, our own 'I'. It is through the soul that we overcome our separateness from others.

The World of Individuality

Within World 24, but hidden from us by our own selves, is World 12. Gurdjieff said that this is the world to which the saint is admitted, so it is not easy of access. Because the energy of consciousness can be concentrated, the whole of reality is seen quite differently. It is not unlikely that every one of us has at some time experienced a *hāl* bringing us under the laws of World 12, probably through some external shock, painful or joyful. As we are, such an intense experiencing would hardly be comprehensible; we would not be able to see it for what it is. In World 12, there is no need to assert ourselves, to have anything, even to be anything: all our ordinary concerns with who we are, what we are doing, and what we have no longer have any meaning. In contrast with World 24, the center of the stage is no longer occupied with our own selves but with our own 'I'. This is a state of spiritual reality where we are effectively returned to the commitment to existence with which our own conception began. We have realized our freedom and are self-created beings.

The real freedom of a man is not only in being able to be himself but also in being able to be not-himself; that is, to be able to put himself in the place of other people. This is what Gurdjieff refers to in *Beelzebub's Tales*, when he says that written over the entrance to the Holy Planet Purgatory are the words:

'Only-he-may-enter-here-who-puts-himself-in-the-position-of-the-other-results-of-my-labours'. The ability to see others as oneself marks the transition from World 24 to World 12. It is the mystery of the true individual: he is able to be altogether himself and yet he is able to be entirely at one with others. When Jesus, in choosing two commandments which together summarized the whole of the law and the prophets, said, 'Love the Lord thy God with all your heart, with all your soul, with all your mind and with all your strength and love your neighbor as yourself', he was referring to this mystery. The unity and wholeness that we find easy to picture is that of a sum of parts. Such a whole is quite separate from other wholes because it has different parts from them. The wholeness and unity of World 12 does not separate one 'I' from another 'I'. It is really the wholeness of humanity that flows through all 'I's, making each one whole just as one shared life flows through all the members of our body. There is only the one life, not a collection of lives fitted together.

In the one life, each of the members has an individual identity. The state of union of World 12 is like that also. In the perfect union of man and woman there is a oneness of being and a oneness of will, but the man and the woman retain their separate identities. The more perfect the union, the more the man is perfectly and fully a man and the more the woman is perfectly and fully a woman. This kind of union goes beyond anything that the selfhood can ever attain. Becoming liberated from the laws of the selfhood is 'losing oneself'. What is discovered is who one is. This is 'I Am', which is quite apart from anything of our selves, and which we represent as 2-3-1*, where the middle term refers to the common life and will of all humanity.

For the man who has a soul, many things are possible that are entirely inaccessible to us. He attains eternal reality, a timelessness in which past and future are an open field and not, as they are with us, the track of successive events along which we are forced to travel. He can manifest in space and time quite independently of the position of his physical body. He sees time and space for what they are - part of the restrictions under which the lower worlds exist. Birth and death are not as they are with us, the beginning and the end of life; they are part of a pattern in which there is real freedom. He is no longer 'in' time and space, but exists according to a higher level of order. The soul or body of consciousness is no longer subject to what the Buddhists call *dukkha,* the constraints of the lower worlds which lead to suffering, wearing out, and dissolution. It is immortal, deathless; there is no longer any need to undergo death and rebirth, to be subject to *samsara,* the turning of the wheel of existence. In the *Bhagavad Gita* and the *Upanishads* is it said that the Self is not born, neither does it die. In Saint Paul's letters we read about the difference between living under the law of our lower nature, under the sentence of death, and living according to the spirit. All the great traditions speak of this immortality in their own way. In our own terminology, it is a matter of becoming free from the separateness of space and time, the conditions of existence in the lower worlds.

To go from a lower world to a higher one we have to cease to be under the action of laws that hold us in the lower worlds. This can be equated with the creation in ourselves of higher functions and organizations of higher energies which are able to respond to the workings of higher laws. The man who has his own 'I' has within him a second body that gives him power over the whole of his selfhood. He can also acquire a third body, or soul, that is connected with the Source of all. It is through this that he becomes free of space, time and number, even though he retains a distinct identity. Only with the perfection of the third body does a man go 'beyond his own 'I''.

Coming to understand the difference between World 48 and World 24 is possible for everyone. We can 'taste' the difference. In World 48 we are in a heavy and constrained state. As long as we are in that world, it is taken as the norm. Once we begin to get the taste of World 24, however, we can see how dull the world of personality is, and how shut in we are. In the world of essence, we

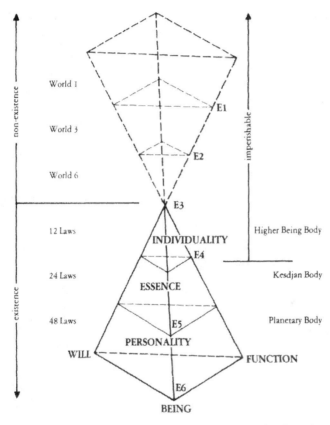

Note: The upper pyramid represents the spiritual realms the 'other side' of creativity: creative energy is the action in which existence and non-existence marry. The reader should refer to Bennett's *A Spiritual Psychology*.

INTERPRETATION OF HUMAN EXISTENCE
FIG. 8.3

can breathe more freely, be aware of what is about us, and be in contact with ourselves. The difference between the two worlds can be learned fairly quickly, even though it may take a long time before we really establish in ourselves the independent being of World 24. The case of World 12 is not so simple. The world of individuality is already something supernatural, and to reach it we quite literally have to go beyond our own nature.

The problem is not that World 12 is far away but that it is hidden by our own selves. Even so, within our experience that reality is there and it is not true to say that we are always without exception locked up inside our own selves. For example, under the laws of World 12, the interaction we have with others is an interaction of will. In this, we are all equal. No one will is more or less than another. It is possible to have a taste of this even though it is very quickly distorted by turning it into a personal experience.

In the Gospels there is the parable of the two women working at their spinning and the two men plowing in the field. In each case, one of the two is taken and the other left. If we ask how it is that two people in the same place apparently doing the same thing should be separated like this, the answer is that they are really in different worlds. One of them is left in the dream world and the other taken into the world of reality. Outwardly, they are both in the physical world, World 48, but inwardly, one is in World 24 and the other in World 12. It is not enough to awaken from the dream world of the personality. It is ultimately necessary to awaken from the illusion of being oneself.

With the perfection of the soul, the individual, now a sacred individual, comes under the laws of World 6. Here it is that the distinction between One and Many is dissolved. The commitment to existence by which the individual life began is transcended. There is no longer any need of a contact of wills because all wills are the same. In this world there is the direct working of the purpose of the creation (Figure 8.3).

The Universal World

To come to this world, one's own will must be drowned in the abyss of the whole. This is very difficult for us to understand. As we are, we look at the world of essence as the place of our fulfillment: there we can be ourselves. World 12 demands that we should become free of ourselves and become individuals;

that is, that we should enter a world of decision where we are no longer carried by the pattern of our own nature. World 6 demands that this freedom of will be overcome in the universal working. What is hard even to put into words is that the creation is not like a machine. Those who enter World 6, the world of the creation, are not abandoning their freedom for immersion in the 'mechanics of stars'.

According to the law of evolution 2-1-3, the created has something to bring to the Creator. The return of the creature to its Source is the very means by which the purpose of the creation is fulfilled. It is the drawing of love. What ultimately returns is not the personality, is not the essence, and is not even the 'I': it is the fruit of all the ascent through the worlds by which unity and oneness are possible. None of this can even enter our consciousness, and all we can hold before us are images that are taken from what has been revealed to mankind.

The culmination of Objective Reason, the function of the highest being part, or soul, is to see the world not from oneself but as God sees it. In that seeing there are no separate wills, that is, different centers of experience; there is the Whole, the Megalocosmos, from which nothing is excluded, no one thing is any more important than any other, and there is no separation. In all our experience, communication is always something between two different wholes. We can say that in the Megalocosmos there is no need of any communication because everything is at once everything else. Throughout, there is the working of the divine reconciling force which sustains an ocean of being that is not divided. The wholeness and unity that is here is not attained by the exclusion of variety but by all-inclusion. But the diversity of the Megalocosmos is not to be understood as the diversity of many things, of many beings, but as the creative action of the six fundamental laws.

Nothing can exist that is not a part of World 6. The universal laws which govern this whole are present in all the worlds. The law of cosmic involution, 1-2-3, is the law of creation by which the issuing forth of the divine affirmation sustains the existence of the whole. Creation is in reality continuous, the creative will 'always' at work. Cosmic evolution, 2-1-3, is the fulfillment of the purpose for which the hazards of the creation were undertaken. It is the return from the creation to the Source, the connection of everything that exists with the Source from which it came. The universal identity, 2-3-1, is the

'thusness' of all that exists. The reconciling force at the center
of the triad proclaims the reconciling will of God as the power
that preserves and sustains everything that is, and enables it to
occupy its place in the whole. By this law, the universe itself is
enabled to be what it is.

The universal law of interaction 1-3-2 is the interaction between all the parts of the creation which in *Beelzebub's Tales* is
called the 'common cosmic *ansanbaluiazar*'. This law assures
the connection of everything with everything; that everything
prehends, is affected by, everything else. It is the universal process. The universal law of order, 3-1-2, issues in a limitless receptivity which is the condition of all possibilities. In ancient myth, it
is the Universal Mother in which everything has its being. It is the
separation of the possible from the impossible which places the
whole under the operation of universal laws.

The universal law of freedom, 3-2-1, can be called the universal law of impossibility, the door that is left open to enable
existence to return to its Source. It is the law of freedom which
enables beings in the lower worlds to come under the action of
higher laws, and enables the mistakes which are inherent in the
limitations of existence to be rectified. It acts to secure the redemption of the whole universe. It reconciles the will of God with
his creation.

In Sufism, the phrase *bhāti-bud-yud* stands for the oneness of
substance that is World 6. In Mahayana Buddhism, the man who is
able to enter this world is called the *Bodhisattva*, the compassionate one, because he is able to enter into all beings. One who has
entered this world can love with impartial, objective love. What is
ordinarily called love is merely our own state, and there is a distinction between the lover and the beloved. To enter the world of
objective love, or compassion, this distinction must go. In Sufism
there is a well-known story of the nature of real love. The lover
comes to the place of his beloved and knocks. When he is asked,
'Who is there?' he replies, 'It is I'. The beloved answers him,
'Then go away: there is no room for two of us here'. It is only
when the lover is able to knock and reply to the same question, 'It
is Thou', that the beloved will give him admission. In this world,
there is no *other*.

The Ultimate Worlds

What lies beyond World 6 is totally outside the range of any psychological language, and we have to approach the two remaining worlds through cosmological ideas. The first thing we can say about World 3 is that it is beyond the creation. There is only a World 6 when there is a creation. The transition from World 3 to World 6 is described in *Genesis*. The spirit of God, *elohim*, moves over the waters of chaos, *tohu-bohu*, and separates light from darkness, heaven and earth, and so on until out of the chaos there emerges an orderly world. The chaos is the incomprehensibility of World 3, and all that we perceive as the order and laws which govern our existence are a result not of an 'improvement' on this 'chaos' but of a series of ever more drastic limitations on it. Our ordinary pictures of some creative intelligence constructing order out of the chaotic material makes it all appear as a gradual improvement. In reality, the movement is downward toward greater limitation, and the formless chaos is the higher state. The reason that we no longer see this correctly is that the key to the wisdom which shaped this symbolism has been lost. It was partly for this reason that Gurdjieff put together his own symbolism in *Beelzebub's Tales*, and avoided as far as possible the use of familiar material. What follows is the barest summary of the chapter entitled 'The Holy Planet Purgatory'.

Before anything else was, our Endless Creator had the place of his being on the Holy Sun Absolute. Having discovered that the Sun Absolute was, though almost imperceptibly, diminishing in volume due to the effect of the Merciless Heropass, or the flow of time, our Endlessness decided to forestall the disappearance of his dwelling by means of the creation of an independent world which could restore the loss. To this end, he altered the functioning of the two sacred fundamental laws, the law of three and the law of seven,[22] so that the various forces or impulses could work only in combination, and not independently. The modified laws were directed outward from the Holy Sun Absolute into the

---

22 The law of seven is the law whereby one kind of thing changes into another. We can understand it best from our perspective as the Law of Hazard. The idea of hazard is one of Bennett's major realizations. It implies that things are so arranged that openings occur which can be realized by acts of will. The opening is in the lower world and the act of will is from a higher world. In this way, the worlds are married. According to Gurdjieff, the 'pure' law of seven involves no hazardous step: it is the absolute harmony of all possibilities.

space of the universe in an emanation called the *theomertmalogos*, or Word-God. The result issuing from this emanation was the concentration of definite existences, the 'second-order suns'. Establishing in their turn their own functioning of the two sacred laws, these second-order suns also began to produce results. Any one of these suns transmitted the affirming force toward which all the other suns taken together transmitted the corresponding denial. The theomertmalogos then took the role of the reconciling force. Then were concentrated the 'third-order suns', or what we know as planets. With this the law of seven, 'having lost half the force of its vivifyingness', began to produce results called 'similarities-to-the-already-arisen', which effectively brought the outer cycle of the creation to an end. Then followed the start of an 'inner cycle', to do with the emergence of life, and the creation of possibilities for an individual transformation liberating free intelligence within the creation.

All of this has, in fact, a great deal to say about the psychology of transformation, but for the moment we are interested in the cosmological meaning. The Holy Sun Absolute corresponds to World 1 and the theomertmalogos to World 3. The second-order suns, taken before they exercise individualized action, represent World 6, the universe of stars, the Megalocosmos. The individual sun, such as the star of our solar system, corresponds to World 12. Third-order suns or planets belong to World 24, and the conditions of existence of the 'similarities-to-the-already-arisen' correspond to World 48. A rough correspondence can also be worked out between this and the scheme of worlds in *In Search of the Miraculous*. We have to be careful with all these correspondences, however, because every presentation approaches the whole problem in a special way, and we have to understand the value of different approaches, and not confuse them.

Gurdjieff's cosmology gives us a new insight into the working of the higher laws. The very first action described, in which Our Endlessness directs the modified laws into 'surrounding space', represents the cosmic law of involution 1-2-3: the first force, the cosmic affirmation, is the will of Our Endlessness; the second force, the cosmic denial, is the world then in process of creation, and the third force, and what unites the two other forces, is the theomertmalogos. It is in the nature of the triad of involution that the third force that issues carries in its turn the affirmative quality. This is where Gurdjieff begins his description.

With the arising of the second-order suns there is introduced another set of laws, those relating to the secondary creative power of separate parts of the Megalocosmos. Each of the suns transmits an affirmation of its own. Side by side with the cosmic creation there is now a solar creation peculiar to each of the suns. This is symbolized as 1-2-3*, where the term 3* represents the limited creative power of the individual sun, just as it represents the limited creative power of the man who has his own 'I'. The actions issuing from this secondary creation originate in World 6, while those of the primary creation originate in World 3. In World 12, there are the six pure laws which govern the whole of the creation and also six laws which result from the limitations of individual existence.

The further condensation of the third-order suns, or planets, results in yet another set of laws, those of the tertiary creation. The planets (as a whole) transmit the creative working of their sun and of the primary creation into the visible world that we know. This gives what we can recognize on the psychological level as the distinctions between higher and lower selves, the instruments of manifestation, by which a further twelve laws are added. It is from the world of planets that we derive our fate, or pattern of manifestation, while it is from the sun that we receive our destiny. The sun is our creator as individuals. There is also in us the creation that is from the Source of all, through which it is possible to go beyond ourselves altogether. Then there is the tertiary influence of the planets in our selfhood.

Every sun has its own pattern, its own destiny, its own possible contribution to the whole. When the solar world comes into being, Gurdjieff describes how the forces combine in a triad of order: 3-1-2*. The reconciling term is the theomertmalogos, the affirmation that of the particular sun, and the denial comes from the field of the other suns. This law represents the destiny of the particular sun. We can say that it is given a task to fulfill *within the limitations of existence.*

Where the fundamental law of seven loses 'half the force of its vivifyingness', we have the dependent laws of World 48, which correspond to existence on the surface of planets. This is where our bodies are formed. It is flatland. (See figure 8.4).

WORLD 1	SUN ABSOLUTE	ENDLESSNESS ·

WORLD 3	THEOMERTMALOGOS	CREATIVE ACT

WORLD 6	MEGALOCOSMOS	UNIVERSE

——————— PURGATORY ———————

WORLD 12	SECOND ORDER SUNS	STAR

WORLD 24	THIRD ORDER SUNS	PLANET

——————— MICROCOSMOS ·· ———————

WORLD 48	SIMILARITIES TO THE ALREADY ARISEN ···	PLANETARY SUR-FACE

· cf. *Talks on Beelzebub's Tales*, 1977, p. 83
·· Living cell, or unit of sexual life.
··· Apparatuses with no inner life of their own

SCHEME OF WORLDS IN RELATION TO DE-SCRIPTIONS IN BEELZEBUB'S TALES
FIG. 8.4

The Manifestation of Higher Worlds to Us

In all that we have said about worlds, energies, function, being, will, and so on, something very important has been omitted. Our picture of the possibilities of transformation will be incomplete unless we bring into it how it is that we receive *help* in the lower worlds. We can talk about struggling, observing, working, and even about receiving guidance and instruction from more experienced people than ourselves. All of this is right. But none of it can begin, and none of it can lead anywhere, unless something enters into us which can draw us toward the higher worlds. Such a thing can come only from the higher worlds themselves. The *work* that we have been speaking about is not just some manner of making efforts; it is a reality in its own right that originates from a source we cannot directly experience.

The mystery of the work is the same as the mystery of sacred individuals, such as the founders of the great religions and teachings of the world. From time to time there appear on this earth individuals who come from the world of great compassion. Such sacred individuals *are* the whole, so that while they are incarnated in a physical body and become breathing living beings, such as ourselves, they are within themselves free from all the laws that estrange this world. *They* do not eat and breathe and sleep; that is only what their physical bodies do. The nature of sacred individuals is described by Gurdjieff in his character Ashiata Shiemash. At the beginning of the legominism of Ashiata Shiemash, entitled 'The Terror of the Situation', he says, 'To me, a trifling particle of the whole of the Great Whole, it was commanded from Above to be coated with the planetary body of a three-centered being of this planet and to assist all other such beings arising and existing upon it to free themselves from the consequences of the properties of the organ kundabuffer'. What 'Above' refers to here is World 3. The place of Ashiata Shiemash himself is in World 6.

These sacred individuals know the purposes for which the creation has come into being. Together with this they bring into this world the working of the freedom that belongs to the higher worlds. They are the source of our help, but they cannot give us freedom. Not even God can give us freedom. They give us help that we have to learn how to accept, how to put ourselves under. The events which surround their incarnation and their mission on the earth are quite beyond us. They are altogether outside space and time, cause and effect, and are totally invisible to ordinary people. For that reason, a 'bridge' has to be made so that something can flow between the different worlds. Here specially prepared people who have attained to World 12 play an important role. They are able to come under the action of the laws of World 6, and through this cooperate in the transmission of help to ordinary people. There is always a period in the life of a sacred individual when he is forming a group of companions or disciples around him and preparing them for participation in the high event. This event will not even touch World 24 or the lower worlds. It is a new entry of the *theomertmalogos* or Word-God. When it is completed, there will be a new source of redemption for the world, a new creative power, but for people of the lower worlds to benefit, something must be formed which they can actually experience. It is in this that the disciples of the sacred one have their work. Their task is the creation and presentation of a *sacred image*; partly an image of the individual and partly an image of his teaching or gospel. People are able to turn toward an image of a person, or toward a 'sacred book', and when they turn their attention in this way toward the image, something can come into them. The power behind the image comes from the high and invisible event that would be unendurable and incomprehensible to ordinary people if they were to come into direct contact with it.

We can take Muhammad as an example. He is represented as the Messenger of Hope. Beginning with the words *Bismillah ar-Rahman ar-Rahim*, 'In the name of God, the Compassionate, the Merciful', the Qu'ran presents the message that, in spite of what man has done, God's compassion will outweigh it all. The power underlying this message is such that it arouses in the believers the confident hope that the promise of the Qu'ran will be fulfilled for them. They are given the confidence that it is sufficient to live in the way that was prescribed by Muhammad, transforming their energies according to the code of behavior that is given, to assure their eternal welfare. Anyone who has lived in a Muslim country can recognize this sense of hope, even today after so many centuries have passed and so much has degenerated. It is the sacred image that takes away their doubts. They do not even have the fear of death that other people have because they feel sure that if they live according to the teaching they will have their reward after this life.

The sacred image makes it possible to return to the Source. Because people's aspirations are directed toward the image, a concentrated flow of energy is produced. For those who can transform their energies with sufficient intensity and purity of intention, through their prayers and disciplines, it is possible to pass beyond and become directly connected with the source of the image. If there is not sufficient purity and intensity, the energies will only rise to a certain height, between Worlds 24 and 12. It is in this way that there accumulate reservoirs of this sort of energy centered on the focal points of prayer and devotion. Mecca is an example. This energy can be used by those who have entered upon their transformation, provided that they are willing to accept the obligation of service that this entails.

While all the various religious teachings purport to show how their founders taught their disciples, and what they actually did, such a thing is utterly impossible. All that is transmitted is the external side of the work. At the same time, besides the transmission of this public message by which people are drawn toward the sacred image, the reality is also transmitted. According to Gurdjieff, the real meaning of the mission of sacred individuals is handed down from generation to generation by 'genuine initiated beings'. What really happened during the lifetime of Muhammad, for example, is quite different from the story which is presented in orthodox Muslim teaching. The same is true about the life of Christ and the life of Buddha.

A 'genuine initiated being' is someone who has come into his own individuality. We are not talking about some 'secret teaching', another set of words, which simply gives a different version of the same incidents. The true story cannot even be seen from a perspective lower than that of World 12. This is where the Revelation of Divine Love is brought, so that something can then enter into the life of this earth and help men to liberate themselves from the slavery of their state. Because World 12 is the focal point of the transmission, it appears to us that those who are 'sent from Above' are only individuals. In reality, the revelations are beyond individuality. We see Muhammad, Christ, Buddha, and Lama as separate individuals, but they are not like that. As long as we continue to look upon them only as individuals, we will fail to understand why there should be the multiplicity of faiths which often appear to contradict one another. The contradictions and distinctions that we see are in our own perceptions, not in the revelations themselves. There are not many sacred individuals. They are not divided. There arc not Jesus, Muhammad, Moses, Abraham, Krishna, and so on; these are but images given to us of the One Word-God, the Theomertmalogos which unites the whole, Creator and Creation, which has manifested in this world. When something in us is able to enter World 12 we see immediately how it is that all the teachings and religions come from the One Source, and all sacred individuals are the One Sacred.

The Divine Action is timeless. It is always completely present here and now. Christ said, 'Behold, I am with you always, even unto the end of the world'.

The Man Divine

We have tried to present many different images of the whole man, the 'man of the resurrection'. He is the man who has become one, made in the image of God. As we work in this life, the image of God is made real in us. Meister Eckhart said of the man divine, 'All that Christ has by nature, he has by grace'. He participates in the Divine Act by which the Word-God descends into the world to make our transformation possible, so that we may return to the Source. Having abandoned himself, he now works from the Work itself. This is beyond our understanding as we are; but there is before us the possibility of the work here and now 'on ourselves'. This we can taste, we can verify, and we can practice.

There are in reality no special people, and in work on ourselves we are all equally beggars, equally beginners, must all start from where we are here and now. The choice confronting us is simple enough to live like animals and die like dogs or to work on ourselves in order to become men. Then we can begin to live from a practical understanding of what we are and what we can become. But for this to come to pass, we have to commit ourselves, here and now, to work and to come at *life*: this is the strait gate and the narrow way - there is no other.

PART THREE

WORLDS

INTRODUCTION

In February and March of 1974, J.G. Bennett gave a series of talks to students of the Third Sherborne Course. These talks were based on a scheme of four worlds derived from the Sufi tradition. He used this scheme a great deal in his teaching and it appears in the last book that he wrote, *The Masters of Wisdom.* He had intended to write two other books, one on man and one on time. From a synopsis we have of the last book, it seems that Bennett had plans to use the four-world scheme as part of his basic framework of ideas. In *The Masters of Wisdom,* very little of the scheme is explained. For that reason, the material of the early 1974 talks is valuable.

The talks were exploratory in nature and I have severely edited them. I have tried to extract the material that is new and tried to avoid or smooth over what is confusing. I have also tried to show how this scheme ties in with the ideas of Parts 1 and 2 of this book, which came from the talks he gave to the Fourth Sherborne Course in October and November 1974.

Always the ideas were being worked with and always Bennett was at pains to show how some really concrete understanding of the great traditions could be found. In his view, the old ideas had become almost 'philosophized out of existence'. He took it as a real responsibility to get important ideas across in such a way that people neither felt them to be remote nor felt that they could come near them without work on themselves. The last thing he wanted was to fill people's heads with more useless ideas. At times, he would take one basic notion and with enormous pains try to get people to recognize what it meant in the reality of life. At other times, he would plunge people into a melee of ideas so that the pigeonholing mechanism of the formatory apparatus could not possibly cope.

The work on the Sufi ideas was, I feel, left incomplete. That is how it should be. In a series of talks on *The Dramatic Universe,* Bennett gave a most wonderful analysis of the meaning of the four worlds, using the transfinite arithmetic of Georg Cantor.[23] In the early 1974 talks, he concentrated more on the side of psychological experience, and he said many things useful for understanding his vision of the nature of man. To reconcile his scheme of

23 J.G. Bennett *Creation*, Coombe Springs Press 1978

four worlds with the traditional Sufi scheme of five worlds or five presences.we can take the fifth world, the 'human' one as where the other four meet.[24] My 'smoothing over' does not amount to removing all contradictions. Bennett himself felt that one should do all one can to be coherent and orderly the better to reveal what is beyond the boundaries of reason. Where I have seen a difficulty for the reader I have made some reference to other parts of this book or to traditional sources so that he can do his own research. It is useful to have some mental picture of the four worlds to start with. I will deliberately make it as crude as possible. From the 'bottom' we have:

World of bodies: things; causality; personality. The 'outer world'.

World of spirits: psyche; non-causal laws; essence. The 'inner world', where an 'inner body' can be formed.

World of possibility: will; beyond time and space; individuality. The ;spiritual world' where a third 'body' can be formed. The world where reality is totally creative.

Unfathomable world: void; ultimate reality; beyond God.

Up to a point, it is easy to fit this scheme with the various other schemes presented in Parts 1 and 2 of this book. This I have done, including drawing parallels with Gurdjieff's cosmology. Where it is not so easy, I have tried to say so.

Bennett, like Gurdjieff, saw that an enormous amount of misunderstanding had been generated by the belief that ordinary man has a soul or inner body. Traditional schemes invariably seem to assume that everyone has a soul as a birthright, that is, a substantial existence in the inner world. The idea that we have to make a soul seems to be relatively recent. This may be because it is connected with practical techniques that have in earlier times been kept hidden, and transmitted only through personal contact. Where this idea is lacking, all thought of entering higher worlds is no more than a dream. Traditional schemes, as written about in books, seem to concentrate on the station of the saints or realized

---

24 These are the Five Divine Presences as explained by Ibn al'Arabi's foremost disciple [Qunawi]: the (1) Divine, (2) spiritual, (3) imaginal, (4) sensory and (5) all-comprehensive, human levels." Note that the Perfect Human (the *insan al-kâmil*) merits a Presence all by itself (level 5), and encompasses all preceding stages.

people and ignore the situation of people who are in the process of transformation. The distortion produced is horrendous.

It may be that religion could not afford to destroy the hopes of people by revealing that their probable fate was dream and dissolution. It is important not only for mankind but also for all life that as much as possible is done in the human race to transform energies belonging to the inner world. This is. one of the great themes of Gurdjieff's *Beelzebub's Tales.*[25]. Morality, discipline, belief, and recitation of sacred texts all contribute enormously to this inner work of transformation. Only now, when religion has lost its power, can a more realistic picture of human life be made available - because it is needed.

If we do not have a substantial place or presence in the inner world, there is nothing there able to respond to higher influences; nothing to receive and bear the impulses of conscience and sacred emotion; nothing able to live in such a way that knowledge of the Will of God, or objective reason, is a possibility. Work on oneself is necessary in in order to form a bridge between the outer world of causal events and the world of possibility, the free creative world where we can 'dwell in God'.

Anthony Blake, 1977

---

25 I remember Mr. Bennett saying how strange it is that we have to work through all kinds of complicated ideas just in order to begin to see the point of practices which were taken for granted by traditional societies. For example, even until recent times, African tribes practised breath control, which is crucial for the nourishment of the inner body.

CHAPTER NINE

What is this Inner World?

We have to be clear what this physical world is like, and what sort of experience belongs to it. It is the world of our own bodies, the objects around us, including other people and living things, and all the visible states of matter that we can detect through our senses and instruments. We know that we are on the surface of a planet, and we can call the physical world we live in a state of 'terrestrial existence'. The kind of experience we have is largely determined by the condition of being on a planetary surface. There are solid, liquid, and gaseous states of matter and also radiant energy. Everything in this world consists of these four media, which in ancient times were given the names earth, water, air, and fire. Our own bodies have a solid structure, a liquid internal form in blood and other bodily fluids, and they breathe air. Radiant energy or 'fire' corresponds internally to the energy of our nervous system and externally to the heat and light that sustain our activity.

Most of the experience we have has to do with the awareness that relates to this condition of existence. What we know is what we can look at or touch or sense in some way or other. All that we are aware of in that way is external and separate because there has to be some energy exchange that makes contact possible. These exchanges come under the laws of conservation and laws of exclusion, so that we have the experience of separated bodies and things going on 'in time', and of a succession of events so connected together that what *has* happened may entirely determine what *will* happen.

If we put these three ideas together - of planetary existence, of the four states of matter, and of subjugation to deterministic laws - we can form some picture of what the Sufis meant by the *world of bodies*, the *ālam-i ajsām*. In this world there are nothing but bodies and the laws pertaining to bodies. There arc no minds or anything like that. It is the visible world of our senses, and it is also the world of our ordinary thinking, which is nothing but a reflection of the nature of this bodily world. It is a terribly restricted sort of existence. Everything is just another composition of the four states of matter, whether it is material, living, human or cosmic. In fact, no differences can be experienced between the living and the non-living, and we are incapable of being aware of other people as beings. We can have no inner life and no contact with ourselves.

Our existence in this world is a reality and it is important, but 'we ourselves' cannot really be contained in it. What is in it corresponds to its laws. Here is the 'man-machine' which has associations, reactions, and reflexes and produces a simulation of a human being but is not such a being.

What else is there besides this world? We can easily be tempted to say that there is nothing else. We talk glibly about a 'mental world' but it is for most of us just a figure of speech: we picture it as existing side by side with the bodily world but with no substance of its own; we see it as accompanying the events of bodily existence, but in itself it appears to be nothing at all. We know that the nervous system and the structure of the brain condition the experience we have, and it is difficult to see what it is that could be independent of the brain or other parts of the body and have a life of its own. People who are eager to believe that there must be something else too easily tend to imagine that this is very like the sort of feeling and thinking that ordinarily goes on in us. This is a very flimsy idea because it is pretty obvious that the ordinary sort of mental experience we have depends very much on stimulation from the bodily world. If this were taken away all that would be left would at best consist of memories and associations about things.

We have to find something which corresponds to a mental world that is not simply a reflection of external events and which really has something different about it. In fact, this is not so hard to find. There are widely known experiences of events different in kind from those of the bodily world, which come to pass when we have been, so to say, 'uncoupled' from the bodily world.

Most people know that when they dream at night the things that happen are not under the same restrictions as when our experience is coupled to the activity of the body, but very few seem to notice the significance of this. For example, it is very common that in dreams we do not experience the force of gravity—we may even fly—and 'up' and 'down' do not have the same meaning as they do when we are awake. Why should this be so? So many other things are the same in dreaming as in waking; we can have all kinds of physical sensations, thoughts, and feelings while dreaming, but not this one of weight. This is just one of the significant differences between the outer and the inner worlds. There is also an extremely important difference in the sense of time, which we shall say more about later. In all this, it is not true to say that dreams are chaotic or random: they obey laws of their own, but these are not the same as those of the ordinary experience of the waking state.

It is also now commonly known that people can come to very intense experiences through drugs or illness. It is easy to say that these are 'just hallucination'. Whatever we call them, they are real *experiences* and they can be far more vivid, more impressive and lasting in their effect, than anything of the bodily world. On the physiological level, parts of the nervous mechanism are temporarily put out of action, but what then comes in and produces the experiences? They can be so different from ordinary experiences that no memories could provide what they are made of. *Something* comes in from somewhere; it does not just happen.

If we are talking about experience while uncoupled from the bodily world, we should mention 'out of the body experiences'. I remember leaving my body when I was wounded in 1918. I was watching everything that was going on around my body, which was in a state of coma. I also remember a very special occasion during the time that I used to read from *Beelzebub's Tales* before the meals in Gurdjieff's flat, which used to happen twice a day. The place was full of cigarette smoke and Gurdjieff, as usual, was sitting facing me in his chair. Suddenly I found myself up in the corner looking at my body - which continued to read as if nothing had happened. I remember thinking to myself, 'How intelligently he reads even when I am not there.' Then Mr. G. looked up at me and gave me a look—so—and I closed my eyes and found myself back in my body, still reading.

One thing we have to be very clear about: nearly all of our life is lived automatically, as a machine. The man-machine can produce the most complex behavior without there being any experience at all—at least, any inner experience. When we are in this automatic state, we are shadows, ghosts, with no inner substance. Then it is quite legitimate to say that the inner world is a sort of flotsam on the surface of external bodily events.

In our practical inner exercises, we are learning how to work with the material of the inner world. This material consists of four media, just as the bodily world consists of four media. They are four energies. There is thought, feeling, and sensation. The fourth, which is on a different level, is *consciousness*. In both the bodily and the inner world, the fourth medium is a link with the next highest world. Light or radiant energy links the bodily world with the inner world. Consciousness links the inner world with the truly spiritual world, the third world. What we mean by 'spiritual' is that which is beyond form.

At this point, we can look at the terminology we shall be using for different worlds, which is derived from the Sufi traditions. There are many different names and descriptions of various worlds, but in all of them there is something equivalent to the distinctions I want to make between the bodily, inner, and spiritual worlds. The Arabic word for world is *ālam* and the scheme is as follows:

ālam-i ajsām – world of bodies

(the word *ajsām* is derived from the word *jasm*, simply meaning 'body')

ālam-i arvāh – world of spirits

(the word *arvāh* is the plural of *ruh*, which means 'spirit')[26]

The ordinary way of taking this is that there is a world peopled by spirits - good spirits, bad spirits, human spirits, nature spirits, and so on. The wrong kind of picture comes about, in which these spirits are represented as beings. This is not right, in spite of the

---

26 *ruh* has a variety of meaning, just as the English word *spirit* does. We have, for example, both in Islam and Christianity, the idea of:

1. Holy uncreated spirit, the *ar ruh-i lahi*, or the Holy Ghost. In Gurdjieff's writings, this is the mystery of the Third Force.

2. The individual spirit. This is the 'spark of divinity' in every man. Bennett writes of this as Individual Will, and associates spirit - in the triad: body, soul and spirit – with the will; soul with being and body with function.

3. The vital spirit, intermediate between 'soul' and 'body'. This represents the base of the *ālam-i arvāh*, the bottom layer. In Bennett's terminology, it is the sensitive energy.

Bennett was concerned to 'fill in' the middle realm between body and will by speaking of the role of the conscious energy. This is the world of light, and corresponds to *Malakūt*, the celestial and angelic kingdom. It is significant for grasping how fluid these categories are that some people speak of *Malakūt* as the animistic realms, the life realm. It is the realm of action, or 'doing', but not of the outer effects in the causal *ālam-i arvāh*.

fact that it is true that there are spirits, including non-human spirits, which have a kind of reality. The point is that they are not like people. They have no bodies and the kind of organization they have is very hard to see objectively. For a moment, it is better to think of this world in terms of the four energies, which we can grasp through our own practical work: sensation, feeling, thought, and consciousness. But we must remember that we are only just beginning to be able to recognize the feeling energy and have not really begun to grapple with the energy of thought. Also, sensation, feeling, and thought are forms of the sensitive energy which we can become conscious of. The conscious energy itself is on a higher level. It is a very great thing to realize the true nature of consciousness.

ālam-i imkān – world of the possible

(the word *imkān* derives from *mumkin*, meaning 'possible')

It is the truly spiritual world and does not really correspond to a state of existence at all. It is beyond the hold of space and time, and is associated with the working of the divine will. Its energies are beyond life.

There is a fourth world which is sometimes given the name *lāhūt* , the 'boundless': *la* means 'not' and *hut* means 'measurable'. In my own terminology, this is the *Unfathomable*.

What is very difficult to get hold of is that these other worlds are not somewhere 'over there', across some kind of spiritual Atlantic. They are here and now - in fact, more really here and now than our ordinary experience allows us to be. In the ordinary state, we do not have the means of perceiving them. The 'personality' —which belongs to the *ālam-i ajsām*—cannot enter into them. As long as we remain attached to the perceptions of our personality, we remain closed to what they contain.

As we said, under the influence of various disturbing factors, such as injuries, illness, great weakness, various drugs, great emotional strains, and so on, we can have an extraordinary change in the kind of experience we have. There is the physiological side, but there is also some kind of medium which permits this kind of experience. It is not less than ordinary experience, it is more: we go into a world where there is a greater freedom of experience. The inner world, the *ālam-i arvāh*, is not under the same laws as the world of bodies, the *ālam-i ajsām*. Even while not physically asleep, we can wander off somewhere and find ourselves in another place. Usually we fail to notice the significance of this and call it simply a 'daydream', and we can hardly credit that in reality we have gone to another place or another time in a way that is impossible through our bodies.

Related to this relative freedom from time and space are all the phenomena of precognition. Once we have seen that these phenomena are a reality, how can we account for them? There is nothing in the world of bodies which can give us access to future events as an experience. The same is true of postcognition, which is really equally outside the laws of the *ālam-i ajsām*. I myself have many times unmistakably gone into past events, and learned things that I could not otherwise have learned; things which subsequently have been verified.

This movement between events which is quite impossible in the physical world leads us once again to the possibility of experience without a physical body at all. When I had that experience of being out of my body while reading, I still remember the sly look that Gurdjieff gave me, and how it is to be outside of this physical world and yet able to look on at what takes place in it. Even the same kind of thinking can go on as when in a body - one can even wiseacre! To get a taste of this we can try to represent to ourselves when we are listening, reading, or actively working at something that we ourselves are somewhere else. It is no good doing this unless we are *actually fully engaged* in something - otherwise it is only useless thinking. It is just possible to get ourselves to produce something quite apart from the activity which, ordinarily, would occupy all our attention. When we work with the creation of thought forms, what are we doing? It is possible, though difficult, to see that something is really created in another world. Then we realize that the second world does not differ from the first world in many respects. There are shapes and places and motions, and events take place.

Once or twice I have had the experience of knowing what it is like to be dead, when all the life functions have ceased. One is still somewhere, and I am sure that this is the same world as one is in when dreaming. All these things - dreaming, drug experiences, precognition, out of the body experiences and so on - are the superficial manifestations of the *ālam-i arvāh*. They suggest that there is another world, subject to different laws, in which experience of a different kind is possible.

In ancient times, this other world was universally recognized, but it is important to understand how it was pictured. In general, the disembodied state was looked at as less real than the embodied one. It was called the 'world of shades', *sheol* in Hebrew, the world of ghosts. In the Homeric poems, especially the *Odyssey*, there are some marvelous insights. What is particularly interesting is the distinction made between the state of the mass of people and the states of special men, such as heroes, and particularly the seers, who had gone beyond ordinary perceptions, like Tiresias. A similar distinction is made by the psalmist in the Old Testament between the ordinary people and those who had been gathered into the bosom of the Fathers Abraham, Isaac, and Jacob. The psalmist laments how in the world of shadows we can no longer worship God because we have no lips with which to sing his praises.

The ancient ideas became discredited with the Western Christian belief that there would be a resurrection in which the physical body would return and physical existence would be regained. This was a prospect so much more appealing than descending into the world of shadows that the old ideas were put aside. The immediate state after death before the time of resurrection was then pictured as in the phrase 'rest in peace', and death came to be seen as sleep. The options open to men were whether to dream in a disturbed state and be in 'hell' or to dream peacefully and be in 'heaven'. The possibility of not dreaming at all was considered to be such an unknown quantity that it was left alone as too daunting in its implications. If we consider it possible to become a substantial being who does not need to dream when disembodied then this must become the most urgent thing of our lives.

In Tibet, the possibility of going beyond the dream-world became an obsession. It is vividly portrayed in the *Tibetan Book of the Dead*. Because of this obsession, many men followed the way of the monk, and went into the homeless life - at one time there were said to be 300,000 monks to 600,000 laymen. All that mattered to them was to prepare for the next life, and this life did not matter at all. Probably it was all a terrible exaggeration and something very important was not properly understood. There was a great decline from the seventeenth century onward, when this dominance of otherworldly attitude really took hold.

For ourselves, we have to learn how to take the second world into account, and how to live with it. It is a world as varied but much deeper than this physical world. The real difference is that it is under different laws: It has its own various 'places' in the bodily sense. When Gurdjieff speaks about all this, he does so in terms of the body kesdjan. Kesdjan means 'vessel of the spirit' in Persian, and describes the kind of being or organization that is able to 'move' in the *ālam-i arvāh*. In other words, the kesdjan body is more than a dream; it is a substantial reality that can be acquired or developed in us. Contrary to many current beliefs, this inner body is not born with us, neither does it form automatically. It cannot be produced in the world where our personality is dominant.

At the moment of death - which Gurdjieff calls the first 'sacred rascooarno' - there is a separation of the body kesdjan from the planetary or physical body. Then, according to Gurdjieff, this other body rises to the sphere corresponding to its 'density of vibrations'. I came to this idea myself from mathematical and physical studies, in which I came to see that there were other dimensions than space and time. What I call eternity is a fifth dimension in which the inner body 'rises' to its corresponding place. This movement is away from the restrictions we meet with in the physical world, toward a freer state. There are different levels in eternity corresponding to different degrees of freedom. The formations that come into existence in the spirit world are not subject to the disruptive influences of the first world and they have vastly more potential. It is in this way that the second world can have an organizing effect on the first world but, sooner or later, everything formed in the second world also disintegrates.

What is 'up' and 'down' in the inner world has nothing to do with the gravitational field of the earth. It is up and down in eternity. Our language makes it very difficult to talk about events in the *ālam-i arvāh* simply because they are not subject to time. The dimension of eternity is, so to say, at right angles to time, yet we are bound to talk in such terms as 'life after death', as if it were something that continued in time and could be measured in days and years like life in the bodily world. Yet we know, even through the superficial evidence that dreams provide, that time completely changes in the inner world. A 'very long' sequence of dream experience can correspond to a fraction of a second in which a sound has brought us awake. Displaced in eternity, a second can seem like a lifetime. We know from moments of intense experience that an infinitesimal duration can be filled with so much experience that it seems to last an age. This has tremendous importance for us in our relations with those who are dead.

When a dead person passes into the spirit world, he may have nothing more than a dream existence. Literally, his state is that of a dream. I myself made some simple experiments to do with communicating with people while they were dreaming, just in order to understand this better. More recent experiments have been much more sophisticated. I also experimented with people under hypnotic trance, which helped me in my research. I found that if one adapts - without any hypnosis - to what is going on in the dream state of a person, that it is possible to get them to respond without waking them up. I believe that this corresponds to what happens in what are called 'spiritualistic communications' with the dead. What we have to realize is that it is all a very low-level functioning. Some people whom I know have worked for many years with communications of this sort, and have come to see that they do not get anywhere because it is all to do with dreaming. Others do not accept that it is as limited as I say.

I believe that all the events that correspond to these states are very limited in character. That is why it is undesirable to have very much to do with them, and I will go even further and say that concentrating on them can be a great disservice to those who are dead. Attempts at communication such as I have described can attract and hold the soul of the dead person, and even persuade him that he has reached a very high state of existence and has accomplished something. This is a terrible deception. Little by little the potential for dreaming will diminish until the soul passes into a dreamless sleep and disintegrates.

Unless a contact has been made with the 'higher principle' - that which belongs to the spiritual world and is capable of return to the Source - this principle will simply return empty-handed, without having accomplished what it was embodied to do.

If people have lived in such a way that they have been dependent on the external world for their perceptions and thinking, then they can hardly recognize what has happened to them when they die. Their thinking, which has been dependent on sense perception and words, is *derouté*, thrown out of gear, and they become muddled. Those who have lived very much in the thinking part find it hard to realize that they are dead at all. This is one of the reasons why work with sensation in this life is so very important. It is necessary to learn what it is to have contact with this physical body. If this is not learned, after death sensation is almost nil. Only one thing remains a little free and that is the *feelings*.

Feeling is much less dependent on the physical body than sensation, and much less dependent on the external world than thinking. Those who are dead, if they have any possibility of development, have much more of a feeling life. That is why what we can do for the dead is from our feelings. It is quite rightly and correctly taught that we should not grieve for the dead. Someone near to us who has died will feel our grief as their own and this is a terrible burden for them to bear. What they need to feel is love and confidence and all the positive emotions that we can transmit. This is the duty that we have to those who have died: not to allow ourselves the self-pity of grief, because they will suffer for it, but to be in a state of positive feeling to give them strength.

In Gurdjieff's third series of writings, he describes an interesting ancient practice in which all the faults and misdeeds of the dead were brought to one's awareness. This was a Tibetan practice, too. The purpose of it was to help the soul of the dead person to awaken from the dream-world by making its dreams uncomfortable, so that it could liberate itself from hankering after a kind of simulation of the life state. It is very difficult to bring oneself to undertake this practice. One needs to have a very great confidence in the condition of the dead person: that they will be able to free themselves from their own egoism and enter the third world, the *ālam-i imkān*.

The help we can bring to the dead is not subject to time. We can help those who have been dead for twenty, forty, a hundred years. The connection with someone who died fifty years ago is as close as the connection with someone who died five minutes ago *in the inner world*.

We are in that world all the time when we are alive, but our attention is constantly being drawn out into the physical world. We attach so little importance to the inner world. Yet in this inner world, not only perceptions are different but the kind of actions and events that can take place are different. It is highly probable that all the important discoveries or insights have originated from it. I remember talking to Lawrence Bragg, who, with his father William, was one of the great pioneers in understanding the structure of crystals. They were working in the Cavendish Laboratories in Cambridge, making measurements and trying to form a picture of how the atoms could be arranged in the crystals they were studying. For a long time, they could not get anywhere. Lawrence Bragg finally decided to give it all up and do something else, and he was walking along when in a flash - how, he could not tell - the whole solution came before him, and he saw how the whole theory of crystals had to be reconstructed. It was a very great step in understanding the structure of matter. At this moment of letting go, he saw things 'from eternity', in a moment out of time and place.

The truth is that if this were not possible for us we would be totally powerless to change or innovate anything. If we existed entirely in the world of bodies, everything in us would be governed by cause and effect. Every relatively free and creative moment is a moment of liberation into the *ālam-i arvāh*. So here we have this strange and contradictory thing that the world of dreams, in which it is not possible to do anything, is yet the world without which creative moments would not be possible. The truth is that the *ālam-i arvāh* can be very much more than the realm of dreams and shadows and ghosts. If we made an excursion into the spirit world, and were able to see all its modes of existence, we might take them all for ghosts because we could not tell which of them had something different in them. In reality, some of them are very much stronger than anything in the physical world, but to see this, we would have to be able to see in eternity.

We have to realize how little the nature of the spirit world is understood. It would be very useful if children were taught some things about it while their perceptions are pure enough for them to be able to see it. At least, it would be an advantage if, when they do see things about it, they were not so severely discouraged or talked down to, as they usually are.

The spirit world is the world of the imagination, but for us, for most of the time, imagination is something destructive and harmful. We can apply the saying 'evil is good in the wrong place' and say that ordinary imagination is dreaming when dreams are not appropriate. We have to deal with the physical world. To deal with that world as if it were the inner world is negative imagination. Our bread and butter has to be earned in the physical world, and it cannot be got by dreaming. When we replace the action required in the world of bodies by what we call 'building castles in Spain', we fall into an inverted world, a world of delusion, which is really below the physical world.

In Gurdjieff's language, the world of delusion is called World 96. For a long time I puzzled about the nature of this world 'under ninety-six laws'. During World War II, in the summer of, I think, 1942, we were experimenting with the use of producer gas to replace petrol - something we may return to before we die. On the pretext of testing certain of our prototypes, we got around the restrictions on travel and took a party to Snowdon, in Wales. I was thinking very hard about the nature of the laws of World 96 during that trip. Then I was called away to Glasgow to attend a meeting to do with my job. I found myself waiting in a railway station drinking strong tea at two o'clock in the morning. The place was full of soldiers and everything was very vivid, as it tended to be at that time. Then suddenly, sitting at that metal-topped table, I saw the whole thing: how this world of delusion is not simply negative but a travesty of everything in the real world. Imagination is the very mockery of creativity. Identification is the very mockery of the freedom of commitment. Self-love is a mockery of real respect for one's individuality. Sometimes it is all hideous in World 96. When we live in it, we are much less than the animals.

Real work in the inner world is totally different from delusion, and totally different from dreaming. I have mentioned the four media of which it is made - sensation, feeling, thought and consciousness. When we are embodied, a substance composed of these media enters into us. When we die, eventually this substance returns to where it came from, which in *The Dramatic Universe* I called the *soul-stuff pool*.[27] Now I see that something more than just a pool or reservoir of energies is involved, but this picture of a pool of energies is useful for understanding how it is that these substances are a limited resource, like petroleum. The material for all human souls and, indeed, all *life* is drawn from a common source, though it has different layers to it. For one-brained beings, only simple sensation material is drawn out; for two-brained beings, sensation and feeling; and for three-brained beings, sensation, feeling ,and thought plus consciousness, the equivalent of bodily light. This substance, while it is in us, picks up something from our lives, and that is why experience goes on after death. After a certain 'time' it is no longer able to sustain experience and it dissolves and is *recycled*. This should not disturb us any more than the dissolution of the body. The inner substance is no more what we really are than our body is. It is what is liberated at the *second* rascooarno or death that really matters. This is our will. The will is the immortal undying part of man, and if it becomes conscious it is able to dispense not only with the body but with the psyche also.

Because the pattern of experiences is carried back into the soul-stuff pool, it is possible for people to have 'memories of other lives'. This is due almost entirely to the recycling of material in the *ālam-i arvāh*. What is carried over has nothing to do with the individuality or will. True reincarnation is very rare.

The possibility is given to us of forming a vessel which will cross the *ālam-i arvāh* and reach the spiritual world. Then it can

27 *The Dramatic Universe*, Vol 3 pp. 171-4; Vol 4, p. 204

be discarded. This vessel is the body kesdjan. Gurdjieff describes the state of the substance of the inner world in ordinary man as like a cloud. It is amorphous, without any coherence of its own. It temporarily takes up the 'shape' of whatever physical part is attracting our interest. At one time it is a mouth, at another an eye, at another an anus, and so on. If life is lived like that, then only the very barest kind of organization is produced, because without the body it is always in a state of dream. Many of the exercises that we do are aimed at producing some coherence in this substance. We learn how to use our attention to separate and blend the various energies of which it is made. This is what is meant by alchemy. Besides this active work, it is also necessary to practice meditation or something of the kind, in which we do not try to do anything. If we can become quiet enough, the energies settle into their appropriate places in us and can coalesce to form the second body. We can call whatever state this substance is in the 'soul', but we have to remember that this is a relative term: some souls are much more substantial than others.

There are various ways in which the soul can separate from the body at the moment of death. If there has been a very long illness, it can separate long before the body dies. If people then try to keep the body alive, they can be dealing simply with a physical object, for the soul has left and may be looking on and saying to itself, 'What on earth are they doing with this body? Why can't they leave it alone?' If it is in a relatively free state, it will know that all these manipulations being done on the body have nothing to do with itself. I have also seen dying people whose souls have been with them to the very moment of death and others whose souls have remained in the body for some time after it has stopped breathing.

If I am right in saying that there is a limited substance from which all human souls are drawn, then this raises some very serious questions. For example, we can see that abortion is just the same as infanticide - the embryo is associated with a certain soul-stuff, just as the child is. For us, infanticide is morally repugnant, but it was not always so. Infanticide was practiced in the Turkish imperial family right up to the late nineteenth century. It was too inconvenient for a number of reasons to have too many princes of the same blood. Once an heir was assured by a certain number of sons, any new male child was killed. For us, this seems a horrible practice, but we may be wrong. Again, at one time wholesale massacre was a way of life. In the *Old Testament* it is clear that everyone massacred whenever they got the chance. Inscriptions were put up by kings describing the mass killings they perpetrated as a sign of what splendid kings they were. Nowadays, we think it is dreadful to kill people *en masse*; but in fifty years' time it may be considered a virtue as the only way to restore the world to normality. I cannot know. I hope it is not the case. What is pretty certain for me is that no human potential is wasted: it all goes back to the common pool. Perhaps that is why people in the East seem to have much less concern for preserving life than we do in the West.

I say quite categorically that I do not know this, but it may be that there is only enough potential for normal life for a thousand million people on the earth, whereas at the present time we have three times that number. This means that there are two thousand million people without adequate potential. It is not entirely a simple quantitative thing like that, but to be sure the potential available is *finite*. Maybe the potential of the human race was exhausted when the population reached a million. It all raises questions that are hair-raising. There is nothing absurd about the notion that we have overpopulated the earth, and that it is not possible for all people to have normal souls any more.

In the Christian religion there was the doctrine of 'election', that only a certain number of people are chosen to be 'saved'. If this is right, then it corresponds to what I have been saying. We cannot tell. Even inspired revelations are capable of gross misinterpretation. What remains is that we have to contemplate the possibility that we have gone beyond the potential which is permitted to man. People who believe that the end of the world is very near believe in something like that.

For us, there is a simple practical proposition: if we do not wake up from the dream-world in this life, it is unlikely that we shall ever awaken, but we shall continue to dream until the substance of our souls dissolves. Gurdjieff said, 'It is necessary to work on oneself in this life; otherwise, early-lately, one will perish like a dirty dog.'

PREFACE TO CHAPTER TEN

One of the many remarkable men that Bennett met was Hasan Shushud. Shushud taught Bennett practical techniques of *zikr* and fasting. He also introduced him to *itlak yölü*, the way of absolute liberation. In this way, the search is for nonexistence. Shushud writes in his book *Hacedan Hanadani*, The Masters of Wisdom, 'In order to reach this goal, no other way but annihilation is open'. Annihilation is *fanā*. It is essentially a loss of conditioning. From the perspective of the lower worlds, this is a loss of existence. . *Fanā* has four main gradations.

1. *fanā-i akhām*   *annihilation of judgement*
2. *fanā-i afāl*   *annihilation of acts*
3. *fanā-i sifāt*   *annihilation of attributes*
4. *fanā-i zāt*   *annihilation of essence*

1. is liberation from the spell of the outer world.

2. is a realization in the inner world, the spirit world, that we 'cannot do'.

3. is a realization in the inner world that our existence is not our reality, and opens the way to the third world.

4. is abandonment of any separateness form the Source.

According to Shushud, the fourth world is 'Absolute Perdition', where it is realized that all perceptions, no matter how subtle, are 'illusory'. The largest and most difficult step is the first: from being under the spell of the bodily world, *hukum*, to living by the laws of the inner, spirit world.

Shushud claimed to follow the path of the Northern Sufis, whose aim is self-extinction, as opposed to the Southern Sufis, whose aim is absorption into states of higher being. Bennett took this distinction very seriously, and made much use of it in his book, *The Masters of Wisdom*.

Anthony Blake, 1977

CHAPTER TEN

Death and Resurrection

According to the Sufi tradition, God is not able to act in the physical world - the *ālam-i ajsām* or world of bodies - because there is no freedom in it. It is entirely under natural laws which, although they originated from the same creative source, are too dense to allow a direct creative action. To come under the power of God[28] it is also necessary to go beyond the next world – the *ālam-i arvāh* or world of spirits. It is this power that draws us on, that produces an attraction in us, but it belongs to a truly spiritual world, the *ālam-i imkān.*

We can very easily form a wrong picture of the different worlds by believing that we are something, and that it is this something that passes from one world into another. It is not at all like that. In each of the worlds, we ourselves are made out of the material or nature or media of the world itself. We are a part of the world we live in. The first world, the *ālam-i ajsām*, is really everything on the surface of this planet, all living and non-living things, including ourselves. What we are is something made out of the material of the earth's surface, including the oceans, the atmosphere, and the radiant energy that falls on it.

The word *alam*, which means 'world', is also connected with the words *ilm*, knowledge, and *alim*, knower. This is very important because each of the worlds is associated with a certain mode of perception or cognition. We are aware of ourselves according to the world that we are in. In the ordinary state, we cannot be aware of ourselves in other worlds. If we live, let us say, in the 'world of society' we recognize ourselves, feel ourselves through the social relationships which make up this world. To be cut off from those relationships means to be cut off from ourselves. We do not want to know any other kind of world; perhaps we feel that in other worlds we would not be anything at all.

---

28 This is the nature of *Jabarūt*, or the 'Kingdom of Heaven'.

It is very much like that in the bodily world. We have sense experience, with its accompaniment of pleasure and pain, and it gives us the sense of immediate reality. We say to ourselves, 'this is solid reality; these things are really happening. I must be something to experience all this.' Any prospect of another world appears very thin, and people do picture other worlds as something ethereal and abstract. This is largely because we do not take notice of other kinds of perceptions which come about in us and that they can be so very much stronger and penetrating than anything of this world.

We all know that thinking goes on in us but we do not ask where the substance of this thinking comes from. For most people, thinking is simply an activity that happens; they do not look at thought as a kind of stuff that has a 'turnover'. In reality, thought is one of the materials out of which the second world is made. We can draw a parallel between the air of the bodily world and the thought of the spirit world. Something in us is living in thought and 'breathing' in thought, just as our bodies are living in air and breathing in air. Thoughts flow through 'us' as air flows through us. We fail to ask whence thoughts come and where they go. It is the same with feelings; they come and they go and we simply take this as something happening in us, without grasping the fact that some material or other is coming and going in us. If feelings are the 'water' of the spirit world there must be a world of feeling like the world of the oceans. There must be something like a heart that pumps our feelings around in us. In many teachings it is said that we have both a bodily and spiritual heart, *qalb.* There is so much material in sacred literature, fairy tales, and legends about all this, but we fail to put it together.

The word *ruh,* besides meaning spirit, also means 'breath'. The connection between breath and spirit is found in nearly all languages. This has an important practical significance because what we call 'conscious breathing' is the way in which the inner life is nourished. It is all connected with developing different kinds of perceptions. The different worlds merge and touch one another and we can have more experience of the second world than we take into account. When I was writing *The Dramatic Universe* I did not realize that we were in fact living in the spirit world; only our perceptions of it are all conditioned and constrained by sense experience. The development of different perceptions is needed not only for the sake of 'waking up' in this life so that we can die consciously, or something like that, it is needed for this very life. Mankind will need this very much. In the next stage of development of man there is going to be a big return to realizing the importance of our connection with the second world.

At the moment we have a very strange relationship with it - we are continually turning our backs to it and looking out upon the bodily world. We do not know how to use other kinds of perception, so we come to depend more and more on our senses. We ascribe all sorts of things to bodies that they cannot possibly have, and we try to change the physical world as the answer to our problems. But real change is not possible in the bodily world: it is *under too many laws*. It cannot give us what we need. It is the sense of this that leads us to search for some way of inner development.

Disillusionment with the possibilities of the external bodily world is the first freedom. In Sufism it is given the name *fanā-i akhām*. *Fanā* is translated as 'annihilation', and this corresponds to disillusionment. The world *akhām* is derived from *hukum,* which means the state of being dominated by laws. We blindly accept the limitations imposed on us by the bodily world, yet they prevent us from achieving anything real for ourselves. We constantly need to be in two places at once, but this is impossible with a body. We need to know the future and draw directly on the experience of the past, but we cannot do it. We need to communicate with each other directly so that we can really share in experience and come to accept each other, but we are dependent all the time on what goes through our bodies. We are forced to make contact with people through behavior and words, and all this gets in the way.

Through knowledge of the laws that condition the physical world, we are able to manipulate it. At the present time, man is very successful at doing this, but he fails to realize that this does nothing for his being and even takes him further away from contact with *life*. Besides all this, there are the destructive influences of the laws of delusion, which Gurdjieff called the 'maleficent consequences of the properties of the organ kundabuffer'.[29] In spite of it all, we cling to this world and we do not want to leave it. We maintain what Gurdjieff calls our 'self-calming' through the other 'disease of tomorrow': tomorrow things will be different; someday things will work out properly.

Fanā-i akhām is total disillusionment with the bodily world and all the perceptions and thinking that go with it. It is the realization that this world cannot satisfy us and no combination of

29 The negative laws of World 96; see Chapter 7, 'The World of Delusion'.

events in this world can ever satisfy us. It gives us the possibility of entering the spirit world, but in Sufism it is said that it is not a true liberation. We can be disillusioned in this way but in ourselves remain unchanged: through our personality we can be just as dependent upon the opinion of other people as before, and we can remain subject to negative states, though we know that the world in which our personality lives can give us nothing. When we go into the spirit world, it is only a temporary state, a *hāl*.[30]

Disillusionment with this world does not mean rejection. It means that we realize what it is that this world by its very nature cannot give. A man who has the freedom to live in the second world does not on that account turn his back on the physical world. If he did this he would be repeating, but in reverse, the mistakes from which he has just been liberated. He has got himself free of turning away from the spirit world to look only at the bodily world. For him to look now only at the spirit world and turn his back on the bodily world would be to fall into another kind of illusion, another kind of despair. It is the freedom to live in the second world that enables us to live rightly in the first world.

I have spoken before a lot about dream states and dreaming. I think we can all recognize what it means when it is said that in order to get into the second world we must *wake up*. This is something we can understand through our own experience much better than we can through any story or image. The taste of waking up is unmistakable. In a moment, we are aware that everything is different; not only seeing and hearing but the whole of our state is changed. We feel that a dimension has been added to our experience. To say much more than that leads to distortion. For example, if l start saying, 'In that state, I am aware of myself', I realize that it is not true, that it is not really a state of self-awareness. If I say, 'I am aware of the world', this is partly true, but I was aware of the world before. I came into this room and opened the door and was aware that it was there and that it was a solid object that had to be moved; but I was not awake. What is the difference? All we can say is that some extraordinary change comes over us suddenly.

We have got to make sure that we do not distort this experience in us. I believe that I can talk about it in the right way if l say that it is a transition into the second world. In the dreaming state we are only in the bodily world. When the transition comes we are also aware of the second world. Because of that everything is different.

30 See the distinction made between *hāl*, state and *makām*, station, in Chapter 8, sections 'The Facts of Experience' and 'The World of Selves'.

For example, *we are able to see with our eyes*. Why is that? It is because the second world is made of the stuff of seeing and hearing and thinking and feeling, and when we are not in that world these things are all happening *without our participation*.

It is not right to say that in dreaming we do not experience. If we said that, then we should have to use the word experience in a special way and say that we hardly ever have an experience. But we see and feel and think in the ordinary state. Something is going on. We can remember what has happened. But the point is that there is no depth in it, no true power of judgment, and no freedom of choice. All these things come only through the second world.

The very last sentence of Gurdjieff's Third Series, at the end of the chapter 'The Outer and Inner World of Man', says that man who 'works on himself' lives in two worlds and he can become a 'candidate for another life' and have three worlds. This summarizes the whole thing. A man who works on himself is coming under the action of the third world, the *ālam-i imkān*.

We do have life in the two worlds in the ordinary state, but there is no connection between them, and for this reason the second world becomes for us the stuff of dreams. When a connection is made, it turns seeing into *seeing*, thinking into *thinking*. We have to make sure that in talking about these things we do not turn it all into a dream again. We have to find out what it is that is unmistakable. For me, one of the most useful marks of this change is in our physical state. We feel ourselves to be physically different. Simultaneously, we are more aware of our bodies, and more free from them. Quite by itself in that moment, relaxation comes over us.

One of the most important practices we have is 'sensing'. If we are able to understand sensing and have mastery over it, it brings us to the threshold of the inner world, not as a dream but substantially. On the one side of sensation there is the external world and the consequences of an inner life. On the other, there is experience itself, the inner life. Sensation is really the interface between the two worlds.

What is in the first world is dead, inanimate, inert. The state of mental inertness is that state that we call 'sleep'. We need to look at and really treasure the moments of awakening because little by little they create in us the conviction that another way of living is possible.

But if the body world cannot satisfy us, can the spirit world? Although the *ālam-i arvāh* has perhaps only half the constraints that the bodily world has[31] it is still a conditioned world. There is not the same kind of time, but there is a time, and because of that there is decay and nothing there is really permanent. It is still separated from the Source. That is the terrible hardship of the spirit world: it is neither an environment where there is external support in the form of a body, nor is it a world of light in which there is strength and support from above. For there to be permanence, we have to go into the third world, the *ālam-i imkān;* it is the world that the Will of God is able to reach directly, without having to pass through intermediaries.

What we have called the second or kesdjan body does not provide us with a permanent home. It is rather like a boat which can carry us over the sea. Sooner or later we have to jettison it. It is a very great thing to acquire a second body, but then it is supremely important that we are able to 'throw it away' when it has done its job.

Every movement from one world to another is a death and resurrection or, in Sufi terminology, *fanā-baqā,* annihilation-becoming. Something goes or is lost and then something of a different order can enter. Liberation from the first world is disillusionment with this world of laws and bodies. Liberation from the second world is really disillusionment with oneself and what one can do. It is possible to pass into the third world only when one is thoroughly disillusioned with one's ability to achieve anything by oneself; when one sees that, whatever one does, it is self-frustrating and even *has* to produce its own opposite. This disillusionment is called the *fanā-i afāl ,* where *afāl* is the plural of the world *fils*, which means action or doing. It is the end of the belief that one can achieve anything from oneself.[32]

We can get a taste of this if we really work at asking ourselves in the midst of life, 'There are thoughts, but who is thinking these thoughts? There are actions, but who is doing these actions?' It is possible really to glimpse and see for a moment that there is no one thinking and no one acting. When this is *established*, it is the second *fanā*. We can be quite disillusioned with the body world yet still believe in ourselves, and what we can achieve for our

---

31 In the triadic system of worlds, the body world is under forty-eight laws, while the spirit world is under only twenty-four laws. See Chapter 8, section 'The Taste of the Natural World'.
32 See Chapter 4, section, 'The Divided Self'.

own satisfaction. If we come to the *fanā-i afāl* we realize that real change is not in our power, that we have no power, that everything is connected together in the spirit world by laws that we cannot command. This is the beginning, but only the beginning, of the realization that life in the spirit world is something transitory and cannot be otherwise.

The *fanā-i afāl* is not a rejection of oneself but the acceptance of one's own nature. To think that one can reject oneself is an illusion. There are all kinds of false things that can happen here - various kinds of despair, revolt, and rejection - that still leave one with the illusion that one is something. The rejection of oneself is a trap, not a liberation. One can be desperate because one cannot do what one wants to do, or because one has acted in a way that is felt to be disgusting or disappointing, but all this arises because one still believes that one is something and could have done otherwise. The *fanā-i afāl* is a real liberation and something changes in us. The first *fanā* can leave us unchanged and with no basis for another kind of life. With the second *fanā,* a new light comes. One no longer feels separate from other people and one is really aware that 'we are all in the same boat'. But for something really to change in us in this way, there must be *something*, the body kesdjan in which such a change can be established.

For a man who has his kesdjan body, death makes practically no difference because he is completely himself with or without his physical body. The kesdjan body gives a man powers beyond those of the physical world. As we are, we are so very much tied up in satisfying our own needs and desires that if we form this body *without being disillusioned* with our power to achieve things, we will use our powers to strengthen ourselves instead of to lose ourselves. This kind of thing does happen and it produces what Gurdjieff calls a '*hasnamuss*'. For this reason, the work has to be rightly conducted, so that the formation of the body kesdjan and freeing ourselves from illusions go together.

It is a very great thing to enter into the second world. The quality of being in that world is so much greater than in the world of bodies. When once one has had a taste of it one knows how everything else in comparison is like a dream. Everything that is described as Paradise and Hell belongs to the second world: they are there. The thing is how to get through this world safely with all its allures and all its terrors.

One of the key moments in my life was when I was with Gurdjieff in Vichy, in 1949. I knew by certain signs that my body kesdjan was formed. Gurdjieff said to me, 'Now you can have paradise, but not be satisfied. Necessary go to *soleil absolu*. The *soleil absolu* is his Holy Sun Absolute, about which he writes in *Beelzebub's Tales* in the chapter called 'The Holy Planet Purgatory'. It corresponds to something beyond even the third world, the *ālam-i imkān*.

In the Purgatory chapter, Gurdjieff describes the two deaths, or *rascooarnos*.

The first death is the separation of the soul-stuff from the physical body. If the soul-stuff is organized, it rises to the sphere corresponding to its density. All this is in the *ālam-i arvāh*. Eventually, there comes the second separation, which is of the higher spiritual part or will from the soul-stuff. The will is the seed of the higher-being body, the body that can live in the *ālam-i imkān*. If this has been formed, it is this which passes to the planet Purgatory, where it can be completely purified of its residual egoism, without which it is impossible to return to the Ultimate Source, the Sun Absolute, the fourth world. In Sufism, this world is called *lāhūt ,* the unfathomable; also *huvviyet,* the state of union.

The state of Purgatory makes possible a very high *fanā*, but it is worthwhile digressing to talk about Gurdjieff's insistence, in all his writings, on the need for disillusionment, and in particular for the first *fanā.* At the end of the chapter in *Beelzebub's Tales* on War, for example, he tells a story concerning an attempt made to stop wars. A society is formed called 'The Earth Is Equally Free for all' and it dedicates itself to this aim of world peace. One day its members are highly discomfited to learn from the most learned being among them, the Kurd Atarnakh, that energies are produced by death, and that nature has need for the energies produced by the destruction of human life in war. In spite of the fact that the society consisted of elderly people who were good in character with considerably less egoism and ambition than ordinary people, they could not see the situation as it really was. Gurdjieff writes how, '... certain of them it seems had not yet acquired enough ground to be convinced of the nonactualizability of their dreams - which they owed to that notorious education of theirs - with the result that they were still not sufficiently disillusioned to be able to be fully impartial and just'.[33] They were thrown into confusion by what Atarnakh had to say and had to be rescued from their predicament by the 'Assembly of the Enlightened'. Gurdjieff does not say much about this Assembly, which I believe is a reference

33 *Beelzebub's Tales*, pp. 1096-7

to a historical group of people [34] but clearly they were people who had passed into the world of light, and could see things as they really are.

Gurdjieff's reference to education is very important. The whole of our bringing up of children is directed toward making them believe in the *ālam-i ajsām* as the real world. They are trained to think that problems can be solved in that world and by the instruments that are available in it. It is not possible for them to be impartial.

When Gurdjieff spoke of three worlds, the third world, the *ālam-i imkān*, is the world of the Work. It is from this world that all the positive forces come into our inner world, such as the 'sacred impulses' of wish, hope, and so on. These are free from the laws of existence and they help us to be free.

The first thing we have to learn is to see our own personality - that it is an artificial production of the first world which enables us to live as though we existed, as though we already had something in the second world. When cracks come in the shell that covers us, we begin to see things differently. At first it may be very painful, but it helps us to put away the illusions of our 'somethingness'. When experiences come of seeing things as they really are, it is very desirable to have someone at hand who has traveled that way before, otherwise such experiences can be denied or rejected, or their importance exaggerated.

Through the *fanā-i afāl* one no longer believes in one's ability to do anything from one's own intelligence and powers, but one still remains attached to oneself. One is prepared to accept that one does not have anything, but one is still not prepared to accept that one is not anything. But this separate existence of ours is nothing at all, or it is no more than something equivalent to an isolated page out of a book. We are nothing at all as separate individuals. To see this is to come to the *fanā-i sifāt* . The word *sifat* can be translated as 'personality', but this does not mean the same thing as the personality of the body world. If we say that this *fanā* is disillusionment with oneself, we have to understand that this is with oneself as being anything at all. It is liberation from one's psyche, mind, or self and opens the door toward nonexistence, the *ālam-i imkān*.[35]

---

34 *The Masters of Wisdom*, p. 197
35 See Chapter 8, section 'The World of Individuality'.

First there is *fanā,* annihilation, and then *baqā,* coming into being, or re-emergence. As we said, in Christianity it is called death and resurrection. In Buddhism it is detachment and enlightenment. It happens on all scales. There are moments when something in us dies and something in us is born again. When it happens in a bigger way, we may find that we have lost confidence in one world and have not found confidence in another. We need to have some kind of confidence. In the Sufi terminology there is *yakin*, certainty, which has different degrees. First of all, we need to know for ourselves unmistakably that there are different states, and that they are sharply different, not merely more or less, but different. This is the beginning of the first degree of *yakin.* It arises out of disillusionment with the body world, and when we begin to see what it is, this disillusionment turns into acceptance. We are able to say, 'Yes, it is what it is and I am what I am', and then a certain kind of confidence comes. It feels like a resurrection: I was dead and I am alive again; I was lost and I am found. This is a real acquisition but it is not a guarantee that we will find our way in this life. This comes only after the second *fanā*, the *fanā-i afāl .*

The third *fanā,* the *fanā-i sifāt ,* comes when one sees that there is no need even to exist. This existence is all too dependent to be trusted. The time comes when one is really ready to let it all go. Then one sees that there is something else. This is the germ of the higher-being body. It is neither self nor not-self; neither I nor not-I. It does not fit into anything that we can understand and there is no possibility of answering the question, 'Who am I?' There is something much more important than ever before, yet one can neither call it 'I' or 'mine'.

When we begin to get rid of the illusions which surround the world of bodies and the illusions of 'I am the doer' and 'I am something', then something other comes. One of the things that *we* can hope for is to come to have confidence in the *Work*. It does take many years and very many experiences, some very agonizing and some very wonderful, before this can take possession of us ,and we are really confident that the one thing that is absolutely to be trusted is the *Work* and that it is possible to live a fully satisfying life as long as we trust ourselves to it. It is really the same as the *yakin* that comes after the *fanā-i afāl .* One completely loses confidence in oneself and then completely and finally regains confidence in the *Work*. I know perfectly well that without the Work there is nothing I could do. I would make just the same mistakes and have just the same wrong attitudes as twenty, thirty, or forty years ago.

The disillusionment we have to come to is not only with things but with people. Nothing can be trusted and no one can be trusted. This does not mean any rejection of the world or of people. It really means that we stop expecting things from people and we stop making demands on them and judging them. All of this is to do with liberation from the world of bodies. Then there is liberation from the world of minds and the belief in our own doing, and then can come the liberation from oneself. In all of this nothing is rejected. Everything has its place.

The process of transformation is not moving from one world to another but of something emerging which can accept all the different things and be able to live in these different ways. One of the things, for example, we have to learn is how to conserve the substance of the inner world and not use it up for the sake of satisfactions in the bodily world. We need to be able to separate the needs of the inner world from those of the outer world. To enter the third world means to be prepared to lose everything, but then something is born which rediscovers the whole. Those who attain that in this life are saints. They do not act from themselves, but the Spirit of God acts through them. They are under the direct action of the Will of God and they carry the burden of transmitting influences from the spiritual world to the rest of mankind.

Still, it is not finished. The saint has attained the state of *zat,* his very essence, his own real place,[36] but there is still a separation from the Source, and this is the meaning of *purgatory.* Gurdjieff describes how everything on the planet Purgatory is everything that is desirable for existence but that it is an intolerable state because there is a full awareness of what it means to be separated from the Source. Until this state is reached, the awareness of separation is attenuated, diluted by all the other illusions that are in us. It is one of the forms of suffering to know that something is possible and to realize that we are not yet able to have that - for example, to know that the only thing that matters is to be the instrument of some higher power. This belongs to one of the very high stages of work on oneself. It does not come about through effort or struggle. It comes about through the awakening of an insight, a perception of what it is to be deprived of our own real nature. These sorts of experiences, which can come to us even

---

36 In Gurdjieff's terminology, this is World 12. It is the World of Individuality.

while we live in the lower worlds, are very much weaker than the direct experience of Purgatory.

To pass beyond the *ālam-i imkān* and reach the Holy Sun Absolute, there must come the *fanā-i zāt* , the annihilation of essence. In my own terminology, this is the abandonment of the individual will. Purification is needed because the experience of separate existence could, so to say, 'carry over' into the higher worlds and produce a disturbance in the cosmic balance.[37]

I talk about this as the final goal and I have talked about different stages. This is bound to raise questions such as 'Can this be done in one lifetime? If it needs many lifetimes, how is it all worked out?' These may sound like questions which can be answered, but they are not. They are wrongly worded and we can only get from them wrongly worded answers. Our minds are stuck with looking at things as processes which start at one point and end at another at a later time. It looks as if there is a movement from the world of bodies to the final state of union. But it is possible to say that it is all a self-realization, a removal of veils to reveal what has been hidden to us but was always there.

In Sufism, it is possible to distinguish between two treatments of the higher states of realization. In Southern Sufism, there is a tendency toward the idea of union of being, which is connected with the view that in some way 'God is everything'. This was the approach of lbn Arabi. In Northern Sufism, especially that of central Asia around Bukhara and Samarkand, there is a tendency to look beyond Being, probably through the influence of Buddhism. This is the approach of the *Khwajagan,* the Masters of Wisdom.[38]* **

Jalal ad-din Rumi put the Northern view very bluntly: 'Whoever says that all of this is God is a blockhead!' The manifestations of God are not God; God is altogether beyond understanding. We can all too easily slip from the direct feeling that God is *in* everything to the thought that God *is* everything. For me, the Northern Sufis seem to have understood how it is more clearly. They say that there is a barrier between the creation and God that cannot be passed by any finite being, and whatever we say, we are not talking about God; we are only talking about the images that we have on this side of the barrier that separates us. This is the thing

---

37 This notion gives an objective meaning to Purgatory. Purgatory is the place of transition from separate being to Union. It is a real 'place' in the universe, and Gurdjieff referred to it as a 'planet'.

38 Hasan Shushud was a proponent of Northern Sufism.

that we have really to get hold of if we are ever to make sense of the worlds beyond existence, the *ālam-i imkān* and the *lāhūt*.

All the worlds are states of existence, or modes of being, or simply conditions of more or less constraint. They are not different places peopled with different beings. Most Sufis talk about the ordinary world of humanity as having the character of being cut off from the direct action of the Divine Will. It is called *nasūt*. In this state we can get revelations given to us and we can interpret what our senses tell us of nature, and from this we can derive some picture of other worlds; but we do not see anything directly.

Then there is another condition, another world, called *Jabarūt*. This is the region under the Will of God. The word *jabar* means 'compulsion'. We can include in the *Jabarūt* the world of angels. They respond directly and have no power to do otherwise. That is why the Sufis often talk of awakening our own angelic nature, which is able to respond *directly* to the Higher Will. We can also call *Jabarūt* the *kingdom of heaven*, where God's will is done. In the Lord's Prayer we ask that 'Thy will be done on earth (*nasūt*) as it is in heaven (*Jabarūt*).[39]

When a man is awakened in the *Jabarūt* he becomes aware of his destiny, of God's Will for him. For this, something has to be prepared. There is little in the Sufi teaching that makes clear what this is, but Gurdjieff says something very important about it. He states categorically that the planetary body cannot have objective reason. Objective reason is awareness of the Will of God. To have objective reason it is necessary to have the second body, the body kesdjan. Only when this body is formed can a man begin to acquire the awareness of what is required of him without anyone having to tell him or teach him from outside. It is the kesdjan body which is the seat of *conscience*, which cannot find a place in us while our soul-stuff remains incoherent. Clearly, conscience in Gurdjieff's teaching is man's link with the *Jabarūt*.

There is no need to speak of the world of compulsion or the Divine Will in either personal or impersonal terms, or we are free to use them both. In Buddhism, there is no reference, of course, to the Will of God, but they speak of the awakening of the 'divine eye', the *dibbha chakku*, which is able to see reality. All the different Sufi schools talked about this sort of thing in their various

---

39 *Jabarūt* can be connected with the *ālam-i imkān*. The term emphasizes the relation to the Higher Will rather than the state of the individual. In a sense, individuality is overwhelmed by the presence of God. This can be the end, but there is a further stage, a 'going beyond God'.

ways, but what they said was not expected to be understood without personal contact with a teacher.

What is beyond concerns the *higher being body* and the possibility of entering into the absolute Godhead,[40] the 'source of God', or *nirvana*. Gurdjieff meant his idea of being taken into the Holy Sun Absolute to be taken seriously. But we will find many difficulties in orienting ourselves toward this ultimate world. In Southern Sufism, they talk of merging into the being of the whole, in the awareness that one has not, is not, and never will be separate from one's source. It is the final beatific vision: one has returned to the place one has never left. In Northern Sufism, it is more connected with notions of death, nothingness and non-existence. A similar difference is to be found between Western and Eastern Christianity. The notion of union with Christ is stronger in the West whereas the notion of the need to die in order to be born again—death and resurrection—is stronger in the East. I do not mean to say that the two deny each other; it is just that the emphasis is different. It is one of the reasons why Easter occupies such a dominant place in the Eastern church.

In Sufism, the difference of emphasis is reflected in the doctrine of *fanā*, annihilation. In the West and South, *fanā* is absorption into a person, into a being. There is *fanā-i shaikh*, which means to annihilate oneself in one's teacher; to lose oneself and find oneself again in him. There is *fanā-i pīr*, annihilation in the founder of the tradition, and *fanā-i rasūl*, annihilation in the Prophet and ultimately annihilation in and union with God, *Allah*. It is all very personal, and the responsibilities of the teacher are very great. In the North and East, the teacher is much less important. What matters is the death of illusion, rather like the Buddhist ending of ignorance, *avijja*. I have already spoken about the *fanā-i akhām*, *fanā-i afāl* , *fanā-i sifāt* and *fanā-i zāt* . What really matters in all this is the annihilation of belief in oneself, that one exists at all.

When we come to the *lāhūt*, and say that it is without limit, we are once more tempted to say that it includes everything. It is quite unlike that. It is not even a state of being. It is beyond being. I have found that one very good way of representing the *lāhūt* is as a vacuum. This vacuum draws everything in and needs to be

---

40 A Christian mystic who saw this was Meister Eckhart, who often talked about what was 'beyond God'. He may have seen these things directly, or they were revealed to him. It is unlikely that he had any contact with eastern teachings. He describes quite explicitly how the Trinity arises in order to complete what is needed.

filled. There is a difference between an infinite ocean of being in which we can be merged, and a nothingness which is drawing us to it. One Sufi teacher described it like this: 'this *lāhūt* offers its breasts for whoever is able to drink it to relieve its own over-flowing nothingness'. This may seem a fancy way of talking, but represents a real insight.

The ones who enter into the ultimate are very rare; destined for this before they are born. They bring great blessings to mankind. It is no longer possible to distinguish between them and the Supreme Will. Many verses of Rumi's *Masnawi* speak about the ultimate world. He says: 'If you want to enter into that place leave your existence behind. If you want to find the worker, go into the workshop; the workshop is nothingness'. The ultimate is represented not simply as the final destination of man but as the Source of everything. It is close to the ancient Taoist tradition: Tao cannot be described, what can be described is not Tao, it is nothing in itself, but everything comes into existence because of it.

Those who go beyond the *Jabarūt* into the *lāhūt* are the rarest of the rare, but even those who come fully into the *Jabarūt*, and live wholly in conformity with the Divine Will, are very rare. They are called *abdāl*, transformed people.

All this may sound very remote. What is its relevance for us? The point is this. We are not required to disappear into an ocean of beatitudes or go into some paradise or state where nothing more is required of us. To the extent that he or she is able, the individual being can give back something to the Source, which needs it because it is empty.

We have to see how it is that all of us can serve. The spirit world, the *ālam-i arvāh*, has many different regions in it. If we can become liberated from the dream state and cease to be obsessed with things, then we can enter an immensely freer mode of existence. The experiences belonging to the higher spheres of the spirit world are not only for individual satisfaction; they serve a purpose. The different levels are needed for the whole harmony of the cosmos.

It is not necessary for people to go the whole way. Those who do not go the whole way receive all that is possible for them, and they are not deprived. Some people I know have had a vision of this and it is very important and real. No work, no endeavor, is wasted. There is no black and white about it, no absolute salvation or absolute damnation, nor anything remotely like that. There are the higher regions in which there is an awareness of the proximity of God because that is where the second world merges with the *ālam-i imkān*. This can be thought of as Paradise, but one of the important things about the Sufi teaching is that Paradise is not anything ultimate and final, and there is the far harder step of passing into and even through the *ālam-i imkān*.

The world of bodies is the world of quantity and it is the domain of measurement and constraint. The world of spirits has different levels in it, gradations of existence, but not the same kind of quantitative constraints. When we come to the *ālam-i imkān* there is nothing to be measured. To be in that world means to be free to create. It does not have to do with existence.

The different worlds can be thought of as communities, or 'places of meetings'. If we think of them simply as a hierarchy we can get it all wrong. It is true that the higher worlds are more free, but there is something beyond all this: that each one of us has his or her own perfection. Perfection is perfection; there is no beyond in it. Whoever attains what he is destined for has achieved his perfection and anything else has no meaning. The Work that we hope to enter into is to bring us to our perfection. All the worlds play a part in this. The pattern of it all is quite beyond our minds, but we should have the confidence that if we commit ourselves to the Work, all will be fulfilled and we shall come to our reality here and now in this very life.

Index

W

Made in United States
Orlando, FL
09 January 2022

13212425R00155